WORCESTER WARRIORS
OFFICIAL YEARBOOK 2006/07

Editorial
Amanda Chatterton, Christopher Townend

Sidan Press Team
Simon Rosen, Julian Hill-Wood, Marc Fiszman, Mark Peters, Karim Biria, Robert Cubbon, Marina Kravchenko, Anette Lundebye, Gareth Peters, Janet Callcott, Trevor Scimes, John Fitzroy, Jenny Middlemarch, Anders Rasmussen, Lim Wai-Lee, Emma Turner, Carla Atkins, Tim Ryman, Ronen Dorfan, Humphrey Badia

Statistics
Stuart Farmer Media Services, OPTA

Kick Off Editorial
Amanda Chatterton

Photography
Ian Smith

Sidan Press, 63-64 Margaret St, London W1W 8SW
Tel: 020 7580 0200
Email: info@sidanpress.com

sidanpress.com

Club Directory

Chairman and Directors

Chairman and Chief Executive Cecil Duckworth OBE

Company Secretary Louise Brook

Director Roger Murray

Commercial Director Kathy Leather

Operations Director Mike Robins

Associate Director Jamie Evans

General Manager Charlie Little

Rugby Management

Director of Rugby John Brain

Head Coach Anthony Eddy

Strength & Conditioning Co-ordinator Keir Hansen

Director of Sports Medicine Robert Stewart

Team Manager Tony Boddy

Contacts

Operations & Management
Mike Robins
Tel: 01905 459324
Fax: 01905 459352
Email: Mike@wrfc.co.uk

Commercial Director
Kathy Leather
Tel: 01905 459326
Fax: 01905 459333
Email: Kathy@wrfc.co.uk

Financial Controller
Jamie Evans
Tel: 01905 459344
Fax: 01905 459302
Email: Jamie@wrfc.co.uk

Press & PR Manager
Mark Higgitt
Tel: 01905 459340
Fax: 01905 459352
Email: Mark@wrfc.co.uk

Merchandise Manager
Jane Fudger
Tel: 01905 459308
Fax: 01905 459352
Email: Jane@wrfc.co.uk

Ticket Office Manager
Maxine James
Tel: 0870 9905650
Fax: 01905 459352
Email: Tickets@wrfc.co.uk

Community Development Manager
Dan Zaltzman
Tel: 01905 459314
Fax: 01905 459352
Email: Dan@wrfc.co.uk

Corporate Sales
Tel: 01905 459347
Fax: 01905 459333
Email: Kim@wrfc.co.uk

Marketing
Tel: 01905 459346
Fax: 01905 459333
Email: Chris@wrfc.co.uk

Conference & Banqueting
Tel: 01905 459322
Fax: 01905 459333
Email: Kathy@wrfc.co.uk

Match Day Hospitality
Tel: 01905 459323
Fax: 01905 459333
Email: Helen@wrfc.co.uk

Charity Requests
Email: Kathy@wrfc.co.uk

Sixways Stadium
Pershore Lane
Hindlip
Worcester WR3 8ZE

Phone   01905 454183
Fax   01905 459352
Email   Rugby@wrfc.co.uk

Contents

Sixways Conference Centre

All the room you need, all the facilities you could want!

Our centre is available for weddings, parties, conferences, presentations, training workshops, team-building events: all and more are catered for to an exceptionally high standard by the dedicated and experienced Sixways Conference Centre team.

Whatever the occasion or celebration, one of the major strengths is to ensure that planning your special day is as easy as possible.

With the versatility of lounges and suites capable of hosting from 2 to 300 people in comfort and style, Sixways Conference Centre is tailor-made for parties and celebrations of all shapes and sizes – from New Year to Christmas.

Another key word in the success of Sixways catering is versatility. Set menus are provided but virtually any taste and request can be satisfied, including vegetarian and special diets.

Fine dining, traditional fare, silver service, snacks, barbecues, finger buffets, full banquets: you name it, Sixways Conference Centre can do it.

So whether you come to Sixways for business or pleasure, you'll be well looked after – and you won't have to compromise on room space, facilities, service, organisational skills or any other limitations which lesser venues so often impose.

Quote YB1 to receive 10% discount on all room hire rates.

Applies to all Season ticket holders.

Chairman and Chief Executive's Message
Cecil Duckworth OBE

Looking back on the Season 2005/6 we have to be pleased with the progress we made. We started the season exceptionally well but unfortunately had a difficult Christmas and the second half never did quite live up to the first half's expectations. However, we made progress and played some fantastic rugby at times, though we did not always win, when clearly we were the better team. For example, the Gloucester games at the end of the season were close and we were winning 10 minutes before time in each game but ended up losing on both occasions.

Looking forward John Brain and Anthony Eddy have again strengthened the squad and therefore, we should be more competitive during the coming Season 2006/7.

We have also embarked on a significant amount of development to the ground to lift the capacity to 13,500 by 1 September 2007. The work we have carried out during the Summer has provided a substantial improvement to changing rooms and rehab facilities for the players. The main pitch has been completely overhauled with a new fibre sand pitch which will provide us with one of the best pitches in the country. It will also have the added advantage of being more durable during the season. The old pitch had deteriorated substantially during the season to such an extent that it was no longer really suitable for Premiership rugby. The East Stand has been extended and re-built to provide built-in toilets, bars, food-outlets and a retail shop which will considerably enhance the comfort levels and enable supporters to have a drink with friends inside, instead of being outside in the freezing cold. The capacity of the stand is increased by 500 seats, bringing the ground capacity to 10,200 for the coming season 2006/7.

The above is a considerable step forward to ensuring the Warriors have the best training facilities and are one of the best prepared teams in the country, together with continuous improvements in the facilities for our supporters. The next phase of the development will, of course, significantly improve the car parking, access and exiting of the ground but we will have to be a little patient for another year. I look forward to your understanding in this direction.

I hope you all have an enjoyable and exciting season.

Message From the Coaching Staff
John Brain & Anthony Eddy

▶ John Brain, Director of Rugby

The 2006/07 season is already upon us as the squad returned to training on Monday 26th June 2006. The majority of the team enjoyed a well earned six week break, however several players earned representative honours and as a result continued to play and train during the break.

Congratulations must be extended to Pat Sanderson on his selection as England Captain, Kai Horstmann and Shane Drahm on their selection for England 'A', however, unfortunately Shane was forced to withdraw as a result of an ongoing injury. Tavita Taumoepeau spent the off season representing Tonga in the Pacific 5 Nations Tournament.

The 2005/06 season is perhaps best described as 'reasonably satisfying', as we certainly improved as the season went on, however we hope to improve further in the 06/07 season, with consistent performances and be a real threat to the top premiership teams. The team played some outstanding rugby towards the end of the season and it is hoped that we start the new season playing the style of game we finished with in 05/06.

There are a number of new players coming to the Club, and we would like to extend a warm welcome to them, as we are sure they will contribute to the ongoing success of Worcester Rugby.

▶ Anthony Eddy, Head Coach

Miguel Avramovic	Centre
Lee Best	Fullback / Wing
Marcel Garvey	Wing
Ben Gotting	Hooker
Darren Morris	Prop
Ryan Powell	Halfback
Gavin Quinnell	Lock / Backrow

As well as the new players we would also like to welcome Keir Hansen (Strength and Conditioning Co-ordinator), Bob Stewart (Medical Co-ordinator) and Mike Hall (Performance Analyst and Kit Manager). Keir, Bob and

Mike all have a wealth of experience in their respective areas and we are delighted to have them as part of our team.

We would also like to make special mention of our supporters and thank them sincerely for their support during last season. We consider our loyal supporters to be the best in the premiership and would encourage you to be even more vocal during the 2006/07 season.

Worcester Warriors 15
Gloucester Rugby 15

Premiership Home Record vs Gloucester Rugby					
Played	Won	Drawn	Lost	For	Against
2	**0**	**1**	**1**	**28**	**33**

Player of the Match

10 **James Brown**
Outside half

Worcester Warriors took two points from their opening match in the GUINNESS PREMIERSHIP 2005/2006 season against local rivals Gloucester, despite finding themselves 6-0 down to Gloucester within the first ten minutes.

In front of a record 9726 crowd, Jonny Hylton made his first Premiership start for the club since picking up a knee injury the previous season and showed signs of his former self throughout this highly charged derby.

Despite making a slow start, Worcester picked up their game on the half hour mark and edged into the lead thanks to three penalties from James Brown, making the score 9 – 6. The Warriors looked like they were going half time with a narrow lead, but Gloucester's Ludovic Mercier took an impressive penalty kick from near the half way line which sailed over the bar making it nine a piece on the half time whistle.

The second half saw Worcester take the lead again when Brown made it 12-9 two minutes in, but this was short lived when Mercier added another penalty before his opposite number put Worcester back in front with 15 minutes to go.

Chris Fortey and Shane Drahm replaced Andre Van Nierkerk and James Brown and then a penalty from Ludovic Mercier levelled the score at 15-15. Drahm later watched a penalty kick fall agonisingly short while Gloucester squandered a half chance to edge the lead again. This local derby finished honours even.

Venue:	Sixways		Referee:	Ashley Rowden - Season 05/06
Attendance:	9,726		Matches:	0
Capacity:	9,726		Yellow Cards:	0
Occupancy:	100%		Red Cards:	0

Worcester Warriors
Gloucester Rugby

Starting Line-Ups

○ Worcester Warriors		Gloucester Rugby ○
Delport	15	Goodridge
Hylton	14	Foster
Rasmussen	13	Tindall
Lombard	12	Paul
Hinshelwood	11	Thirlby
Brown	10	Mercier
Powell	9	Richards
Windo	1	Collazo
Van Niekerk	2	Azam
Horsman	3	Vickery
Collier	4	Eustace
Gillies	5	Brown
Vaili	6	Boer
Sanderson (c)	7	Hazell
Hickey	8	Balding (c)

Replacements

Le Roux	22	Allen
Drahm	21	McRae
Runciman	20	Thomas
Horstmann	19	Buxton
Murphy	18	Cornwell
C Fortey	17	Powell
Taumoepeau	16	Davies

Event Line

TC	Try Converted		P	Penalty
T	Try		DG	Drop Goal

Min	Score Progress		Event	Players
2	0	0	⇄	○ Buxton > Boer
4	0	3	DG	○ Mercier
7	0	3	⇄	○ Cornwell > Balding
11	0	3	⇄	○ Boer > Cornwell
12	0	6	P	○ Mercier
36	3	6	P	○ Brown
39	6	6	P	○ Brown
40	9	6	P	○ Brown
40	9	9	P	○ Mercier
Half time 9-9				
42	12	9	P	○ Brown
51	12	9	⇄	○ Davies > Azam
57	12	12	P	○ Mercier
59	12	12	⇄	○ Powell > Collazo
60	12	12	⇄	○ Murphy > Collier
68	15	12	P	○ Brown
69	15	12	⇄	○ Drahm > Brown
69	15	12	⇄	○ Fortey > Van Niekerk
72	15	12	⇄	○ Thomas > Richards
74	15	12	⇄	○ Le Roux > Rasmussen
74	15	15	P	○ Mercier
84	15	15	⇄	○ Taumoepeau > Horsman
Full time 15-15				

Match Stats

	Worcester	Gloucester
Tackles	32	48
Missed Tackles	6	4
Ball Carries	50	41
Metres	230	204
Defenders Beaten	4	6
Passes	47	57
Clean Breaks	0	2
Pens Conceded	15	22
Turnovers	8	9
Breakdowns Won	39	32
% Scrums Won	75%	57%
% Line-Outs Won	89%	75%

Scoring Statistics

○ Worcester Warriors

by Situation	by Half

▶ TC:	0	▶ first:	60%
▶ T:	0	▶ second:	40%
▶ P:	15		
▶ DG:	0		

○ Gloucester Rugby

by Situation	by Half

▶ TC:	0	▶ first:	60%
▶ T:	0	▶ second:	40%
▶ P:	12		
▶ DG:	3		

Premiership Table

Team	P	W	D	L	F	A	BP	Pts
5 Sale Sharks	1	1	0	0	26	25	0	4
6 Worcester Warriors	1	0	1	0	15	15	0	2
7 Gloucester Rugby	1	0	1	0	15	15	0	2

London Irish 15
Worcester Warriors 20

Premiership Away Record vs London Irish					
Played	Won	Drawn	Lost	For	Against
2	**1**	**0**	**1**	**35**	**40**

Despite the five point deficit with 4 minutes to go, Worcester came out on top in a closely contested match which saw Warriors' Shane Drahm light up the stadium with a stunning drop goal.

Player of the Match

8	**Drew Hickey**
	Back row

An unusual fumble by James Brown on his 22 allowed Irish to take the lead through a Scott Staniforth try, which was converted by Barry Everitt. The Worcester fly-half was then replaced by Shane Drahm after picking up an injury.

Worcester seemed slightly off the pace with the Exiles dominating periods of the game but were given a lifeline when prop Tony Windo forced the ball over the line from a driving maul and Drahm kicked the conversion. Their fight back was shortlived when Staniforth sprinted over the line to put the Exiles ahead again. Everitt missed the conversion and London Irish went in at half-time with a 15-10 lead.

Worcester came out in the second half looking more positive, showing power in their play and looking hungry to try and win the game. Kieran Dawson appeared to have taken the ball over the line, only for the referee to award a scrum due to an infringement in play. Worcester's quick thinking paid off opting for a scrum to force the ball over, leading to a penalty try which Drahm converted. He then later added a moment of sheer brilliance with a stunning drop goal.

Worcester dug deep and showed great strength and resilience in preventing a determined Irish side to get back into the game and came away worthy winners.

Venue: Madejski Stadium
Attendance: 7,118
Capacity: 24,104
Occupancy: 30%

Referee: Martin Fox - Season 05/06
Matches: 0
Yellow Cards: 0
Red Cards: 0

London Irish
Worcester Warriors

Starting Line-Ups

O London Irish		Worcester Warriors O
Armitage	15	Delport
Staniforth	14	Hylton
Penney	13	Rasmussen
Catt (c)	12	Lombard
Bishop	11	Hinshelwood
Everitt	10	Brown
Willis	9	Gomarsall
Hatley	1	Windo
Russell	2	Van Niekerk
Hardwick	3	Horsman
Casey	4	Murphy
Roche	5	Gillies
Magne	6	Vaili
Dawson	7	Sanderson (c)
Murphy	8	Hickey

Replacements

Geraghty	22	Tucker
Hodgson	21	Drahm
Gustard	20	Powell
Strudwick	19	Horstmann
Skuse	18	Collier
Flavin	17	C Fortey
Collins	16	MacDonald

Match Stats

Tackles	84	55
Missed Tackles	10	6
Ball Carries	62	81
Metres	300	383
Defenders Beaten	6	9
Passes	86	100
Clean Breaks	6	6
Pens Conceded	12	13
Turnovers	18	16
Breakdowns Won	41	64
% Scrums Won	82%	90%
% Line-Outs Won	72%	63%

Premiership Table

Team	P	W	D	L	F	A	BP	Pts
4 London Irish	2	1	0	1	42	31	2	6
5 Worcester Warriors	2	1	1	0	35	30	0	6
6 Gloucester Rugby	2	1	1	0	36	33	0	6

Event Line

TC	Try Converted		P	Penalty
T	Try		DG	Drop Goal

Min	Score Progress		Event	Players
5	0	0	⇄	O Flavin > Russell
10	7	0	TC	O Staniforth / Everitt
24	7	0	⇄	O Drahm > Brown
28	7	7	TC	O Windo / Drahm
30	12	7	T	O Staniforth
34	12	10	DG	O Drahm
40	15	10	P	O Everitt

Half time 15-10

41	15	10	⇄	O Skuse > Hardwick
46	15	10	⇄	O Gustard > Dawson
47	15	10	▮	O Horsman
52	15	10	⇄	O Fortey > Van Niekerk
52	15	10	⇄	O MacDonald > Vaili
55	15	10	▮	O Armitage
56	15	10	⇄	O Dawson > Gustard
59	15	10	⇄	O Vaili > MacDonald
65	15	10	⇄	O Gustard > Murphy
65	15	10	⇄	O Collins > Hatley
68	15	10	⇄	O Powell > Gomarsall
68	15	10	⇄	O Horstmann > Vaili
76	15	10	⇄	O Collier > Murphy
76	15	10	⇄	O Strudwick > Roche
77	15	17	TC	O Pen Try / Drahm
82	15	17	⇄	O Geraghty > Armitage
84	15	20	DG	O Drahm
89	15	20	▮	O Sanderson

Full time 15-20

Scoring Statistics

O London Irish

by Situation   by Half

▶ TC:	7	▶ first:	100%
▶ T:	5	second:	0%
▶ P:	3		
▶ DG:	0		

O Worcester Warriors

by Situation   by Half

▶ TC:	14	▶ first:	50%
▶ T:	0	second:	50%
▶ P:	0		
▶ DG:	6		

Worcester Warriors 25
Saracens 24

Premiership Home Record vs Saracens					
Played	Won	Drawn	Lost	For	Against
2	**1**	**0**	**1**	**43**	**43**

Worcester Warriors grabbed a second league win of the season – and first at Sixways – as they edged a nail biting Guinness Premiership clash.

Player of the Match

15 | **Nicolas Le Roux**
Wing/Full back

Saracens' Scarborough opened the scoring before their scrum half and Worcester's Andre Van Niekerk were sent to the sin bin for their part in a brawl which was sparked by Saracens' Kris Chesney.

The Warriors edged their noses in front when a penalty try was awarded after David Seymour picked the ball up in an offside position. Shane Drahm added the conversion.

Richard Haughton then powered over and when Castaignede crossed within three minutes of the re-start the home side faced an uphill battle.

However the Warriors dug deep and when Pat Sanderson off-loaded the ball to Drew Hickey, the number 8 stormed over in the corner to set the comeback rolling.

A Drahm penalty edged the home side ahead before a second try from Dan Scarborough six minutes from time looked to deny the Warriors.

But a battling display was richly rewarded when Tony Windo and Shane Drahm combined to add a memorable finale.

Venue:	Sixways
Attendance:	9,140
Capacity:	9,726
Occupancy:	94%

Referee:	Dave Pearson - Season 05/06
Matches:	2
Yellow Cards:	2
Red Cards:	0

Worcester Warriors
Saracens

Starting Line-Ups

O Worcester Warriors		Saracens O
Le Roux	15	Scarbrough
Hylton	14	Haughton
Rasmussen	13	Castaignede
Lombard	12	Sorrell
Hinshelwood	11	Bailey
Drahm	10	Jackson
Gomarsall	9	Dickens
Windo	1	Yates
Van Niekerk	2	Byrne
Horsman	3	Broster
Murphy	4	Chesney
Gillies	5	Vyvyan (c)
Vaili	6	Sanderson
Sanderson (c)	7	Seymour
Hickey	8	Skirving

Replacements

Delport	22	Powell
Trueman	21	Rauluni
Powell	20	Russell
Horstmann	19	Randell
Collier	18	Raiwalui
C Fortey	17	Lloyd
Taumoepeau	16	Cairns

Match Stats

Tackles	67	122
Missed Tackles	17	17
Ball Carries	110	70
Metres	535	446
Defenders Beaten	14	17
Passes	109	94
Clean Breaks	3	8
Pens Conceded	10	13
Turnovers	14	13
Breakdowns Won	88	49
% Scrums Won	100%	100%
% Line-Outs Won	94%	82%

Premiership Table

Team	P	W	D	L	F	A	BP	Pts
2 Sale Sharks	3	2	0	1	73	49	2	10
3 Worcester Warriors	3	2	1	0	60	54	0	10
4 Bristol Rugby	2	2	0	0	35	30	0	8

Event Line

TC	Try Converted			P	Penalty
T	Try			DG	Drop Goal

Min	Score Progress		Event	Players
2	0	0	⇄	O Rauluni > Dickens
4	0	0	⇄	O Dickens > Rauluni
17	0	5	T	O Scarbrough
23	0	5	▪	O Chesney
23	0	5	▪	O Dickens
23	0	5	▪	O Van Niekerk
25	0	5	⇄	O Fortey > Vaili
25	7	5	TC	O Pen Try / Drahm
28	7	5	⇄	O Lloyd > Yates
31	7	12	TC	O Haughton / Jackson
33	7	12	⇄	O Vaili > Fortey
40	10	12	P	O Drahm
Half time 10-12				
44	10	17	T	O Castaignede
50	15	17	T	O Hickey
52	15	17	⇄	O Yates > Broster
57	15	17	⇄	O Fortey > Van Niekerk
57	15	17	⇄	O Powell > Gomarsall
57	15	17	⇄	O Randell > Yates
57	15	17	⇄	O Cairns > Byrne
61	15	17	⇄	O Collier > Murphy
61	15	17	⇄	O Raiwalui > Chesney
67	15	17	⇄	O Horstmann > Vaili
67	15	17	⇄	O Rauluni > Dickens
67	18	17	P	O Drahm
72	18	17	⇄	O Trueman > Lombard
74	18	24	TC	O Scarbrough / Jackson
80	18	24	⇄	O Taumoepeau > Horsman
80	25	24	TC	O Windo / Drahm
Full time 25-24				

Scoring Statistics

O Worcester Warriors			
by Situation		by Half	
TC:	14	first:	40%
T:	5	second:	60%
P:	6		
DG:	0		

O Saracens			
by Situation		by Half	
TC:	14	first:	50%
T:	10	second:	50%
P:	0		
DG:	0		

London Wasps 34
Worcester Warriors 20

Premiership Away Record vs London Wasps					
Played	Won	Drawn	Lost	For	Against
2	**0**	**0**	**2**	**37**	**66**

Player of the Match

1 | **Tony Windo**
Prop

It wasn't the start that the Warriors had hoped for with Raphael Ibanez picking up the ball from a move instigated by Matt Dawson and raced it over the line.

Wasps' kicker Mark Van Gisbergen added the conversion and Worcester found themselves 7-0 down within the first two minutes. Despite being on the back foot, Worcester responded with a Pat Sanderson try putting them back in the game. Shane Drahm stepped up to convert making it honours even.

Worcester enjoyed bouts of pressure throughout the first half with Warriors' diminutive French man, Nicolas Le Roux, showing signs of sheer brilliance. Thanks to a Drahm penalty Worcester went into half-time with a well-deserved lead.

The turning point of the match came early on in the second period. Jonny Hylton unusually miss kicked the ball and Tom Voyce charged it over the line.

Van Gisbergen scored two penalties in quick succession making the score 20-10 giving the hosts a comfortable lead. Despite a Shane Drahm penalty, Wasps came back at the visitors with a Joe Worsely try, taking the game out of Worcester's reach.

Worcester supporters were given something to cherish – a late try scored by Nicolas Le Roux. Nicolas picked up the ball and sprinted effortlessly down the wing, showing the kind of pace that wins gold medals.

Venue:	Causeway Stadium	Referee:	Sean Davey - Season 05/06
Attendance:	8,720	Matches:	1
Capacity:	10,200	Yellow Cards:	1
Occupancy:	85%	Red Cards:	0

London Wasps
Worcester Warriors

Starting Line-Ups

○ London Wasps		Worcester Warriors ○
Van Gisbergen	15	Le Roux
Sackey	14	Hylton
Erinle	13	Rasmussen
Abbott	12	Lombard
Voyce	11	Hinshelwood
King	10	Drahm
M Dawson	9	Gomarsall
Payne	1	Windo
Ibanez	2	Van Niekerk
J Dawson	3	Horsman
Purdy	4	Murphy
Birkett	5	Gillies
Hart (c)	6	Vaili
Worsley	7	Sanderson (c)
Lock	8	Horstmann

Replacements

Waters	22	Delport
Brooks	21	Trueman
Reddan	20	Powell
O'Connor	19	Tu'amoheloa
Chamberlain	18	Collier
Bracken	17	C Fortey
Gotting	16	Taumoepeau

Match Stats

Tackles	88	101
Missed Tackles	11	28
Ball Carries	87	79
Metres	414	305
Defenders Beaten	28	11
Passes	93	69
Clean Breaks	1	0
Pens Conceded	11	17
Turnovers	17	9
Breakdowns Won	73	70
% Scrums Won	83%	75%
% Line-Outs Won	82%	100%

Premiership Table

Team	P	W	D	L	F	A	BP	Pts
4 Sale Sharks	4	3	0	1	113	81	3	15
5 Worcester Warriors	4	2	1	1	80	88	0	10
6 London Irish	4	2	0	2	69	82	2	10

Event Line

TC	Try Converted		P	Penalty
T	Try		DG	Drop Goal

Min	Score Progress		Event	Players
2	7	0	TC	○ Ibanez / Van Gisbergen
5	7	7	TC	○ Sanderson / Drahm
30	7	10	P	○ Drahm
36	7	10	⇄	○ Gotting > Ibanez
Half time 7-10				
43	14	10	TC	○ Voyce / Van Gisbergen
48	17	10	P	○ Van Gisbergen
50	20	10	P	○ Van Gisbergen
54	20	13	P	○ Drahm
55	20	13	⇄	○ Fortey > Van Niekerk
57	20	13	⇄	○ Taumoepeau > Horsman
57	20	13	⇄	○ O'Connor > Lock
59	20	13	⇄	○ Powell > Gomarsall
59	27	13	TC	○ Worsley / Van Gisbergen
63	27	13	⇄	○ Collier > Murphy
68	27	13	⇄	○ Brooks > King
70	27	13	⇄	○ Waters > Voyce
70	27	13	⇄	○ Bracken > Dawson
71	27	13	⇄	○ Trueman > Lombard
78	27	20	TC	○ Le Roux / Drahm
82	27	20	⇄	○ Delport > Hinshelwood
82	34	20	TC	○ Payne / Van Gisbergen
Full time 34-20				

Scoring Statistics

○ London Wasps

by Situation		by Half	
TC:	28	first:	21%
T:	0	second:	79%
P:	6		
DG:	0		

○ Worcester Warriors

by Situation		by Half	
TC:	14	first:	50%
T:	0	second:	50%
P:	6		
DG:	0		

Worcester Warriors 7
Northampton Saints 22

The Warriors turned their attention to the Powergen Cup but there was to be no dream start as the Sixways outfit crashed to defeat.

Player of the Match

6 | Kai Horstmann
Back row

Northampton put the Warriors under pressure in the early stages of the first half and it took a moment of magic from Spencer to unlock the Worcester defence. The Kiwi star floated out wide and took a tackle before releasing Cohen to coast into the corner – his first try since February. Bruce Reihana added the extras for an early 7-0 lead.

Worcester forced their way into Northampton territory, but were hit with a counter-attack just before the half hour. A stolen line-out allowed the Saints to release their backs and after an initial break from Sean Lamont the ball again found Cohen who demonstrated his finishing skills giving Saints a 12-0 half-time lead.

Worcester bravely battled to get back into the game in the early stages of the second half with Pat Sanderson and Gary Trueman making breaks only to be hauled down. However, Saints continued to pile up the points with Reihana adding a penalty before Jon Clarke broke clear in midfield and offloaded to Harding who dived under the posts for a 22-0 lead.

Worcester hit back when the pack flexed its muscles to show why they have the reputation of being one of the most feared set of forwards in the land. Mark Soden was sin-binned for a high tackle and with the extra man Worcester crashed over with Johnny Tuamoheloa touching down. Shane Drahm's conversion cut the lead to 22-7.

But there was to be no late fight-back as the Saints and Cohen celebrated victory.

Venue:	Sixways	Referee:	Martin Fox		**Worcester Warriors**
Attendance:	7,561				**Northampton Saints**
Capacity:	9,726				
Occupancy:	78%				

Starting Line-Ups

O Worcester Warriors		Northampton Saints O
Le Roux	**15**	Reihana (c)
Hylton	**14**	Lamont
Rasmussen	**13**	Clarke
Trueman	**12**	Quinlan
Tucker	**11**	Cohen
Drahm	**10**	Spencer
Powell	**9**	Robinson
Windo	**1**	Smith
Van Niekerk	**2**	Richmond
Taumoepeau	**3**	Noon
Collier	**4**	Boome
Gillies	**5**	Dm Browne
Horstmann	**6**	Thompson
Sanderson (c)	**7**	Fox
Hickey	**8**	Soden

Replacements

Lombard	**22**	Mallon
Whatling	**21**	Davies
Gomarsall	**20**	Howard
Tu'amoheloa	**19**	Harding
Murphy	**18**	Lord
Clunis	**17**	Budgen
MacDonald	**16**	Hartley

Event Line

TC	Try Converted		P	Penalty
T	Try		DG	Drop Goal

Min	Score Progress		Event	Players
9	0	7	TC	O Cohen / Reihana
20	0	7	⇄	O Tu'amoheloa > Hickey
25	0	7	⇄	O Budgen > Noon
28	0	12	T	O Cohen
Half time 0-12				
49	0	15	P	O Reihana
50	0	15	⇄	O Murphy > Collier
50	0	15	⇄	O Harding > Fox
50	0	22	TC	O Harding / Reihana
56	0	22	⇄	O Howard > Robinson
61	0	22	▪	O Soden
65	7	22	TC	O Tu'amoheloa / Drahm
66	7	22	⇄	O Gomarsall > Powell
66	7	22	⇄	O Lombard > Trueman
66	7	22	⇄	O Lord > Browne
66	7	22	⇄	O Davies > Quinlan
70	7	22	⇄	O Clunis > Van Niekerk
80	7	22	⇄	O Whatling > Rasmussen
81	7	22	⇄	O Mallon > Thompson
Full time 7-22				

Match Stats

Tackles	77	66
Missed Tackles	21	10
Ball Carries	70	105
Metres	376	691
Defenders Beaten	9	22
Passes	94	108
Clean Breaks	9	18
Pens Conceded	11	16
Turnovers	14	17
Breakdowns Won	44	58
% Scrums Won	92%	83%
% Line-Outs Won	59%	67%

Scoring Statistics

O Worcester Warriors

by Situation | by Half

- TC: 7 — first: 0%
- T: 0 — second: 100%
- P: 0
- DG: 0

O Northampton Saints

by Situation | by Half

- TC: 14 — first: 55%
- T: 5 — second: 45%
- P: 3
- DG: 0

Powergen Cup Table

Team	P	W	D	L	F	A	BP	Pts
1 Northampton Saints	1	1	0	0	22	7	0	4
2 Newport Gwent Dragons	1	1	0	0	24	15	0	4
3 Leicester Tigers	1	0	0	1	15	24	0	0
4 Worcester Warriors	1	0	0	1	7	22	0	0

19

Leicester Tigers   42
Worcester Warriors 16

Player of the Match

8 | **Kai Horstmann**
Back row

Worcester's domestic cup run came to end as they suffered a five-try defeat at a wet and windy Welford Road.

The Warriors initially looked to be in for a long afternoon when Irish debutant Ian Humphreys converted tries from George Chuter and Leon Lloyd and kicked two penalties to put the Tigers ahead after 27 minutes.

Missing inspirational captain Pat Sanderson and a number of key players, Worcester fought courageously and refused to yield.

Despite the sin-binning of Thomas Lombard, Worcester dragged themselves back from the brink thanks to three penalties from Shane Drahm and a try from Ben Hinshelwood, who was sent over the line by a pass from Kai Horstmann. The visitors managing to claw back from 20 – 3 down to move within four points of the hosts at the break.

But Leicester came roaring out of the traps at the start of the second half which proved too much for the visitor's with a fifteen minute spell that yielded a point a minute.

Austin Healey and Harry Ellis crossed the line in the space of a minute. Replacement Andy Goode kicked a penalty and then converted Tom Varndell's try to ensure the win and end any hopes of a famous victory.

However Worcester refused to roll over and fought on to the final whistle with Uche Oduoza, the right wing, being denied twice with the try line in sight. As such the lop-sided nature of the scoreline failed to reflect the part the Warriors played in the match.

Attendance: 8,642
Capacity: 16,815
Occupancy: 51%

Starting Line-Ups

O Leicester Tigers		Worcester Warriors O
Murphy	15	Hylton
Lloyd	14	Tucker
Hipkiss	13	Hinshelwood (c)
Vesty	12	Lombard
Tuilagi	11	Oduoza
Humphreys	10	Drahm
Healey	9	Gomarsall
Rowntree	1	Sparks
Chuter	2	C Fortey
White	3	Taumoepeau
Kay	4	Collier
Cullen	5	O'Donoghue
Skinner	6	Vaili
Jennings	7	Tu'amoheloa
Corry (c)	8	Horstmann

Replacements

Goode	22	Lennard
Varndell	21	Robinson
Ellis	20	Powell
Deacon	19	Hickey
Deacon	18	Blaze
Holford	17	Keylock
Buckland	16	Mullan

Match Stats

Tackles	93	37
Missed Tackles	12	3
Ball Carries	43	75
Metres	318	345
Defenders Beaten	3	12
Passes	55	110
Clean Breaks	9	5
Pens Conceded	13	21
Turnovers	11	16
Breakdowns Won	33	55
% Scrums Won	100%	83%
% Line-Outs Won	89%	72%

Event Line

| TC | Try Converted | | | P | Penalty |
| T | Try | | | DG | Drop Goal |

Min	Score Progress		Event	Players
7	7	0	TC	O Chuter / Humphreys
10	7	3	P	O Drahm
16	10	3	P	O Humphreys
24	17	3	TC	O Lloyd / Humphreys
27	17	6	P	O Drahm
28	17	6	■	O Lombard
29	20	6	P	O Humphreys
33	20	6	■	O Hipkiss
34	20	9	P	O Drahm
40	20	9	⇄	O Deacon > Kay
40	20	16	TC	O Hinshelwood / Drahm
Half time 20-16				
41	20	16	⇄	O Goode > Humphreys
48	23	16	P	O Goode
53	30	16	TC	O Healey / Goode
55	30	16	⇄	O Ellis > Healey
55	30	16	⇄	O Blaze > O'Donoghue
55	35	16	T	O Ellis
57	35	16	⇄	O Deacon > Skinner
63	35	16	⇄	O Lennard > Tucker
63	35	16	⇄	O Buckland > Chuter
67	35	16	⇄	O Powell > Gomarsall
68	35	16	⇄	O Hickey > Vaili
68	35	16	⇄	O Varndell > Tuilagi
71	35	16	⇄	O Holford > Rowntree
73	42	16	TC	O Varndell / Goode
75	42	16	⇄	O Healey > Ellis
Full time 42-16				

Scoring Statistics

O Leicester Tigers	
by Situation	by Half

▶ TC:	28	▶ first:	48%
▶ T:	5	second:	52%
▶ P:	9		
DG:	0		

O Worcester Warriors	
by Situation	by Half

▶ TC:	7	▶ first:	100%
▶ T:	0	second:	0%
▶ P:	9		
DG:	0		

Powergen Cup Table

Team	P	W	D	L	F	A	BP	Pts
1 Northampton Saints	2	2	0	0	54	14	1	9
2 Leicester Tigers	2	1	0	1	57	40	1	5
3 Newport Gwent Dragons	2	1	0	1	31	47	0	4
4 Worcester Warriors	2	0	0	2	23	64	0	0

Worcester Warriors 22
Leeds Tykes 15

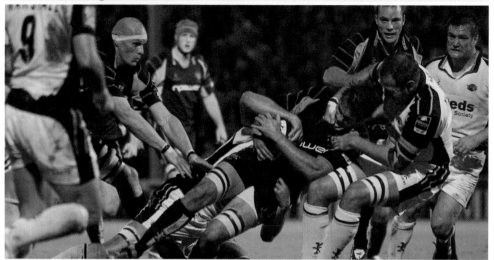

Premiership Home Record vs Leeds Tykes

Played	Won	Drawn	Lost	For	Against
2	2	0	0	44	30

The Warriors returned to winning ways with a workmanlike victory over struggling Leeds Tykes at a packed Sixways.

Player of the Match

4 Phil Murphy
Lock

Pat Sanderson and Aisea Havili were among a host of changes to the side and the captain was typically in the thick of the early exchanges. Havili looked bright on his debut and integrated with the team well, delighting the Sixways' crowd.

It was Leeds, though, who took the lead on 11 minutes when Roland De Marigny landed a penalty. But Worcester hit back hard on 20 minutes when Thinus Delport rounded off a flowing move that had switched from left to right. Drahm missed the conversion but kicked his second penalty of the half to leave the Warriors 8-3 in front at the break.

Drahm and De Marigny, the Italian international, traded three-pointers at the start of the second half before Vaili, the replacement back-rower, scored the try that finally extended Worcester's lead, giving them some breathing space.

Despite the home side's possession, Worcester had missed opportunities on either flank in quick succession but they made no mistake with a rumbling rolling maul that led to Vaili being propelled over. Unfortunately Drahm missed the conversion and then saw his opposite number cut the arrears with his fourth penalty of the match. Drahm added a penalty to claim a well deserved win.

Venue:	Sixways	Referee:	Sean Davey - Season 05/06		**Worcester Warriors**
Attendance:	9,626	Matches:	2		**Leeds Tykes**
Capacity:	9,726	Yellow Cards:	1		
Occupancy:	99%	Red Cards:	0		

Starting Line-Ups

O Worcester Warriors		Leeds Tykes O
Le Roux	15	Stimpson
Havili	14	Biggs
Hinshelwood	13	Vickerman
Lombard	12	Jones
Delport	11	Doherty
Drahm	10	De Marigny
Gomarsall	9	Marshall (c)
Windo	1	Isaacson
C Fortey	2	Bulloch
Horsman	3	Gerber
Murphy	4	Morgan
Gillies	5	Palmer
Horstmann	6	Thomas
Sanderson (c)	7	Parks
Hickey	8	Crane

Replacements

Trueman	22	Rees
Brown	21	Ross
Powell	20	Care
Vaili	19	Hyde
Collier	18	Murphy
Keylock	17	Rawlinson
Taumoepeau	16	Kerr

Match Stats

	Worcester	Leeds
Tackles	37	90
Missed Tackles	6	2
Ball Carries	85	46
Metres	373	207
Defenders Beaten	2	6
Passes	138	53
Clean Breaks	2	1
Pens Conceded	16	13
Turnovers	13	6
Breakdowns Won	80	34
% Scrums Won	100%	70%
% Line-Outs Won	90%	69%

Event Line

TC	Try Converted			P	Penalty
T	Try			DG	Drop Goal

Min	Score Progress		Event	Players
10	0	3	P	O De Marigny
20	5	3	T	O Delport
36	8	3	P	O Drahm
40	8	3	⇄	O Ross > De Marigny
40	8	3	⇄	O Vaili > Horstmann
Half time 8-3				
41	8	3	⇄	O Kerr > Isaacson
41	8	3	⇄	O De Marigny > Ross
46	8	3	⇄	O Murphy > Morgan
46	8	3	⇄	O Horstmann > Vaili
46	11	3	P	O Drahm
48	11	3	⇄	O Taumoepeau > Horsman
55	11	6	P	O De Marigny
56	11	6	⇄	O Rawlinson > Bulloch
56	11	6	⇄	O Ross > Stimpson
56	11	6	⇄	O Hyde > Thomas
57	11	6	⇄	O Vaili > Horstmann
63	16	6	T	O Vaili
65	16	9	P	O De Marigny
66	16	9	⇄	O Powell > Gomarsall
70	16	9	▣	O Fortey
71	16	9	⇄	O Collier > Murphy
71	16	12	P	O De Marigny
73	19	12	P	O Drahm
76	19	15	P	O De Marigny
78	19	15	⇄	O Keylock > Vaili
80	19	15	⇄	O Vaili > Keylock
82	22	15	P	O Drahm
Full time 22-15				

Scoring Statistics

O Worcester Warriors				O Leeds Tykes			
by Situation		by Half		by Situation		by Half	
TC:	0	first:	36%	TC:	0	first:	20%
T:	10	second:	64%	T:	0	second:	80%
P:	12			P:	15		
DG:	0			DG:	0		

Premiership Table

Team	P	W	D	L	F	A	BP	Pts
4 Gloucester Rugby	4	3	1	0	105	66	1	15
5 Worcester Warriors	5	3	1	1	102	103	0	14
6 London Irish	4	2	0	2	69	82	2	10

Worcester Warriors 36
Montpellier 18

Player of the Match

9 | Andy Gomarsall
Scrum half

Worcester Warriors kicked off their European Challenge Cup campaign in true style with a five try spectacular to seal a win against the towering French side.

Worcester took the lead early on, slotting over a penalty with three minutes gone. The French side responded when Bortolussi kicked his way through and Oduoza was forced to make a try saving tackle to keep Worcester in the lead. However, Montpellier brought the score even when Andy Gomarsall infringed at a scrum which led to the French side scoring a long range penalty.

On 19 minutes the Warriors really came to light. Craig Gillies claimed the line out on the edge of the visitor's 22 and Drahm rounded off a slick move with a superb try, his first in a Worcester shirt and he converted to make it 10-3 to the hosts. However, Montpellier were dangerous from turnover ball and brought the scores level when winger Sebastien Kuzbic touched down and Bortolussi converted.

Once again Worcester responded in fine form in a move that lead to skipper Pat Sanderson ploughing over from a line-out drive. A see saw of tries between the two sides followed until Worcester were awarded a penalty try after Montpellier infringed for a third time at the scrum. Drahm converted and sent Worcester into a 22-15 lead at the break.

Montpellier narrowed the scoring early on in the second half thanks to a penalty scored by Lespinas, but Worcester showed character with a breathtaking move instigated by Lombard. Oduoza, who had put in a sterling performance throughout, ran the ball over the line. Drahm added the stunning conversion to extend Worcester's lead. With minutes to go, Worcester added their fifth try when Andy Gomarsall went round the back of the maul and burrowed over.

Venue:	Sixways	Referee:	Carlo Damasco
Attendance:	6,078		
Capacity:	9,726		
Occupancy:	62%		

Worcester Warriors
Montpellier

Starting Line-Ups

O Worcester Warriors		Montpellier O
Le Roux	15	Bortolussi
Hylton	14	Logerot
Hinshelwood	13	Crane
Lombard	12	Stoica
Oduoza	11	Kuzbik
Drahm	10	Lespinas
Gomarsall	9	Tomas
Windo	1	Magrakvelidze
C Fortey	2	Caudullo
Taumoepeau	3	Decamps
Blaze	4	Gorgodze
Gillies	5	Nouchi
Vaili	6	Durand
Sanderson (c)	7	Bost
Hickey	8	Russel (c)

Replacements

Tucker	22	Benazech
Brown	21	Mercier
Runciman	20	Aucagne
Tu'amoheloa	19	Mathieu
O'Donoghue	18	Bert
MacDonald	17	Brugnaut
Clunis	16	Diomande

Event Line

TC	Try Converted		P	Penalty
T	Try		DG	Drop Goal

Min	Score Progress		Event	Players
2	3	0	P	O Drahm
15	3	3	P	O Bortolussi
19	10	3	TC	O Drahm / Drahm
29	10	3	⇄	O Brugnaut > Decamps
30	10	10	TC	O Kuzbik / Bortolussi
33	15	10	T	O Sanderson
37	15	15	T	O Magrakvelidze
40	22	15	TC	O Pen Try / Drahm
Half time 22-15				
48	22	15	⇄	O Benazech > Bortolussi
48	22	15	⇄	O Bert > Gorgodze
51	22	18	P	O Lespinas
54	29	18	TC	O Oduoza / Drahm
56	29	18	⇄	O Mercier > Tomas
58	29	18	⇄	O Diomande > Caudullo
59	29	18	⇄	O Aucagne > Logerot
61	29	18	⇄	O Logerot > Kuzbik
69	29	18	⇄	O Tucker > Lombard
69	29	18	⇄	O Kuzbik > Logerot
72	29	18	⇄	O Mathieu > Bost
76	29	18	▣	O Mathieu
77	36	18	TC	O Gomarsall / Drahm
78	36	18	⇄	O Brown > Drahm
Full time 36-18				

Euro Challenge Cup Table

Team	P	W	D	L	F	A	BP	Pts
1 Connacht	1	1	0	0	62	17	1	5
2 Worcester Warriors	1	1	0	0	36	18	1	5
3 Amatori Catania	1	0	0	1	17	62	0	0
4 Montpellier	1	0	0	1	18	36	0	0

Scoring Statistics

O Worcester Warriors

by Situation	by Half

◗ TC:	28	◗ first:	61%
◗ T:	5	◗ second:	39%
◗ P:	3		
◗ DG:	0		

O Montpellier

by Situation	by Half

◗ TC:	7	◗ first:	83%
◗ T:	5	◗ second:	17%
◗ P:	6		
◗ DG:	0		

Amatori Catania 14
Worcester Warriors 19

Player of the Match

7 | **Drew Hickey**
Back row

The Worcester line were put under pressure from the first whistle as the Sicilians immediately attacked with basic, forceful play.

Once the Warriors got into their stride they dominated possession for the rest of the first half. Both Worcester's first half tries came from their dominance in the scrum. On 12 minutes a five metre put in gave the back row the chance to creep closer to the line and prop Tevita Taumoepeau added the necessary bulk to open the scoring. The second also came from five metres out as number eight Kai Horstmann picked up at the base and despite being tackled by two Sicilians, managed to stretch his long arm out and touch down on the line. James Brown converted to make it two out of two on his return from a knee injury and Worcester were 0-14 up and seemingly on the brink of a powerful performance.

Worcester attacked immediately from the start of the second half with Drew Hickey, who captained the side in the absence of England squad member Pat Sanderson, stealing the ball back from Catania and giving centre Mark Tucker the space to beat his opposite number and cross for try number three. James Brown missed the conversion.

Two slight errors brought the home side back into the match though, on 46 minutes a horizontal kick from Worcester full-back Nicholas Le Roux bounced straight into the hands of Catania left wing and captain Benjamin de Jager who ran 40 metres to dive-in under the posts. Fly-half Barry Irving converted to make it 7-19. Worcester lost the ball after a five-metre scrum on 77 minutes and gave Benjamin de Jager the chance of a second long run and unopposed try, any chances of a fourth try and a bonus point disappeared with it. Once again Irving was on target with the kick and Worcester faced a tense five minutes of injury time as Catania attacked, however to no avail.

Amatori Catania
Worcester Warriors

Starting Line-Ups

○ Amatori Catania		Worcester Warriors ○
Cosa	15	Le Roux
Viassiolo	14	Oduoza
Romagnoli	13	Tucker
Estomba	12	Trueman
De Jager (c)	11	Delport
Irving	10	Brown
Viassiolo	9	Powell
Levaggi	1	Sparks
Alvarez Quinones	2	C Fortey
Condorelli	3	Taumoepeau
Wargon	4	Blaze
Lagarrigue	5	Gillies
Krancz	6	Vaili
Lorenzetti	7	Hickey (c)
Tukino	8	Horstmann

Replacements

Privitera	22	Whatling
Pappalardo	21	Drahm
Grasso	20	Gomarsall
Carbone	19	Tu'amoheloa
Vidal	18	Murphy
Vinti	17	MacDonald
De Bonis	16	L Fortey

Event Line

TC	Try Converted		P	Penalty
T	Try		DG	Drop Goal

Min	Score Progress	Event	Players
13	0 — 7	TC	○ Taumoepeau / Brown
22	0 — 14	TC	○ Horstmann / Brown
30	0 — 14	⇄	○ Vidal > Krancz
Half time 0-14			
41	0 — 19	T	○ Tucker
43	0 — 19	⇄	○ Carbone > Viassiolo
44	7 — 19	TC	○ De Jager / Irving
45	7 — 19	⇄	○ De Bonis > Condorelli
45	7 — 19	⇄	○ Murphy > Blaze
45	7 — 19	⇄	○ MacDonald > Sparks
49	7 — 19	⇄	○ Gomarsall > Powell
60	7 — 19	⇄	○ Privitera > Lagarrigue
66	7 — 19	⇄	○ Vinti > Tukino
66	7 — 19	⇄	○ Tu'amoheloa > Vaili
68	7 — 19	⇄	○ Drahm > Brown
70	7 — 19	⇄	○ Fortey > Fortey
78	7 — 19	⇄	○ Condorelli > Levaggi
80	7 — 19	⇄	○ Pappalardo > Lorenzetti
80	14 — 19	TC	○ De Jager / Irving
83	14 — 19	■	○ Estomba
Full time 14-19			

Euro Challenge Cup Table

Team	P	W	D	L	F	A	BP	Pts
1 Connacht	2	2	0	0	81	33	1	9
2 Worcester Warriors	2	2	0	0	55	32	1	9
3 Amatori Catania	2	0	0	2	31	81	1	1
4 Montpellier	2	0	0	2	34	55	1	1

Scoring Statistics

○ Amatori Catania

by Situation — by Half

TC:	14	first:	0%
T:	0	second:	100%
P:	0		
DG:	0		

○ Worcester Warriors

by Situation — by Half

TC:	14	first:	74%
T:	5	second:	26%
P:	0		
DG:	0		

Worcester Warriors 15
Leicester Tigers 11

Premiership Home Record vs Leicester Tigers

Played	Won	Drawn	Lost	For	Against
2	1	0	1	26	49

A gritty and gallant team performance by the Warriors led to their first victory over Leicester Tigers and four well deserved points to keep them in the top half of the table.

Player of the Match

8 | **Drew Hickey**
Back row

In the absence of skipper Pat Sanderson and Chris Horsman, Tony Windo captained the side with Tevita Taumopeau and Johnny Tuamoheloa slotting into the pack. Leicester were also without several key first team players, however they fielded a strong side that caused Worcester some problems.

Despite conceding a Ross Broadfoot penalty, Worcester responded with two successive penalties within five minutes, superbly taken by Shane Drahm. Leicester's Will Skinner scored the only try but, much to the delight of the Sixways faithful, Broadfoot failed to extend Leicester's lead when he missed the conversion.

On 18 minutes Worcester were awarded a penalty just inside the 22 mark which fell just short, but Drahm redeemed himself on 20 minutes to make it 9-8 to the hosts. Two penalties from the boot of Shane Drahm eased them into a 15-8 lead going into half-time.

Leicester were not prepared to roll over and be beaten but their only points in the second half were in the form of a penalty from the boot of Goode. The final whistle was met with scenes of jubilation at Sixways. The Warriors had clinched a well deserved victory over the East Midlands side.

Venue:	Sixways	Referee:	Roy Maybank - Season 05/06
Attendance:	9,726	Matches:	4
Capacity:	9,726	Yellow Cards:	5
Occupancy:	100%	Red Cards:	0

Worcester Warriors
Leicester Tigers

Starting Line-Ups

O Worcester Warriors		Leicester Tigers O
Le Roux	15	Vesty
Havili	14	Tuilagi
Hinshelwood	13	Lloyd
Lombard	12	Hipkiss
Delport	11	Varndell
Drahm	10	Broadfoot
Gomarsall	9	Healey (c)
Windo (c)	1	Holford
C Fortey	2	Chuter
Taumoepeau	3	Moreno
Murphy	4	Hamilton
Gillies	5	Kay
Horstmann	6	Deacon
Tu'amoheloa	7	Skinner
Hickey	8	Johnson

Replacements

Tucker	22	Goode
Brown	21	Smith
Powell	20	Cole
Vaili	19	Croft
Blaze	18	Cullen
L Fortey	17	Morris
MacDonald	16	Buckland

Event Line

TC	Try Converted		P	Penalty
T	Try		DG	Drop Goal

Min	Score Progress		Event	Players
3	0	3	P	O Broadfoot
6	3	3	P	O Drahm
10	6	3	P	O Drahm
16	6	8	T	O Skinner
22	9	8	P	O Drahm
30	9	8	◼	O Kay
37	12	8	P	O Drahm
40	15	8	P	O Drahm
Half time 15-8				
46	15	8	◼	O Hamilton
50	15	8	⇄	O Goode > Broadfoot
56	15	8	⇄	O Cullen > Hamilton
63	15	8	⇄	O Smith > Lloyd
63	15	8	⇄	O Morris > Holford
69	15	11	P	O Goode
70	15	11	⇄	O Vaili > Tu'amoheloa
Full time 15-11				

Match Stats

Tackles	47	49
Missed Tackles	8	7
Ball Carries	57	58
Metres	221	191
Defenders Beaten	8	8
Passes	88	87
Clean Breaks	3	1
Pens Conceded	12	16
Turnovers	12	15
Breakdowns Won	55	47
% Scrums Won	83%	80%
% Line-Outs Won	94%	88%

Scoring Statistics

O Worcester Warriors

by Situation	by Half

▶ TC:	0	▶ first:	100%
▶ T:	0	▶ second:	0%
▶ P:	15		
▶ DG:	0		

O Leicester Tigers

by Situation	by Half

▶ TC:	0	▶ first:	73%
▶ T:	5	▶ second:	27%
▶ P:	6		
▶ DG:	0		

Premiership Table

Team	P	W	D	L	F	A	BP	Pts
3 Sale Sharks	5	4	0	1	131	91	3	19
4 Worcester Warriors	6	4	1	1	117	114	0	18
5 Gloucester Rugby	5	3	1	1	121	84	2	16

Sale Sharks 24
Worcester Warriors 13

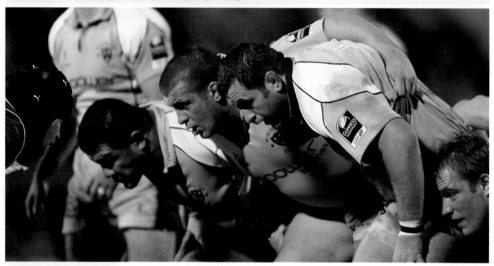

Premiership Away Record vs Sale Sharks					
Played	Won	Drawn	Lost	For	Against
2	**0**	**0**	**2**	**16**	**81**

Sale attacked from the kick-off and it took some time for the Warriors to settle into their rhythm.

Player of the Match

10 | **Shane Drahm**
Outside half

Worcester gave away a number of penalties which obviously lost territory and possession, resulting in a penalty which Sale's full-back Daniel Larrechea converted. The Warriors began to play some useful attacking rugby and Shane Drahm levelled the score with a well taken 30m drop goal.

Worcester then conceded a number of penalties which fortunately weren't converted. Johnny Tuamoheloa was sin-binned after 37 minutes for alleged killing the ball, which resulted in a penalty that Valentin Courrent converted. Worcester were reduced to 14 men and Sebastien Chabal made a cross field run before slipping the ball to Jason Robinson who scored in the corner. Courrent added the extras.

Shane Drahm began the second half with a well flighted kick and after a powerful drive from Thomas Lombard Worcester got within 10m of the Sale line. Andy Gomarsall flicked a pass to Shane Drahm who side stepped through the Sale players and scored under the posts.

A botched Worcester throw in bounced conveniently for Chabal, who fed Robinson to slide in at the corner after 48 minutes. The conversion was missed and a Drahm penalty made the score 18-13 with half an hour left on the clock. Play then turned scrappy and Sale were awarded a penalty which Courrent converted. Robinson later added a drop goal to take the spoils.

Venue:	Edgeley Park	Referee:	Martin Fox - Season 05/06		Sale Sharks
Attendance:	7,056	Matches:	2		Worcester Warriors
Capacity:	10,641	Yellow Cards:	3		
Occupancy:	66%	Red Cards:	0		

Starting Line-Ups

O Sale Sharks		Worcester Warriors O
Larrechea	15	Le Roux
Ripol Fortuny	14	Havili
Taylor	13	Hinshelwood
Todd	12	Lombard
Robinson (c)	11	Delport
Courrent	10	Drahm
Martens	9	Gomarsall
Coutts	1	Windo (c)
Titterrell	2	C Fortey
Turner	3	Taumoepeau
Day	4	Murphy
Schofield	5	Blaze
Carter	6	Horstmann
Lund	7	Tu'amoheloa
Chabal	8	Hickey

Replacements

Mayor	22	Hylton
Foden	21	Whatling
Wigglesworth	20	Powell
Taione	19	Vaili
Anglesea	18	O'Donoghue
Stewart	17	L Fortey
Briggs	16	MacDonald

Event Line

TC	Try Converted		P	Penalty
T	Try		DG	Drop Goal

Min	Score Progress	Event	Players
4	3	0	P	O Larrechea
5	3	3	DG	O Drahm
22	3	3	⇄	O Hylton > Havili
34	3	3	⇄	O Stewart > Coutts
36	3	3	■	O Tu'amoheloa
36	6	3	P	O Courrent
40	13	3	TC	O Robinson / Courrent
Half time 13-3				
41	13	3	⇄	O Anglesea > Carter
43	13	10	TC	O Drahm / Drahm
45	18	10	T	O Robinson
51	18	13	P	O Drahm
55	18	13	⇄	O Powell > Gomarsall
58	18	13	⇄	O Taione > Taylor
59	21	13	P	O Courrent
60	21	13	⇄	O Vaili > Horstmann
68	21	13	⇄	O Foden > Ripol Fortuny
68	21	13	⇄	O Coutts > Turner
71	24	13	DG	O Robinson
73	24	13	⇄	O Wigglesworth > Martens
75	24	13	⇄	O Briggs > Titterrell
Full time 24-13				

Match Stats

Tackles	55	70
Missed Tackles	6	10
Ball Carries	70	58
Metres	428	213
Defenders Beaten	10	6
Passes	76	79
Clean Breaks	4	2
Pens Conceded	5	11
Turnovers	14	10
Breakdowns Won	48	43
% Scrums Won	100%	93%
% Line-Outs Won	85%	79%

Scoring Statistics

O Sale Sharks

by Situation   by Half

▶ TC:	7	▶ first:	54%
▶ T:	5	▶ second:	46%
▶ P:	9		
▶ DG:	3		

O Worcester Warriors

by Situation   by Half

▶ TC:	7	▶ first:	23%
▶ T:	0	▶ second:	77%
▶ P:	3		
▶ DG:	3		

Premiership Table

Team	P	W	D	L	F	A	BP	Pts
5 Leicester Tigers	6	3	2	1	156	106	3	19
6 Worcester Warriors	7	4	1	2	130	138	0	18
7 Saracens	6	3	0	3	152	137	4	16

Worcester Warriors 24
Bristol Rugby 15

Guinness Premiership
18.11.05

Premiership Home Record vs Bristol Rugby

Played	Won	Drawn	Lost	For	Against
1	1	0	0	24	15

It was Bristol, the Premiership new boys' turn to come to the Sixways fortress.

The game began at a fast pace. Bristol's Brian Lima was handed a yellow card for killing the ball and then Shane Drahm kicked the ball across the field, finding Delport who ran it over the line and Drahm converted.

Bristol finally registered on the scoreboard on 37 minutes thanks to a Jason Strange penalty, making it 7-3 at half-time.

Worcester extended their lead immediately after the break as Drahm scored a penalty in front of goal. Worcester took advantage of Bristol's second sin bin, when Sam Cox was yellow carded for stamping on Andy Gomarsall by carving out a spectacular flowing move which Aisea Havili bull dozed over in the corner for a try on 53 minutes. Drahm failed to increase the points deficit, but he soon notched up another three points with a penalty to make it 18-3.

Drahm then slotted another penalty before Bristol flanker Joe El Abd scored a dubious try with Warriors players believing it was a knock on. Jason Strange scored the conversion making it 21-10, and although Bristol's David Lemi took the ball over the line for another try, Worcester still looked very much in control of the game.

A stunning 43-metre penalty by Shane Drahm took the game out of Bristol's reach and when a late kick fell short, Bristol were resigned to leave without even a point.

Player of the Match

13 | **Dale Rasmussen**
Centre/Wing

Venue:	Sixways	Referee:	David Rose - Season 05/06	**Worcester Warriors**
Attendance:	9,726	Matches:	4	**Bristol Rugby**
Capacity:	9,726	Yellow Cards:	8	
Occupancy:	100%	Red Cards:	0	

Starting Line-Ups

O Worcester Warriors		Bristol Rugby O
Le Roux	15	Going
Havili	14	Lima
Rasmussen	13	Higgitt
Lombard	12	Cox
Delport	11	Lemi
Drahm	10	Strange
Gomarsall	9	Perry
Windo (c)	1	Hilton
C Fortey	2	Regan
Taumoepeau	3	Crompton
Murphy	4	Winters
Gillies	5	Llewellyn
Horstmann	6	Salter (c)
Tu'amoheloa	7	El Abd
Hickey	8	Lewis

Replacements

Tucker	22	Stanojevic
Brown	21	Hayes
Powell	20	Rauluni
Vaili	19	Morgan
O'Donoghue	18	Sambucetti
L Fortey	17	Nelson
Hickie	16	Clarke

Match Stats

	Worcester	Bristol
Tackles	71	85
Missed Tackles	11	15
Ball Carries	80	77
Metres	444	391
Defenders Beaten	14	11
Passes	119	94
Clean Breaks	9	3
Pens Conceded	14	15
Turnovers	15	12
Breakdowns Won	68	48
% Scrums Won	100%	100%
% Line-Outs Won	86%	73%

Premiership Table

Team	P	W	D	L	F	A	BP	Pts
3 Leicester Tigers	8	4	2	2	197	150	3	23
4 Worcester Warriors	8	5	1	2	154	153	0	22
5 Gloucester Rugby	7	4	1	2	168	129	3	21

Event Line

TC	Try Converted		P	Penalty
T	Try		DG	Drop Goal

Min	Score Progress		Event	Players
18	0	0	■	O Lima
24	7	0	TC	O Delport / Drahm
35	7	3	P	O Strange
Half time 7-3				
44	10	3	P	O Drahm
50	10	3	■	O Cox
51	15	3	T	O Havili
55	18	3	P	O Drahm
62	18	10	TC	O El Abd / Strange
65	21	10	P	O Drahm
66	21	10	⇄	O Vaili > Horstmann
66	21	10	⇄	O Powell > Gomarsall
69	21	10	⇄	O Stanojevic > Higgitt
70	21	15	T	O Lemi
78	24	15	P	O Drahm
Full time 24-15				

Scoring Statistics

O Worcester Warriors

by Situation	by Half

▶ TC:	7	▶ first:	29%
▶ T:	5	▶ second:	71%
▶ P:	12		
▶ DG:	0		

O Bristol Rugby

by Situation	by Half

▶ TC:	7	▶ first:	20%
▶ T:	5	second:	80%
▶ P:	3		
▶ DG:	0		

Player of the Match

10 | **Shane Drahm**
Outside half

Premiership Away Record vs Northampton Saints					
Played	Won	Drawn	Lost	For	Against
2	**2**	**0**	**0**	**39**	**27**

Worcester Warriors came away from Franklin's Gardens with an inspiring win over the Saints.

Scoring was opened by a Shane Drahm try which he converted. The Warriors controlled the ball, dominated and forced a penalty on 14 minutes which Drahm kicked beautifully extending their lead to 10-0.

On 18 minutes Northampton were awarded a penalty. Reihana regained his kicking form after missing one early on in the match. Worcester replied with another Drahm penalty giving them a ten point lead. Darren Fox peeled from back of a line-out and dived over to score on 32 minutes. Reihana converted Fox's try narrowing Worcester's lead. A penalty from both sides just before half-time meant Worcester went in with a three point lead, 16-13.

Worcester failed to emulate the dream start of the first half when Rhodri Davies finished off a move which was started when Carlos Spencer made a stunning break. Davies scored the try putting the Saints ahead for the first time. Reihana failed to convert the try although he added a penalty shortly after making the score 21-16.

Drahm, who had kicked so well all match, then added another penalty to make it 21-19. With ten minutes to go Worcester regained the lead thanks to a superb Drahm penalty which well deserved to win the match. Northampton were awarded a penalty following Kai Horstmann's sending off on 80 minutes which Reihana kicked wide.

Venue:	Franklin's Gardens		Referee:	Wayne Barnes - Season 05/06		**Northampton Saints**
Attendance:	12,481		Matches:	1		**Worcester Warriors**
Capacity:	13,591		Yellow Cards:	1		
Occupancy:	92%		Red Cards:	0		

Starting Line-Ups

○ Northampton Saints		Worcester Warriors ○
Reihana (c)	15	Le Roux
Clarke	14	Havili
Mallon	13	Rasmussen
Davies	12	Lombard
Cohen	11	Delport
Spencer	10	Drahm
Howard	9	Gomarsall
Budgen	1	Windo (c)
Richmond	2	C Fortey
Barnard	3	Taumoepeau
Dm Browne	4	Murphy
Lord	5	Gillies
Lewitt	6	Horstmann
Fox	7	Tu'amoheloa
Dn Browne	8	Hickey

Replacements

Myring	22	Hinshelwood
Vilk	21	Brown
Robinson	20	Powell
Harding	19	Mason
Gerard	18	O'Donoghue
Harbut	17	L Fortey
Hartley	16	Hickie

Match Stats

Tackles	62	84
Missed Tackles	10	25
Ball Carries	89	70
Metres	559	375
Defenders Beaten	26	10
Passes	108	81
Clean Breaks	10	8
Pens Conceded	15	11
Turnovers	8	12
Breakdowns Won	67	56
% Scrums Won	75%	88%
% Line-Outs Won	67%	88%

Premiership Table

Team	P	W	D	L	F	A	BP	Pts
3 London Wasps	8	6	1	1	213	150	2	28
4 Worcester Warriors	9	6	1	2	176	174	0	26
5 Gloucester Rugby	9	5	1	3	197	162	3	25

Event Line

TC	Try Converted			P	Penalty
T	Try			DG	Drop Goal

Min	Score Progress		Event	Players
7	0	7	TC	○ Drahm / Drahm
14	0	10	P	○ Drahm
18	3	10	P	○ Reihana
24	3	13	P	○ Drahm
31	3	13	▪	○ Horstmann
32	10	13	TC	○ Fox / Reihana
36	10	13	▪	○ Mallon
37	10	16	P	○ Drahm
40	10	16	▪	○ Hickey
40	13	16	P	○ Reihana
Half time 13-16				
48	18	16	T	○ Davies
52	18	16	⇄	○ Harbut > Budgen
54	18	16	⇄	○ Harding > Fox
54	18	16	⇄	○ Robinson > Howard
57	18	16	⇄	○ Powell > Gomarsall
58	18	16	⇄	○ Vilk > Mallon
60	18	16	⇄	○ O'Donoghue > Murphy
60	18	16	⇄	○ Hickie > Fortey
60	21	16	P	○ Reihana
63	21	19	P	○ Drahm
66	21	19	⇄	○ Hartley > Richmond
69	21	22	P	○ Drahm
70	21	22	⇄	○ Budgen > Barnard
73	21	22	⇄	○ Gerard > Browne
80	21	22	▪	○ Horstmann
Full time 21-22				

Scoring Statistics

○ Northampton Saints

by Situation — by Half

▪ TC:	7		▪ first:	62%
▪ T:	5		▪ second:	38%
▪ P:	9			
▪ DG:	0			

○ Worcester Warriors

by Situation — by Half

▪ TC:	7		▪ first:	73%
▪ T:	0		▪ second:	27%
▪ P:	15			
▪ DG:	0			

Newport Gwent Dragons 33
Worcester Warriors 10

Player of the Match

14 Aisea Havili
Wing

Worcester Warriors travelled to Rodney Parade unable to qualify for the next stages of the Powergen Cup, after suffering two consecutive defeats at the hands of Northampton and Leicester Tigers.

Neither team could progress any further in this new look Powergen Cup and both Worcester and the Dragons were without key players. It was a perfect opportunity to give members of the Academy team a chance to step up to the mark.

It never looked to be the Warriors day, when on 20 minutes Worcester found themselves 17-0 down partly thanks to an Adam Black try. Worcester were then penalised for bringing down the ruck, which lead to a five-metre line-out. The Dragons secured the ball and Andrew Hall touched down.

The Dragons led 20-10 at the break and the second half saw two more penalties and an injury time penalty try. However, Worcester did show signs of brilliance when Rasmussen, Worcester's skipper for the match pulled off a fantastic tackle on Richard Fussell, halting the Dragons extending their lead.

Worcester did get back into the game and came within seven points of the hosts, with a superb solo try from wing speedster Aisea Havili running in from 60 metres.

Uche Oduoza made some threatening moves much to the delight of the Warriors faithful, giving them something to cheer about on a rather dark, damp December afternoon. New signing, Tom Harding made his first appearance in a Worcester shirt, but failed to turn the game around which would have been a lot to ask considering the type of game and that a host of first team players were missing.

Attendance: 4,017
Capacity: 11,700
Occupancy: 34%

Newport Gwent Dragons
Worcester Warriors

Starting Line-Ups

O Newport Gwent Dragons		Worcester Warriors O
Hinton	15	Lennard
Wyatt	14	Havili
Tuipulotu	13	Rasmussen (c)
Williams	12	Tucker
Fussell	11	Oduoza
Warlow	10	Brown
Cooper	9	Powell
Black	1	Mullan
Jones	2	Hickie
Robinson	3	MacDonald
Griffiths	4	Collier
Gough	5	O'Donoghue
Hall	6	Mason
Ringer	7	Tu'amoheloa
Bryan (c)	8	Horstmann

Replacements

Smith	22	Delport
Bryant	21	Whatling
Breeze	20	Runciman
Forster	19	Harding
Thomas	18	Blaze
Maddocks	17	Black
Brown	16	Clunis

Powergen Cup Table

Team	P	W	D	L	F	A	BP	Pts
1 Leicester Tigers	3	2	0	1	86	56	2	10
2 Northampton Saints	3	2	0	1	70	43	1	9
3 Newport Gwent Dragons	3	2	0	1	64	57	0	8
4 Worcester Warriors	3	0	0	3	33	97	0	0

Event Line

TC	Try Converted		P	Penalty
T	Try		DG	Drop Goal

Min	Score Progress		Event	Players
2	0	0		O Black > MacDonald
6	7	0	TC	O Black / Warlow
8	10	0	P	O Warlow
11	10	0		O MacDonald > Black
19	17	0	TC	O Hall / Warlow
24	17	3	P	O Brown
29	17	10	TC	O Havili / Brown
34	20	10	P	O Warlow
38	20	10		O Delport > Havili
40	20	10		O Black > MacDonald
40	20	10		O Havili > Delport
40	20	10		O Breeze > Wyatt
Half time 20-10				
49	23	10	P	O Warlow
50	23	10		O Thomas > Jones
53	23	10		O Brown > Robinson
53	23	10		O Harding > Mason
53	23	10		O Blaze > Collier
60	23	10		O Whatling > Brown
60	23	10		O Delport > Lennard
65	23	10		O Forster > Griffiths
66	26	10	P	O Warlow
69	26	10		O Smith > Hinton
70	26	10		O Maddocks > Black
74	26	10		O Bryant > Williams
80	33	10	TC	O Pen Try / Warlow
Full time 33-10				

Scoring Statistics

O Newport Gwent Dragons

by Situation · by Half

TC:	21	first:	61%
T:	0	second:	39%
P:	12		
DG:	0		

O Worcester Warriors

by Situation · by Half

TC:	7	first:	100%
T:	0	second:	0%
P:	3		
DG:	0		

Worcester Warriors 30
Connacht 20

Player of the Match

14 | **Uche Oduoza**
Wing

With nine points a piece, the Warriors and Irish side Connacht were both looking to extend their unbeaten run easing them closer to a quarter final place.

Worcester made the start they were after when on 11 minutes a line-out resulted in a maul, where the ball was released and Thomas Lombard found Nicolas Le Roux who raced over the line. Shane Drahm converted putting the Warriors 7-0 ahead.

Connacht were awarded a penalty on 17 minutes when skipper Pat Sanderson was sent to the sin bin for dissent. David Slemen took advantage and notched up three points for the visitors. Connacht went on to score a try on 21 minutes with Slemen slotting the conversion over the post.

Drahm, who racked up 20 points in the match brought the Warriors back into game when he was passed the ball from Matt Powell and charged across the line. He then kicked the conversion to take Worcester into the break with a 14-10 lead.

The Warriors extended their lead early on in the second half thanks to a Drahm penalty awarded when Connacht players entered the ruck from the side. Slemen narrowed the gap on 50 minutes with a disputed penalty which the referee deemed legal. Connacht edged infront again briefly with a Matt Mostyn try which Slemen converted. However this was short lived as Drahm responded with a couple of penalties in quick succession.

With two minutes to go the Warriors were awarded a penalty and took the decision to go for a try to deny Connacht a bonus point. Number 8 Drew Hickey sealed the win for Worcester as he went under the posts for a try which Drahm converted convincingly.

Venue: Sixways
Attendance: 6,137
Capacity: 9,726
Occupancy: 63%

Referee: Jean-Pierre Matheu

Worcester Warriors
Connacht

Starting Line-Ups

O Worcester Warriors		Connacht O
Le Roux	15	Mostyn
Oduoza	14	Robinson
Lombard	13	Hearty
Whatling	12	Matthews
Delport	11	McPhillips
Drahm	10	Slemen
Powell	9	Keane
Windo	1	Hogan
C Fortey	2	Fogarty
Horsman	3	Knoop
Murphy	4	Short
Gillies	5	Farley (c)
Horstmann	6	Muldoon
Sanderson (c)	7	Lacey
Hickey	8	Rigney

Replacements

Tucker	22	O'Loughlin
Brown	21	Riordan
Gomarsall	20	Tierney
Tu'amoheloa	19	Swift
O'Donoghue	18	Gallagher
L Fortey	17	Clarke
Sparks	16	Merrigan

Euro Challenge Cup Table

Team	P	W	D	L	F	A	BP	Pts
1 Worcester Warriors	3	3	0	0	85	52	1	13
2 Connacht	3	2	0	1	101	63	1	9
3 Montpellier	3	1	0	2	108	67	2	6
4 Amatori Catania	3	0	0	3	43	155	1	1

Event Line

TC	Try Converted		P	Penalty
T	Try		DG	Drop Goal

Min	Score Progress		Event	Players
11	7	0	TC	O Le Roux / Drahm
16	7	0	▣	O Sanderson
17	7	3	P	O Slemen
21	7	10	TC	O Matthews / Slemen
34	14	10	TC	O Drahm / Drahm
Half time 14-10				
44	17	10	P	O Drahm
50	17	13	P	O Slemen
56	17	13	⇄	O O'Donoghue > Murphy
58	17	13	⇄	O Fortey > Horsman
59	17	20	TC	O Mostyn / Slemen
63	20	20	P	O Drahm
65	20	20	⇄	O Swift > Rigney
67	20	20	▣	O Short
69	23	20	P	O Drahm
70	23	20	⇄	O Tu'amoheloa > Horstmann
77	23	20	⇄	O Gallagher > Short
80	30	20	TC	O Hickey / Drahm
Full time 30-20				

Scoring Statistics

O Worcester Warriors

by Situation		by Half	
➤ TC:	21	➤ first:	47%
➤ T:	0	➤ second:	53%
➤ P:	9		
➤ DG:	0		

O Connacht

by Situation		by Half	
➤ TC:	14	➤ first:	50%
➤ T:	0	➤ second:	50%
➤ P:	6		
➤ DG:	0		

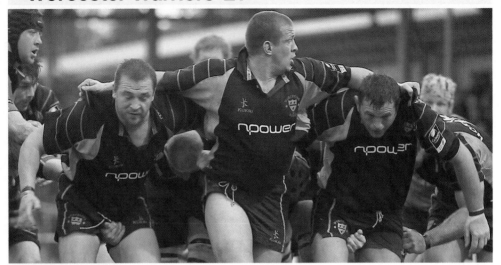

Player of the Match

2 | **Chris Fortey**
| Hooker

This was a match full of silly mistakes, penalties and yellow cards but high on drama and tension.

Both Connacht and Worcester were forced to spend major parts of the match with just fourteen men as the French referee Eric Darriere brandished five yellow cards.

The fly halves Shane Drahm and David Slemen swapped penalties in the opening 15 minutes. Prop Chris Horsman became the first player to spend 10 minutes in the sin bin for killing the ball. Connacht centre Chris Matthews followed him on 18 minutes and Worcester hooker Chris Fortey took advantage of his absence to power over for the game's first try. Drahm added the conversion for a 3-10 lead for the Warriors but when he was sent to the sin-bin just before half-time, Connacht punished the visitors with a second Slemen penalty and a try from Conor McPhillips to lead 11-10 at half-time.

Penalties were swapped again early on in the second half before scrum half Chris Keane got a 10 minute sin-bin and the Warriors finally upped the pressure and gave full-back Thinus Delport the opportunity to cross the line on 56 minutes to give them a narrow one point lead. Drahm missed the conversion but added a penalty just minutes later and the visitors were in sight of a second victory over the Irish side in as many weeks.

The clock ticked down and again and again Worcester got into the opposition's 22 only to come away without any points. When flanker Kai Horstmann was the fifth player to be sin-binned five minutes from time, Connacht sensed that a victory was within their reach. Flanker Matt Lacey touched down for the crucial try in the corner on 79 minutes and, although Paul Warwick missed the conversion, they hung on to the one point lead until the final whistle.

Attendance: 2,300
Capacity: 7,000
Occupancy: 33%

Connacht
Worcester Warriors

Starting Line-Ups

O Connacht		Worcester Warriors O
Mostyn	15	Le Roux
Robinson	14	Oduoza
Hearty	13	Lombard
Matthews	12	Whatling
McPhillips	11	Delport
Slemen	10	Drahm
Keane	9	Powell
Hogan	1	Windo
Fogarty	2	C Fortey
Knoop	3	Horsman
Short	4	Collier
Farley (c)	5	Gillies
Muldoon	6	Horstmann
Lacey	7	Sanderson (c)
Rigney	8	Hickey

Replacements

Riordan	22	Rasmussen
Warwick	21	Brown
Tierney	20	Gomarsall
Swift	19	Tu'amoheloa
Gallagher	18	O'Donoghue
Clarke	17	L Fortey
Merrigan	16	Sparks

Euro Challenge Cup Table

Team	P	W	D	L	F	A	BP	Pts
1 Worcester Warriors	4	3	0	1	106	74	2	14
2 Connacht	4	3	0	1	123	84	1	13
3 Montpellier	4	1	0	3	142	104	4	8
4 Amatori Catania	4	1	0	3	80	189	2	6

Event Line

TC	Try Converted		P	Penalty
T	Try		DG	Drop Goal

Min	Score Progress		Event	Players
4	0	3	P	O Drahm
13	0	3	■	O Horsman
15	3	3	P	O Slemen
22	3	10	TC	O Fortey / Drahm
40	6	10	P	O Slemen
40	11	10	T	O McPhillips

Half time 11-10

Min	Score Progress		Event	Players
41	11	10	⇄	O Warwick > Robinson
49	11	10	⇄	O Swift > Rigney
52	14	10	P	O Warwick
54	14	10	■	O Keane
54	14	13	P	O Drahm
58	17	13	P	O Warwick
62	17	18	T	O Delport
65	17	18	⇄	O Gomarsall > Powell
66	17	18	⇄	O Fortey > Horsman
68	17	21	P	O Drahm
69	17	21	⇄	O Rasmussen > Le Roux
77	17	21	⇄	O Tierney > Keane
78	17	21	■	O Horstmann
80	22	21	T	O Fogarty
82	22	21	⇄	O Clarke > Knoop
82	22	21	⇄	O Merrigan > Fogarty
83	22	21	⇄	O Tu'amoheloa > Hickey
83	22	21	⇄	O O'Donoghue > Gillies

Full time 22-21

Scoring Statistics

O Connacht

by Situation   by Half

TC:	0	first:	50%
T:	10	second:	50%
P:	12		
DG:	0		

O Worcester Warriors

by Situation   by Half

TC:	7	first:	48%
T:	5	second:	52%
P:	9		
DG:	0		

Worcester Warriors 18
Bath Rugby 36

Premiership Home Record vs Bath Rugby					
Played	Won	Drawn	Lost	For	Against
2	**0**	**0**	**2**	**40**	**62**

It was always going to be a tough encounter for the hosts with Bath desperate for points and Worcester keen to keep their good run of form.

Player of the Match

7 | **Johnny Tuamoheloa**
Back row

However, Worcester were kept at arms' length by a strong Bath side but led 13 –10 at the interval. Drahm scored with a penalty after just a minute and Bath were fortunate to score their first try when Chris Malone charged down a ball from Shane Drahm and made a simple run-in from 40 metres. Olly Barkley added the conversion. Bath were now easing themselves back into the game.

Worcester scored again on the 34th minute when they were awarded a penalty which Drahm converted. Barkley then added a penalty though Drahm added another penalty on the stroke of half-time after Duncan Bell killed the ball at the ruck. Worcester failed to capitalise in his absence and Barkley racked up six points.

Worcester responded with a period of pressure which led to a Kai Horstmann try on 50 minutes. Worcester's lead of 18-16 was short lived and as they conceded another penalty which Barkley comfortably converted after Worcester's Simon Whatling found himself sin binned for a similar offence to that of Duncan Bell.

With ten minutes left, Drahm kicked a penalty from just inside the Bath half, but Bath then collected the ball from a Gavin Hickie throw and after a short run Malone dived over by the posts. Gareth Delve put pay to a losing bonus point for the Warriors as he raced over the line to score when a pass found him on the Bath 22.

Venue:	Sixways	Referee:	Sean Davey - Season 05/06		**Worcester Warriors**
Attendance:	9,726	Matches:	8		**Bath Rugby**
Capacity:	9,726	Yellow Cards:	9		
Occupancy:	100%	Red Cards:	0		

Starting Line-Ups

O Worcester Warriors		Bath Rugby O
Le Roux	15	Stephenson
Havili	14	Finau
Lombard	13	Crockett
Whatling	12	Barkley
Delport	11	Maddock
Drahm	10	Malone
Powell	9	Walshe
Windo (c)	1	Barnes
C Fortey	2	Mears
Horsman	3	Bell
Murphy	4	Borthwick (c)
Gillies	5	Grewcock
Horstmann	6	Beattie
Tu'amoheloa	7	Lipman
Hickey	8	Delve

Replacements

Rasmussen	22	Higgins
Brown	21	Davis
Gomarsall	20	Williams
Harding	19	Feau'nati
Collier	18	Short
Taumoepeau	17	Stevens
Hickie	16	Dixon

Match Stats

	Worcester	Bath
Tackles	86	74
Missed Tackles	7	12
Ball Carries	82	82
Metres	473	378
Defenders Beaten	11	7
Passes	128	85
Clean Breaks	8	3
Pens Conceded	14	7
Turnovers	16	16
Breakdowns Won	63	69
% Scrums Won	83%	92%
% Line-Outs Won	69%	80%

Premiership Table

Team	P	W	D	L	F	A	BP	Pts
4 Gloucester Rugby	10	5	1	4	222	194	4	26
5 Worcester Warriors	10	6	1	3	194	210	0	26
6 London Irish	9	5	0	4	179	185	4	24

Event Line

TC	Try Converted		P	Penalty
T	Try		DG	Drop Goal

Min	Score Progress		Event	Players
2	3	0	P	O Drahm
15	3	7	TC	O Malone / Barkley
33	10	7	TC	O Pen Try / Drahm
38	10	10	P	O Barkley
39	10	10	■	O Bell
40	13	10	P	O Drahm
Half time 13-10				
41	13	10	⇄	O Rasmussen > Lombard
41	13	10	⇄	O Taumoepeau > Horsman
42	13	10	⇄	O Stevens > Lipman
43	13	13	P	O Barkley
47	13	16	P	O Barkley
50	13	16	⇄	O Lipman > Bell
50	18	16	T	O Horstmann
53	18	19	P	O Barkley
63	18	19	⇄	O Gomarsall > Powell
63	18	19	■	O Whatling
63	18	22	P	O Barkley
64	18	22	⇄	O Bell > Barnes
65	18	22	⇄	O Hickie > Fortey
65	18	22	⇄	O Collier > Murphy
71	18	22	⇄	O Higgins > Finau
76	18	22	⇄	O Harding > Horstmann
76	18	22	⇄	O Short > Grewcock
76	18	22	⇄	O Williams > Walshe
76	18	29	TC	O Malone / Barkley
80	18	36	TC	O Delve / Barkley
Full time 18-36				

Scoring Statistics

O Worcester Warriors

by Situation   by Half

► TC:	7	► first:	72%
► T:	5	► second:	28%
► P:	6		
► DG:	0		

O Bath Rugby

by Situation   by Half

► TC:	21	► first:	28%
► T:	0	► second:	72%
► P:	15		
► DG:	0		

Newcastle Falcons 21
Worcester Warriors 15

Player of the Match

14 | **Aisea Havili**
Wing

Premiership Away Record vs Newcastle Falcons					
Played	Won	Drawn	Lost	For	Against
2	**1**	**0**	**1**	**36**	**37**

James Brown missed a relatively easy early penalty before Matthew Burke belted over one from over 55 metres to give Newcastle the lead in a lively opening 10 minutes, but the Falcons gave away a string of penalties at the line-out.

Newcastle's line-out transgressions caught up with them when Owen Finegan was sin-binned for pushing. Burke hacked the ball 70 yards down field and was there again when Thinus Delport could not gather and he snapped it up to dive over and then converted from wide out.

Newcastle were stretched when Thomas Lombard kicked and Aisea Havili scrambled to touch down for a try which Brown converted from the touchline. Burke then added his second penalty just before half-time. Newcastle lost two of their own line-outs early in the second half and conceded a penalty to make it 13-10.

Worcester again lost the ball when it looked like they would score and Walder snapped it up when Jonny Hylton could not hang on. Walder raced 80 metres to score. Burke missed the conversion but kicked a penalty when Tony Windo went over the ball right in front of the posts but the Worcester captain made amends when he was driven over for a try from a line-out, although the Falcons players were adamant he had not touched down. There was a nervous finish from both sides but Newcastle were able to run down the clock in the last 10 minutes.

Venue:	Kingston Park	Referee:	Ashley Rowden - Season 05/06	**Newcastle Falcons**
Attendance:	8,864	Matches:	5	**Worcester Warriors**
Capacity:	10,000	Yellow Cards:	6	
Occupancy:	89%	Red Cards:	0	

Starting Line-Ups

O Newcastle Falcons		Worcester Warriors O
Burke	15	Delport
Shaw	14	Havili
Noon	13	Lombard
Mayerhofler	12	Whatling
Tait	11	Maguire
Walder	10	Brown
Grindal	9	Powell
Ward	1	Windo (c)
Long	2	C Fortey
Morris	3	Taumoepeau
Perry	4	Murphy
Parling	5	Gillies
Finegan	6	Horstmann
Woods	7	Tu'amoheloa
Charvis (c)	8	Hickey

Replacements

Flood	22	Hylton
Richardson	21	Gomarsall
Buist	20	Rasmussen
McCarthy	19	Vaili
Grimes	18	O'Donoghue
Thompson	17	L Fortey
Williams	16	Hickie

Event Line

TC	Try Converted		P	Penalty
T	Try		DG	Drop Goal

Min	Score Progress		Event	Players
7	3	0	P	O Burke
29	3	0	■	O Finegan
30	3	0	⇄	O Hylton > Maguire
30	10	0	TC	O Burke / Burke
34	10	7	TC	O Havili / Brown
37	13	7	P	O Burke
Half time 13-7				
41	13	7	⇄	O Grimes > Perry
41	13	7	⇄	O Williams > Ward
41	13	7	⇄	O Thompson > Long
49	13	7	⇄	O McCarthy > Finegan
51	13	7	⇄	O Ward > Williams
53	13	10	P	O Brown
56	13	10	⇄	O Flood > Walder
56	18	10	T	O Walder
61	21	10	P	O Burke
65	21	15	T	O Windo
66	21	15	⇄	O Fortey > Windo
66	21	15	⇄	O Rasmussen > Lombard
72	21	15	⇄	O Hickie > Fortey
72	21	15	⇄	O Vaili > Tu'amoheloa
Full time 21-15				

Match Stats

Tackles	79	68
Missed Tackles	15	13
Ball Carries	75	91
Metres	281	459
Defenders Beaten	13	14
Passes	98	90
Clean Breaks	6	7
Pens Conceded	10	8
Turnovers	12	15
Breakdowns Won	55	58
% Scrums Won	86%	82%
% Line-Outs Won	79%	78%

Scoring Statistics

O Newcastle Falcons

by Situation / by Half

- TC: 7
- T: 5
- P: 9
- DG: 0
- first: 62%
- second: 38%

O Worcester Warriors

by Situation / by Half

- TC: 7
- T: 5
- P: 3
- DG: 0
- first: 47%
- second: 53%

Premiership Table

Team	P	W	D	L	F	A	BP	Pts
5 London Irish	11	6	0	5	218	239	4	28
6 Worcester Warriors	11	6	1	4	209	231	1	27
7 Saracens	10	4	1	5	218	206	5	23

Worcester Warriors 11
Northampton Saints 15

Premiership Home Record vs Northampton Saints					
Played	Won	Drawn	Lost	For	Against
2	1	0	1	32	34

The Warriors were denied their seventh league win of the season by a controversial disallowed try in a thrilling match with Northampton at Sixways.

Player of the Match

5 | Craig Gillies
Lock

Both sides struggled to cope with the tricky conditions and the first half yielded just six points. James Brown and Bruce Reihana traded a penalty a piece while Brown and Carlos Spencer both missed efforts at the posts. The Warriors endured a sustained assault just before the half hour while, at the other end, Havili was beaten to a clever grubber from Brown by the covering Marc Robinson.

Defences remained on top in the first 20 minutes of the second half before the game burst into life in the last quarter. Northampton's hooker, Steve Thompson, sparked the flurry of points by crashing his way over in the left-hand corner.

Drahm, on as a replacement for Brown, cut the deficit to just two points with a 66th minute penalty. But an impressive cross-field kick from Carlos Spencer found Ben Cohen lurking out wide and the England wing rose superbly to gather the kick and touch down under pressure. The points looked to be in the bag when Spencer kicked a touchline conversion but Worcester had other ideas.

A lovely interchange of passes eventually led to Drahm sending Kai Horstmann racing over the try line on 75 minutes to put the match back in the balance. The Warriors threw everything at the Saints in a rousing finale but they were denied maximum points by the referee much to the disappointment of the Sixway's faithful.

Venue:	Sixways	Referee:	Chris White - Season 05/06	**Worcester Warriors**
Attendance:	9,726	Matches:	5	**Northampton Saints**
Capacity:	9,726	Yellow Cards:	0	
Occupancy:	100%	Red Cards:	0	

Starting Line-Ups

O Worcester Warriors		Northampton Saints O
Delport	15	Reihana (c)
Havili	14	Lamont
Rasmussen	13	Clarke
Lombard	12	Kydd
Tucker	11	Rudd
Brown	10	Spencer
Powell	9	Robinson
Windo (c)	1	Smith
C Fortey	2	Thompson
Taumoepeau	3	Budgen
Murphy	4	Dm Browne
Gillies	5	Lord
Horstmann	6	Tupai
Tu'amoheloa	7	Lewitt
Hickey	8	Dn Browne

Replacements

Whatling	22	Cohen
Drahm	21	Vilk
Gomarsall	20	Howard
Harding	19	Seely
O'Donoghue	18	Gerard
L Fortey	17	Emms
Hickie	16	Hartley

Event Line

TC	Try Converted		P	Penalty
T	Try		DG	Drop Goal

Min	Score Progress		Event	Players
10	3	0	P	O Brown
31	3	0	⇄	O Hickie > Fortey
32	3	3	P	O Reihana
35	3	3	⇄	O Cohen > Rudd
Half time 3-3				
41	3	3	⇄	O Fortey > Hickie
51	3	3	⇄	O Drahm > Brown
59	3	3	⇄	O Seely > Browne
59	3	3	⇄	O O'Donoghue > Murphy
59	3	3	⇄	O Gerard > Lord
59	3	3	⇄	O Emms > Smith
61	3	8	T	O Thompson
63	3	8	⇄	O Vilk > Kydd
63	3	8	⇄	O Gomarsall > Powell
65	6	8	P	O Drahm
66	6	15	TC	O Cohen / Spencer
68	6	15	⇄	O Harding > Tu'amoheloa
73	6	15	⇄	O Fortey > Taumoepeau
74	11	15	T	O Horstmann
76	11	15	⇄	O Hartley > Budgen
Full time 11-15				

Match Stats

Tackles	154	92
Missed Tackles	13	10
Ball Carries	73	145
Metres	350	472
Defenders Beaten	8	13
Passes	90	125
Clean Breaks	9	4
Pens Conceded	5	10
Turnovers	11	9
Breakdowns Won	59	112
% Scrums Won	100%	91%
% Line-Outs Won	100%	80%

Scoring Statistics

O Worcester Warriors

by Situation / by Half

TC:	0	first:	27%
T:	5	second:	73%
P:	6		
DG:	0		

O Northampton Saints

by Situation / by Half

TC:	7	first:	20%
T:	5	second:	80%
P:	3		
DG:	0		

Premiership Table

Team	P	W	D	L	F	A	BP	Pts
5 London Irish	11	6	0	5	218	239	4	28
6 Worcester Warriors	12	6	1	5	220	246	2	28
7 Saracens	11	4	1	6	245	240	6	24

Player of the Match

12 Simon Whatling
Centre

The Warriors edged closer to a place in the quarter-finals of the European Challenge Cup with an emphatic win over Amatori Catania.

The only down side to an entertaining game of rugby was seeing Thinus Deplort limp off with a knee injury.

The Warriors took charge early on and continued to dominate throughout. Worcester opened the scoring with a penalty from the boot of Shane Drahm who then added to his scoring on 7 minutes when Worcester were awarded a penalty for breaking off the scrum. Two minutes later Worcester's Dale Rasmussen scored their first try from a move started by Drahm.

Catania did little to help themselves when Mariano Lorenzetti was shown the yellow card mid way through the first half. This opened the flood gates for Worcester who added another two tries thanks to Johnny Tuamoheloa and Drew Hickey.

Catania went into the break buoyed by a last minute try from Allesandro Pinna, with Barry Irving missing the conversion. Worcester had a ten point advantage. Catania added to their scoring early on in the second half thanks to a Barry Irving penalty, but they never looked likely to make an impact and get back into the game.

Worcester responded with a try from Mark Tucker which Shane Drahm converted. Just short of the hour, Catania were a man short again when Juan Pablo Lagariggue was yellow carded and moments later Jonny Hylton went over the line in the far corner, with once again Drahm the provider.

In the dying moments of the game, Andy Gomarsall got his name on the score board with a try, to secure a comfortable win for the hosts.

Venue:	Sixways	Referee:	Peter Allan
Attendance:	5,062		
Capacity:	9,726		
Occupancy:	52%		

Starting Line-Ups

○ Worcester Warriors		Amatori Catania ○
Delport	15	Comuzzi
Hylton	14	Pinna
Rasmussen	13	Estomba
Whatling	12	Romagnoli
Tucker	11	De Jager (c)
Drahm	10	Irving
Gomarsall	9	Viassiolo
Windo (c)	1	Alvarez Quinones
C Fortey	2	Vidal
Taumoepeau	3	Condorelli
O'Donoghue	4	Privitera
Gillies	5	Lagarrigue
Horstmann	6	Krancz
Tu'amoheloa	7	Lorenzetti
Hickey	8	Tukino

Replacements

	22	Gravagna
Brown	21	Pappalardo
Powell	20	Grasso
Vaili	19	Carbone
Blaze	18	Suaria
MacDonald	17	Vinti
L Fortey	16	Levaggi

Euro Challenge Cup Table

Team	P	W	D	L	F	A	BP	Pts
1 Worcester Warriors	5	4	0	1	150	82	3	19
2 Connacht	5	4	0	1	166	94	2	18
3 Montpellier	5	1	0	4	152	147	4	8
4 Amatori Catania	5	1	0	4	88	233	2	6

Event Line

TC	Try Converted		P	Penalty
T	Try		DG	Drop Goal

Min	Score Progress		Event	Players
2	3	0	P	○ Drahm
8	6	0	P	○ Drahm
9	13	0	TC	○ Rasmussen / Drahm
17	13	0	⇄	○ Brown > Delport
26	13	0	▥	○ Lorenzetti
29	20	0	TC	○ Tu'amoheloa / Drahm
34	25	0	T	○ Hickey
40	25	5	T	○ Pinna
Half time 25-5				
43	25	5	⇄	○ Levaggi > Condorelli
46	25	8	P	○ Irving
47	25	8	⇄	○ Fortey > Taumoepeau
51	32	8	TC	○ Tucker / Drahm
55	32	8	▥	○ Lagarrigue
57	39	8	TC	○ Hylton / Drahm
59	39	8	⇄	○ Vaili > Horstmann
72	39	8	⇄	○ Suaria > Vidal
73	39	8	⇄	○ Vinti > Krancz
73	39	8	⇄	○ Pappalardo > Pinna
73	39	8	⇄	○ Blaze > Gillies
73	39	8	⇄	○ MacDonald > Windo
77	39	8	⇄	○ Powell > Rasmussen
77	39	8	⇄	○ Gravagna > Estomba
77	39	8	⇄	○ Grasso > Viassiolo
77	44	8	T	○ Gomarsall
Full time 44-8				

Scoring Statistics

○ Worcester Warriors

by Situation   by Half

▶ TC:	28	▶ first:	57%
▶ T:	10	▶ second:	43%
▶ P:	6		
▶ DG:	0		

○ Amatori Catania

by Situation   by Half

▶ TC:	0	▶ first:	63%
▶ T:	5	▶ second:	38%
▶ P:	3		
▶ DG:	0		

Montpellier 21
Worcester Warriors 31

Photos courtesy of BBC Herefordshire and Worcestershire

Player of the Match

19 | **Saiosi Vaili**
Back row

A fantastic ten minutes of play at the start of the second half spurred the Warriors on to a four-try victory over Montpellier and a place in the quarter finals of the European Challenge Cup.

The Warriors got the first points on the board with a seven-minute penalty from Shane Drahm and then the fly-half added a further try and conversion after the Montpellier tight-head prop was shown a yellow-card on 18 minutes.

The French team looked dangerous with the ball in hand though, and when Jonny Tuamoheloa was sin-binned on 30 minutes they seized the opportunity. A penalty try after numerous collapsed scrums gave Montpellier the lead for the first time and a second score from full-back David Bortolussi saw Worcester go into the break 18-10 down.

Whatever John Brain and Anthony Eddy said at half-time obviously had the desired effect as Worcester emerged from half-time revitalised. Firstly Jonny Tuamoheloa powered over after a 20 metre line-out, catch and drive before quick-thinking from James Brown saw him seize on a loose ball and put centre Thomas Lombard in under the posts.

Shane Drahm converted both tries for an 18-24 lead. Sadly the last 20 minutes of the game were scrappy and unrewarding as first the Montpellier lock Clement Baiocco and then Worcester wing Mark Tucker were sent to the sin-bin, and the home side resorted to brawling. A penalty brought Montpellier back to within 3 points of Worcester, but excellent work in the line-out by Craig Gillies gave Saiosi Vaili the chance to add try number four and the vital bonus point.

Venue:	Stade Sabathe	Referee:	Carlo Damasco		**Montpellier**
Attendance:	2,500				**Worcester Warriors**
Capacity:	6,500				
Occupancy:	38%				

Starting Line-Ups

Montpellier		Worcester Warriors
Bortolussi	15	Brown
Logerot	14	Trueman
Charrier	13	Rasmussen
Stoica	12	Lombard
Kuzbik	11	Tucker
Aucagne	10	Drahm
Buada	9	Gomarsall
Petit	1	Windo (c)
Grelon	2	C Fortey
Baiocco	3	Taumoepeau
Bert	4	Murphy
Nouchi	5	Gillies
Durand	6	Horstmann
Vallee (c)	7	Tu'amoheloa
Macurdy	8	Hickey

Replacements

Montpellier		Worcester Warriors
Arbo	22	Hylton
Lespinas	21	Whatling
Tomas	20	Powell
Mathieu	19	Vaili
Gorgodze	18	O'Donoghue
Decamps	17	MacDonald
Diomande	16	L Fortey

Event Line

TC	Try Converted		P	Penalty
T	Try		DG	Drop Goal

Min	Score Progress		Event	Players
8	0	3	P	O Drahm
10	3	3	P	O Aucagne
19	3	3	▪	O Baiocco
20	3	10	TC	O Drahm / Drahm
27	6	10	P	O Aucagne
31	6	10	▪	O Tu'amoheloa
37	13	10	TC	O Pen Try / Aucagne
40	18	10	T	O Bortolussi
Half time 18-10				
41	18	10	⇄	O Diomande > Grelon
43	18	17	TC	O Tu'amoheloa / Drahm
51	18	24	TC	O Lombard / Drahm
52	18	24	⇄	O Arbo > Kuzbik
60	18	24	▪	O Nouchi
62	18	24	⇄	O Decamps > Baiocco
62	18	24	⇄	O O'Donoghue > Murphy
63	21	24	P	O Aucagne
66	21	24	⇄	O Mathieu > Macurdy
67	21	24	⇄	O Fortey > Fortey
69	21	24	▪	O Tucker
70	21	24	⇄	O Gorgodze > Nouchi
70	21	24	⇄	O Vaili > Horstmann
78	21	31	TC	O Vaili / Drahm
Full time 21-31				

Euro Challenge Cup Table

Team	P	W	D	L	F	A	BP	Pts
1 Worcester Warriors	6	5	0	1	181	103	4	24
2 Connacht	6	4	0	2	190	122	4	20
3 Amatori Catania	6	2	0	4	116	257	2	10
4 Montpellier	6	1	0	5	173	178	4	8

Scoring Statistics

Montpellier

by Situation	by Half

▶ TC:	7	▶ first:	86%
▶ T:	5	second:	14%
▶ P:	9		
DG:	0		

Worcester Warriors

by Situation	by Half

▶ TC:	28	▶ first:	32%
▶ T:	0	second:	68%
▶ P:	3		
DG:	0		

Bristol Rugby 23
Worcester Warriors 26

Premiership Away Record vs Bristol Rugby					
Played	Won	Drawn	Lost	For	Against
1	**1**	**0**	**0**	**26**	**23**

Warriors French flier Nicolas Le Roux was in the thick of it after just 40 seconds.

Player of the Match

As he leaped to claim the ball in the air, his elbow accidentally caught Bristol centre Brian Lima and knocked him out cold.

Wing Lee Robinson then tore Worcester apart with a piercing run and try through the middle. Warriors responded with brute force, Sanderson leading the charge. They turned to Shane Drahm again and he didn't let anybody down, notching a pair of penalties, to reduce the deficit to a single point.

Drahm figured in Worcester's first try. After Craig Gillies won the line-out, it was Drahm who played in Aisea Havili who touched down under the posts. Drahm's conversion and a penalty from each side saw the teams locked at 13-13 on 50 minutes.

14 | Aisea Havili
Wing

At that point, Worcester won a vital turn-over and Havili sped down the touchline and passed to Thomas Lombard who released number eight Drew Hickey for the score. When the conversion went over, it looked like Warriors might take control, but that all changed when Drahm's kick was charged down and Jason Strange scored.

Dale Rasmussen was then sin-binned for cynically taking out David Lemi as he chased his own chip. Strange kicked the penalty but Drahm levelled the scores with a stunning kick from the right-hand touchline. He then slotted what proved to be the winning penalty.

Venue:	Memorial Stadium	Referee:	Sean Davey - Season 05/06	**Bristol Rugby**
Attendance:	9,058	Matches:	10	**Worcester Warriors**
Capacity:	12,000	Yellow Cards:	11	
Occupancy:	75%	Red Cards:	0	

Starting Line-Ups

○ Bristol Rugby		Worcester Warriors ○
Stortoni	15	Le Roux
Robinson	14	Havili
Lima	13	Rasmussen
Higgitt	12	Lombard
Lemi	11	Tucker
Strange	10	Drahm
Perry	9	Gomarsall
Hilton	1	Windo
Regan	2	Van Niekerk
Crompton	3	Taumoepeau
Budgett	4	Murphy
Llewellyn	5	Gillies
Salter (c)	6	Horstmann
El Abd	7	Sanderson (c)
Lewis	8	Hickey

Replacements

Nicholls	22	Maguire
Denney	21	Whatling
Hayes	20	Powell
Short	19	Harding
Sambucetti	18	O'Donoghue
Nelson	17	L Fortey
Irish	16	Hickie

Event Line

TC	Try Converted		P	Penalty
T	Try		DG	Drop Goal

Min	Score Progress		Event	Players
1	0	0	⇄	○ Denney > Lima
5	7	0	TC	○ Robinson / Strange
9	7	3	P	○ Drahm
17	7	6	P	○ Drahm
23	7	13	TC	○ Havili / Drahm
32	7	13	⇄	○ Hickie > Van Niekerk
40	10	13	P	○ Strange

Half time 10-13

41	10	13	⇄	○ Harding > Sanderson
50	13	13	P	○ Strange
55	13	20	TC	○ Hickey / Drahm
58	20	20	TC	○ Strange / Strange
62	20	20	▪	○ Rasmussen
64	23	20	P	○ Strange
66	23	23	P	○ Drahm
73	23	23	⇄	○ Hayes > Stortoni
73	23	26	P	○ Drahm

Full time 23-26

Match Stats

Tackles	61	95
Missed Tackles	6	6
Ball Carries	101	65
Metres	370	339
Defenders Beaten	5	7
Passes	134	63
Clean Breaks	3	5
Pens Conceded	8	16
Turnovers	16	6
Breakdowns Won	90	47
% Scrums Won	88%	92%
% Line-Outs Won	88%	100%

Scoring Statistics

○ Bristol Rugby			
by Situation		by Half	
▸ TC:	14	▸ first:	43%
▸ T:	0	▸ second:	57%
▸ P:	9		
▸ DG:	0		

○ Worcester Warriors			
by Situation		by Half	
▸ TC:	14	▸ first:	50%
▸ T:	0	▸ second:	50%
▸ P:	12		
▸ DG:	0		

Premiership Table

Team	P	W	D	L	F	A	BP	Pts
4 Gloucester Rugby	12	7	1	4	272	210	5	35
5 Worcester Warriors	13	7	1	5	246	269	2	32
6 London Irish	12	6	0	6	243	267	5	29

Worcester Warriors 33
Sale Sharks 48

Guinness Premiership
11.02.06

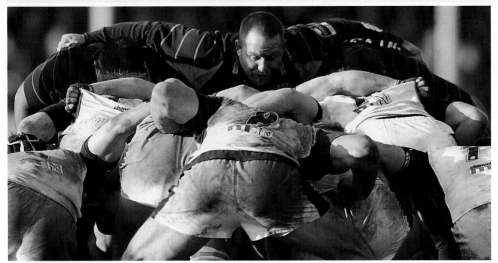

Premiership Home Record vs Sale Sharks					
Played	Won	Drawn	Lost	For	Against
2	**1**	**0**	**1**	**56**	**58**

Worcester played some good rugby during the try-fest and were unlucky to find themselves 17-3 down with just 16 minutes on the clock.

Player of the Match

12 | **Thomas Lombard**
Centre

The north-west side were leading on eight minutes when French fly-half Valentin Courrent kicked a penalty, scored a try and converted in quick succession.

Worcester's first try came in the 24th minute when Shane Drahm broke after a scrum on the Sale 22 and provided Aisea Havili with the scoring pass. Drahm then added to Worcester's points tally by scoring a try himself and kicking the conversion over. Two penalties came from the boot of Drahm just before half-time and Worcester only trailed by four points going into the break.

The Warriors were very much still in the game when they came out for the second half, however the Sharks had other ideas. Sale added two more tries, when England hooker, Andy Titterall latched on to a loose ball and sprinted over the line, then Silio Martens touched down to secure the bonus point.

Worcester refused to lie down when Nicolas Le Roux picked up a long pass and dived down in the corner as the Warriors went in search of a bonus point, much to the delight of another capacity crowd.

Sale's Steve Hanley made it six tries and Worcester were unfortunate not to get something from the game.

Venue:	Sixways	Referee:	Tony Spreadbury - Season 05/06		**Worcester Warriors**
Attendance:	9,726	Matches:	7		**Sale Sharks**
Capacity:	9,726	Yellow Cards:	7		
Occupancy:	100%	Red Cards:	2		

Starting Line-Ups

O Worcester Warriors		Sale Sharks O
Le Roux	15	Robinson (c)
Havili	14	Ripol Fortuny
Rasmussen	13	Taylor
Lombard	12	Todd
Tucker	11	Hanley
Drahm	10	Courrent
Gomarsall	9	Martens
Windo (c)	1	Faure
C Fortey	2	Titterrell
Taumoepeau	3	Turner
Murphy	4	Fernandez Lobbe
Gillies	5	Schofield
Horstmann	6	Jones
Harding	7	Carter
Hickey	8	Chabal

Replacements

Whatling	22	Wakley
Brown	21	Mayor
Powell	20	Wigglesworth
Vaili	19	Bonner-Evans
O'Donoghue	18	Day
Van Niekerk	17	Coutts
L Fortey	16	Stewart

Match Stats

	Worcester	Sale
Tackles	72	137
Missed Tackles	26	25
Ball Carries	158	96
Metres	627	608
Defenders Beaten	25	26
Passes	152	88
Clean Breaks	10	21
Pens Conceded	7	9
Turnovers	12	6
Breakdowns Won	107	56
% Scrums Won	78%	100%
% Line-Outs Won	100%	82%

Premiership Table

Team	P	W	D	L	F	A	BP	Pts
5 London Irish	13	7	0	6	256	276	5	33
6 Worcester Warriors	14	7	1	6	279	317	2	32
7 Newcastle Falcons	13	5	1	7	223	248	4	26

Event Line

TC	Try Converted		P	Penalty
T	Try		DG	Drop Goal

Min	Score Progress		Event	Players
8	0	3	P	O Courrent
10	3	3	P	O Drahm
11	3	10	TC	O Courrent / Courrent
16	3	17	TC	O Schofield / Courrent
18	3	17	⇄	O Vaili > Hickey
21	10	17	TC	O Havili / Drahm
25	10	17	⇄	O Hickey > Vaili
27	10	20	P	O Courrent
29	17	20	TC	O Drahm / Drahm
31	17	27	TC	O Titterrell / Courrent
34	20	27	P	O Drahm
38	23	27	P	O Drahm
Half time 23-27				
42	23	34	TC	O Martens / Courrent
48	23	34	⇄	O Coutts > Faure
49	23	34	⇄	O Van Niekerk > Fortey
52	23	34	⇄	O Bonner-Evans > Carter
54	23	34	⇄	O Stewart > Turner
55	23	41	TC	O Ripol Fortuny / Courrent
58	23	41	⇄	O O'Donoghue > Gillies
60	30	41	TC	O Le Roux / Drahm
63	30	41	⇄	O Mayor > Robinson
65	33	41	P	O Drahm
70	33	48	TC	O Hanley / Courrent
74	33	48	⇄	O Day > Fernandez Lobbe
74	33	48	⇄	O Wigglesworth > Martens
74	33	48	⇄	O Whatling > Lombard
79	33	48	⇄	O Brown > Drahm
79	33	48	⇄	O Vaili > Harding
79	33	48	⇄	O Wakley > Taylor
Full time 33-48				

Scoring Statistics

O Worcester Warriors

by Situation — by Half

▶ TC:	21	▶ first:	70%
▶ T:	0	▶ second:	30%
▶ P:	12		
▶ DG:	0		

O Sale Sharks

by Situation — by Half

▶ TC:	42	▶ first:	56%
▶ T:	0	▶ second:	44%
▶ P:	6		
▶ DG:	0		

Leicester Tigers 28
Worcester Warriors 22

Premiership Away Record vs Leicester Tigers					
Played	Won	Drawn	Lost	For	Against
2	**0**	**0**	**2**	**29**	**78**

Shane Drahm opened the scoring with a penalty on six minutes, easing the visitors into the lead.

Player of the Match

10 | **Shane Drahm**
Outside half

However, the Tigers replied with a well worked try from Ollie Smith. Andy Goode added a conversion and penalty and the hosts were 10-3 up on 20 minutes. Worcester responded in an impressive manner and soon found themselves ahead again. Gavin Hickie, who was enjoying his Premiership debut started the move which lead to Mark Tucker passing the ball out to Dale Rasmussen who went over in the corner. A penalty from Andy Goode just before half-time drew the two teams level with Worcester proving a real match for the East Midlands side.

The Tigers started the second half at a higher tempo and after a powering run by Leicester's Tuilagi lead to a try it looked like it was going to be all one way traffic. With Mark Tucker in the sin bin, Worcester still pressed forward and showed great resource frustrating the hosts. Drahm kicked a stunning penalty from inside his own half and Worcester went ahead again. This was short lived as Matt Cornwell scored what proved to be the winning try on 58 minutes with Andy Goode adding the conversion.

Worcester refused to lie down and were unlucky when the decision went against them as they moved forward with rolling mauls only to be blown up by David Rose for stopping momentarily. Worcester certainly deserved the losing bonus point which may prove a crucial one at the end of the season.

Venue:	Welford Road	Referee:	David Rose - Season 05/06		**Leicester Tigers**
Attendance:	16,815	Matches:	7		**Worcester Warriors**
Capacity:	16,815	Yellow Cards:	14		
Occupancy:	100%	Red Cards:	0		

Starting Line-Ups

○ Leicester Tigers		Worcester Warriors ○
Murphy	15	Le Roux
Tuilagi	14	Trueman
Cornwell	13	Rasmussen
Smith	12	Lombard
Varndell	11	Tucker
Goode	10	Drahm
Ellis	9	Gomarsall
Holford	1	Windo (c)
Chuter	2	Hickie
White	3	Taumoepeau
Hamilton	4	Murphy
Cullen	5	Gillies
Moody	6	Horstmann
Jennings	7	Harding
Corry (c)	8	Hickey

Replacements

Dodge	22	Whatling
Humphreys	21	Hylton
Bemand	20	Powell
Johnson	19	Vaili
Deacon	18	O'Donoghue
Morris	17	L Fortey
Taukafa	16	Van Niekerk

Match Stats

Tackles	89	85
Missed Tackles	10	21
Ball Carries	91	72
Metres	405	286
Defenders Beaten	18	8
Passes	116	63
Clean Breaks	8	6
Pens Conceded	13	13
Turnovers	7	8
Breakdowns Won	70	66
% Scrums Won	100%	100%
% Line-Outs Won	84%	82%

Premiership Table

Team	P	W	D	L	F	A	BP	Pts
5 London Irish	14	7	0	7	262	285	6	34
6 Worcester Warriors	15	7	1	7	301	345	3	33
7 Newcastle Falcons	14	6	1	7	232	254	4	30

Event Line

TC	Try Converted		P	Penalty
T	Try		DG	Drop Goal

Min	Score Progress		Event	Players
6	0	3	P	○ Drahm
10	7	3	TC	○ Smith / Goode
22	10	3	P	○ Goode
24	10	6	P	○ Drahm
32	13	6	P	○ Goode
33	13	9	P	○ Drahm
36	13	16	TC	○ Rasmussen / Drahm
39	16	16	P	○ Goode
Half time 16-16				
44	16	16	◼	○ Tucker
46	21	16	T	○ Tuilagi
50	21	16	⇄	○ Deacon > Hamilton
50	21	16	⇄	○ Vaili > Hickey
50	21	19	P	○ Drahm
54	21	19	⇄	○ Morris > Holford
54	21	22	P	○ Drahm
58	21	22	⇄	○ Powell > Gomarsall
58	21	22	⇄	○ Van Niekerk > Hickie
58	28	22	TC	○ Cornwell / Goode
60	28	22	⇄	○ Bemand > Ellis
68	28	22	⇄	○ Taukafa > Chuter
68	28	22	⇄	○ Whatling > Tucker
76	28	22	⇄	○ Hickie > Van Niekerk
Full time 28-22				

Scoring Statistics

○ Leicester Tigers

by Situation | by Half

▶ TC:	14	▶ first:	57%
▶ T:	5	▶ second:	43%
▶ P:	9		
▶ DG:	0		

○ Worcester Warriors

by Situation | by Half

▶ TC:	7	▶ first:	73%
▶ T:	0	▶ second:	27%
▶ P:	15		
▶ DG:	0		

Leeds Tykes 21
Worcester Warriors 15

Premiership Away Record vs Leeds Tykes					
Played	Won	Drawn	Lost	For	Against
2	**0**	**0**	**2**	**34**	**45**

Player of the Match

4 | **Phil Murphy**
Lock

Worcester Warriors travelled to Headingley to face relegation threatened Leeds.

Youngster Simon Whatling, who came on to replace an injured Shane Drahm in the dying minutes of the game kicked a superb penalty to ensure Worcester went home with a losing bonus point.

Leeds came out looking the more positive side and Worcester found themselves behind after just three minutes thanks to a try scored by Chris Bell. Fortunately for the Warriors Leeds' kicker Roland De Marigny missed the conversion.

Worcester were placed under heavy pressure from the team desperately trying to keep their heads above water. Leeds added their second try of the evening when prop Rayno Gerber unloaded the ball to De Marigny who went over the line. De Marigny then converted his own try and Worcester found themselves trailing 15 – 3 before Drahm added a penalty to ease themselves back into the game.

Worcester had an opportunity to get back into the game early on in the second half and thanks to a drop goal by Shane Drahm. Worcester reduced the deficit but Leeds responded with a penalty from De Marigny.

The Warriors subjected the Leeds defence to a period of pressure and Shane Drahm racked up another three points, his opposite kicker matched the scoring with the third penalty of the game.

Venue:	Headingley Carnegie	Referee:	Martin Fox - Season 05/06		**Leeds Tykes**
Attendance:	3,718	Matches:	7		**Worcester Warriors**
Capacity:	24,000	Yellow Cards:	8		
Occupancy:	15%	Red Cards:	0		

Starting Line-Ups

O Leeds Tykes		Worcester Warriors O
Biggs	15	Delport
Snyman	14	Havili
Bell	13	Rasmussen
Craig	12	Lombard
Rees	11	Tucker
De Marigny	10	Drahm
Marshall	9	Powell
Lensing	1	Windo (c)
Bulloch	2	C Fortey
Gerber	3	Taumoepeau
Hooper (c)	4	Murphy
Palmer	5	Gillies
Dunbar	6	Horstmann
Parks	7	Harding
Thomas	8	Hickey

Replacements

Blackett	22	Whatling
Jones	21	Gomarsall
McMillan	20	Trueman
Hyde	19	Vaili
Murphy	18	O'Donoghue
Rawlinson	17	L Fortey
Shelley	16	MacDonald

Match Stats

Tackles	78	90
Missed Tackles	7	9
Ball Carries	102	56
Metres	472	268
Defenders Beaten	7	5
Passes	95	76
Clean Breaks	8	2
Pens Conceded	11	18
Turnovers	14	10
Breakdowns Won	57	52
% Scrums Won	90%	79%
% Line-Outs Won	67%	87%

Premiership Table

Team	P	W	D	L	F	A	BP	Pts
6 Newcastle Falcons	16	7	1	8	265	283	5	35
7 Worcester Warriors	16	7	1	8	316	366	4	34
8 Northampton Saints	15	6	1	8	312	328	6	32

Event Line

TC	Try Converted		P	Penalty
T	Try		DG	Drop Goal

Min	Score Progress		Event	Players
4	5	0	T	O Bell
19	8	0	P	O De Marigny
22	8	3	P	O Drahm
25	15	3	TC	O De Marigny / De Marigny
34	15	6	P	O Drahm
36	15	6	⇄	O Shelley > Gerber
Half time 15-6				
41	15	6	⇄	O Gomarsall > Powell
54	15	6	⇄	O Hyde > Dunbar
55	15	9	DG	O Drahm
58	15	9	⇄	O Gerber > Lensing
58	18	9	P	O De Marigny
59	18	9	⇄	O Jones > Craig
62	18	9	⇄	O Vaili > Horstmann
68	18	9	⇄	O Fortey > Taumoepeau
68	18	12	P	O Drahm
69	18	12	⇄	O Rawlinson > Bulloch
69	18	12	⇄	O O'Donoghue > Murphy
70	18	12	⇄	O Dunbar > Parks
75	18	12	■	O Vaili
75	18	12	⇄	O Parks > Dunbar
78	18	12	⇄	O Whatling > Drahm
80	21	12	P	O De Marigny
81	21	15	P	O Whatling
Full time 21-15				

Scoring Statistics

O Leeds Tykes

by Situation   by Half

▶ TC:	7	▶ first:	71%
▶ T:	5	second:	29%
▶ P:	9		
DG:	0		

O Worcester Warriors

by Situation   by Half

▶ TC:	0	▶ first:	40%
▶ T:	0	second:	60%
▶ P:	12		
▶ DG:	3		

Worcester Warriors 37
London Wasps 8

Premiership Home Record vs London Wasps					
Played	Won	Drawn	Lost	For	Against
2	**2**	**0**	**0**	**64**	**32**

Worcester Warriors demolished the Premiership Champions at Sixways in a memorable match.

Player of the Match

10 | **Shane Drahm**
Outside half

Shane Drahm was on song but it was a superb team effort with Tony Windo leading from the front, Craig Gillies and Mark Tucker putting in impressive performances.

Worcester made a dream start and a penalty from Shane Drahm eased them into the lead. The Warriors then carved open the Wasps defence with a move started by Mark Tucker who passed the ball to Le Roux, who offloaded it to speedster Havili to make it 8-0 to the hosts. Drahm then kicked a tricky conversion.

Wasps replied with a Jeremy Staunton penalty, reducing the points deficit and could have got back into the game on 23 minutes but the penalty fell short. Drahm then punctured their momentum with a sumptuous 55-metre penalty. Drahm scored another penalty midway through the half and, although Rees hit back for the visitors with a touchdown, the Warriors were awarded a penalty try just before half-time to leave Worcester 23-8 up at the break.

Three minutes into the second half Worcester's pack pushed Wasps back onto their own line and Phil Murphy touched down the third try. Drahm added the conversion with precision and style and Wasps were left shell shocked finding themselves trailing 30-8. Worcester were in pole position and Sixways erupted when Thinus Delport scored their fourth try of the evening which ensured the bonus point. Drahm converted the try and Wasps were made to leave empty handed.

Venue:	Sixways	Referee:	Sean Davey - Season 05/06		Worcester Warriors
Attendance:	9,726	Matches:	13		London Wasps
Capacity:	9,726	Yellow Cards:	14		
Occupancy:	100%	Red Cards:	0		

Starting Line-Ups

Worcester Warriors		London Wasps
Le Roux	15	Van Gisbergen
Havili	14	Sackey
Rasmussen	13	Waters
Lombard	12	Abbott
Tucker	11	Erinle
Drahm	10	Staunton
Gomarsall	9	Honeyben
Windo (c)	1	McKenzie
C Fortey	2	Ward
Taumoepeau	3	J Dawson
Murphy	4	Skivington
Gillies	5	Birkett
Horstmann	6	Leo
Harding	7	Rees
Hickey	8	Lock (c)

Replacements

Delport	22	Hoadley
Whatling	21	Brooks
Powell	20	Laird
Vaili	19	Chamberlain
O'Donoghue	18	Corker
L Fortey	17	Va'a
Hickie	16	Barrett

Match Stats

Tackles	98		73
Missed Tackles	12		7
Ball Carries	75		105
Metres	282		405
Defenders Beaten	7		13
Passes	88		113
Clean Breaks	5		9
Pens Conceded	17		12
Turnovers	12		17
Breakdowns Won	59		77
% Scrums Won	86%		86%
% Line-Outs Won	93%		67%

Event Line

TC	Try Converted		P	Penalty
T	Try		DG	Drop Goal

Min	Score Progress		Event	Players
5	3	0	P	O Drahm
8	10	0	TC	O Havili / Drahm
12	10	0	▪	O Ward
15	10	0	⇄	O Barrett > Rees
17	10	3	P	O Staunton
22	10	3	⇄	O Rees > Barrett
25	13	3	P	O Drahm
27	16	3	P	O Drahm
30	16	8	T	O Rees
40	23	8	TC	O Pen Try / Drahm
Half time 23-8				
43	30	8	TC	O Murphy / Drahm
54	30	8	⇄	O Brooks > Staunton
55	30	8	⇄	O Hickie > Fortey
55	30	8	⇄	O Hoadley > Waters
56	30	8	⇄	O Va'a > McKenzie
62	30	8	⇄	O Vaili > Horstmann
63	30	8	⇄	O Barrett > Ward
68	30	8	▪	O Sackey
69	30	8	⇄	O O'Donoghue > Murphy
69	30	8	⇄	O Fortey > Taumoepeau
70	30	8	⇄	O Corker > Birkett
70	30	8	⇄	O Delport > Tucker
73	30	8	⇄	O Laird > Erinle
73	30	8	⇄	O Chamberlain > Rees
77	37	8	TC	O Delport / Drahm
80	37	8	⇄	O Powell > Gomarsall
Full time 37-8				

Scoring Statistics

O Worcester Warriors

by Situation   by Half

TC:	28	first:	62%
T:	0	second:	38%
P:	9		
DG:	0		

O London Wasps

by Situation   by Half

TC:	0	first:	100%
T:	5	second:	0%
P:	3		
DG:	0		

Premiership Table

Team	P	W	D	L	F	A	BP	Pts
5 London Irish	16	9	0	7	325	316	8	44
6 Worcester Warriors	17	8	1	8	353	374	5	39
7 Newcastle Falcons	16	7	1	8	265	283	5	35

Saracens 29
Worcester Warriors 15

Premiership Away Record vs Saracens					
Played	Won	Drawn	Lost	For	Against
2	**0**	**0**	**2**	**25**	**45**

Saracens meant business from the outset and when Nicolas Le Roux failed to deal with Ben Johnston's kick, Saracens' Tevita Vaikona touched down from the resulting line-out.

Player of the Match

7 | **Pat Sanderson**
Back row

Glen Jackson missed the conversion and booted a penalty wide. Shane Drahm also failed to score from the boot missing a long range penalty in the opening ten minutes. Saracens were awarded a penalty following Pat Sanderson's encounter with Simon Raiwalui, this gave the hosts an eight point cushion.

Worcester, boosted by the return of their skipper showed signs of a comeback with Drahm's superb penalty after half an hour from wide on the left and 55 metres out. They defended well and pressurised the Saracens defence but failed to take their chances and were punished just on half-time when Mark Bartholomeusz dived over. Jackson converted and Saracens went into the break with a 15-3 lead.

The Warriors came out in the second half looking more lively. But after spending over 10 minutes camped inside their 22 they failed to break down the hosts' defence and were punished when the Londoners broke away and racked up two tries in seven minutes.

Despite being 29-3 down, Worcester ended the match the stronger of the two sides as Saracens took their foot off the gas. Two late tries from Siaosi Vaili and Aisea Havili were a consolation for the Warriors who were forced to go home empty handed.

Venue:	Vicarage Road	Referee:	Dave Pearson - Season 05/06	
Attendance:	6,011	Matches:	11	
Capacity:	20,000	Yellow Cards:	23	
Occupancy:	30%	Red Cards:	2	

Saracens
Worcester Warriors

Starting Line-Ups

○ Saracens		Worcester Warriors ○
Bartholomeusz	15	Le Roux
Vaikona	14	Havili
Sorrell	13	Rasmussen
Johnston	12	Whatling
Scarbrough	11	Delport
Jackson	10	Drahm
Bracken	9	Gomarsall
Yates	1	Windo
Byrne	2	C Fortey
Visagie	3	Taumoepeau
Raiwalui	4	Murphy
Ryder	5	Gillies
Chesney	6	Horstmann
Randell	7	Sanderson (c)
Vyvyan (c)	8	Hickey

Replacements

Harris	22	Trueman
Bailey	21	Brown
Rauluni	20	Powell
Barrell	19	Vaili
Broster	18	O'Donoghue
Lloyd	17	L Fortey
Cairns	16	Hickie

Match Stats

Tackles	151	61
Missed Tackles	9	21
Ball Carries	67	155
Metres	414	433
Defenders Beaten	14	7
Passes	92	133
Clean Breaks	14	6
Pens Conceded	15	9
Turnovers	12	21
Breakdowns Won	46	110
% Scrums Won	83%	100%
% Line-Outs Won	81%	96%

Event Line

TC	Try Converted	P	Penalty
T	Try	DG	Drop Goal

Min	Score Progress	Event	Players
3	5	0	T	○ Vaikona
11	8	0	P	○ Jackson
29	8	3	P	○ Drahm
37	15	3	TC	○ Bartholomeusz / Jackson
Half time 15-3			
41	15	3	⇄	○ Rauluni > Bracken
50	22	3	TC	○ Rauluni / Jackson
51	22	3	⇄	○ Trueman > Le Roux
54	22	3	⇄	○ Hickie > Fortey
58	29	3	TC	○ Scarbrough / Jackson
60	29	3	⇄	○ Cairns > Byrne
62	29	3	⇄	○ Barrell > Raiwalui
62	29	3	⇄	○ Vaili > Hickey
64	29	3	⇄	○ Raiwalui > Ryder
66	29	3	⇄	○ Powell > Gomarsall
66	29	3	⇄	○ Fortey > Taumoepeau
66	29	3	⇄	○ Lloyd > Yates
68	29	3	⇄	○ Broster > Visagie
69	29	3	⇄	○ Ryder > Raiwalui
70	29	3	⇄	○ O'Donoghue > Murphy
70	29	3	⇄	○ Harris > Johnston
72	29	3	▪	○ Scarbrough
77	29	3	⇄	○ Bailey > Jackson
78	29	8	T	○ Vaili
80	29	15	TC	○ Havili / Drahm
Full time 29-15			

Scoring Statistics

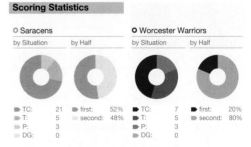

○ Saracens				
by Situation		by Half		
▪ TC:	21	▪ first:	52%	
▪ T:	5	▪ second:	48%	
▪ P:	3			
▪ DG:	0			

○ Worcester Warriors				
by Situation		by Half		
▪ TC:	7	▪ first:	20%	
▪ T:	5	▪ second:	80%	
▪ P:	3			
▪ DG:	0			

Premiership Table

Team	P	W	D	L	F	A	BP	Pts
6 Northampton Saints	18	8	1	9	368	391	7	41
7 Worcester Warriors	18	8	1	9	368	403	5	39
8 Saracens	18	6	1	11	373	415	11	37

Player of the Match

14 | **Aisea Havili**
Wing

Northampton were first to register with a try by Paul Tupai on 13 minutes, but Worcester then dominated possession for most of the first half.

Thomas Lombard touched down under the posts 14 minutes later. Shane Drahm added the conversion. Reihana regained the lead for the Saints on 31 minutes before a sublime series of moves from Worcester saw Havili touch down for the first of his three tries. Kai Horstmann secured possession for Worcester at the re-start and put fellow back-row forward Siaosi Vaili into space before quick, flat passing down the back-line gave right wing Havili a chance to accelerate past the Northampton defence. Drahm then missed the conversion and Worcester's lead proved to be short-lived as the Saints' full-back Bruce Reihana immediately followed up with a converted try of his own from the re-start. But the Warriors struck back once more with a second Havili try to take a 15-17 half-time lead.

The home side started the second half strongly as pressure on Worcester's line saw Chris Fortey sent to the sin-bin and gave Paul Tupai his second score of the afternoon. Despite being down to fourteen men, Worcester's confidence in their own ability was riding high and Drahm regained them the lead. A grubber kick through from the former Northampton fly-half landed sweetly for fellow centre Dale Rasmussen to run in under the posts. Drahm then slotted through the conversion to give Worcester a four point lead over his old club. Drahm added a penalty to stretch the lead before replacement prop Mike Macdonald stole the ball on the Warriors line and released Aisea Havili for Worcester's fifth try and his hat-trick score.

Northampton refused to give up the chance of a Heineken Cup spot next season. Worcester's lead was reduced as Darren Fox went over for the home side's fourth try in injury time and, despite a yellow-card for Johnny Taumoheloa on 48 minutes, Worcester hung on to gain themselves a place in the final four.

Attendance: 9,531
Capacity: 13,591
Occupancy: 70%

Northampton Saints
Worcester Warriors

Starting Line-Ups

○ Northampton Saints		Worcester Warriors ○
Reihana (c)	15	Delport
Lamont	14	Havili
Clarke	13	Rasmussen
Quinlan	12	Lombard
Cohen	11	Trueman
Spencer	10	Drahm
Robinson	9	Powell
Smith	1	Windo
Thompson (c)	2	Van Niekerk
Barnard	3	Taumoepeau
Dm Browne	4	Murphy
Gerard	5	Gillies
Tupai	6	Vaili
Harding	7	Sanderson (c)
Soden	8	Horstmann

Replacements

Rudd	22	Whatling
Kydd	21	Gomarsall
Howard	20	Tu'amoheloa
Fox	19	Blaze
Lord	18	L Fortey
Budgen	17	C Fortey
Richmond	16	MacDonald

Event Line

TC	Try Converted		P	Penalty
T	Try		DG	Drop Goal

Min	Score Progress		Event	Players
14	5	0	T	○ Tupai
28	5	7	TC	○ Lombard / Lombard
32	8	7	P	○ Reihana
33	8	12	T	○ Havili
35	15	12	TC	○ Reihana / Reihana
39	15	17	T	○ Havili
Half time 15-17				
41	15	17	⇄	○ Budgen > Barnard
41	15	17	⇄	○ Fortey > Van Niekerk
48	15	17	■	○ Fortey
48	20	17	T	○ Tupai
53	20	24	TC	○ Rasmussen / Drahm
54	20	24	⇄	○ Fox > Harding
55	20	24	⇄	○ Fortey > Vaili
56	20	24	⇄	○ Lord > Gerard
60	20	24	⇄	○ Vaili > Fortey
61	20	24	⇄	○ MacDonald > Windo
66	20	27	P	○ Drahm
73	20	27	⇄	○ Barnard > Smith
74	20	27	⇄	○ Tu'amoheloa > Vaili
74	20	27	⇄	○ Blaze > Murphy
77	20	34	TC	○ Havili / Drahm
78	20	34	⇄	○ Rudd > Cohen
78	20	34	⇄	○ Kydd > Soden
80	25	34	T	○ Fox
86	25	34	■	○ Tu'amoheloa
Full time 25-34				

Scoring Statistics

○ Northampton Saints			○ Worcester Warriors		
by Situation	by Half		by Situation	by Half	
▶ TC:	7	▶ first: 60%	▶ TC:	21	▶ first: 50%
▶ T:	15	second: 40%	▶ T:	10	second: 50%
▶ P:	3		▶ P:	3	
DG:	0		▶ DG:	0	

Premiership Home Record vs London Irish					
Played	Won	Drawn	Lost	For	Against
2	**1**	**0**	**1**	**26**	**18**

Player of the Match

13 | Dale Rasmussen
Centre/Wing

In the third minute Irish piled on the pressure and the Riki Flutey tormented Worcester's defence and his move gained its reward when Kieran Roche powered over the line in the corner.

Flutey missed the conversion much to the delight of the Warriors supporters and missed the chance to go further ahead when the fly-half sent the penalty wide. It wasn't looking good for the hosts but they responded in a positive manner and Pat Sanderson showed his leadership skills, breaking out from inside his own half and prompting some impressive passing which resulted in Thinus Delport ploughing through the Irish defence for an equalising try. Shane Drahm added the conversion allowing the home side to nudge into the lead. However not long after Thinus Delport found himself in the sin-bin for impeding Delon Armitage.

Worcester continued to pile pressure on Irish at the line-out but a penalty from Drahm clattered into the post on a very blustery afternoon at Sixways. The visitors pulled themselves back into the lead just before half-time when Flutey fed Shane Geraghty for the final try of the game. The Exiles went into break with a narrow lead.

The second half was a scrappy encounter and the referee's decisions didn't seem to help. Drahm closed in on Irish by adding a penalty, failing to grab a late win when his penalty sailed agonisingly wide. Worcester had had to play the final 25 minutes without Thinus Delport, who was sent off after receiving a yellow card for a scuffle with Delon Armitage.

Venue:	Sixways	Referee:	Wayne Barnes - Season 05/06		**Worcester Warriors**
Attendance:	9,726	Matches:	8		**London Irish**
Capacity:	9,726	Yellow Cards:	12		
Occupancy:	100%	Red Cards:	2		

Starting Line-Ups

O Worcester Warriors		London Irish O
Delport	15	Armitage
Havili	14	Ojo
Rasmussen	13	Franze
Lombard	12	Geraghty
Tucker	11	Bishop
Drahm	10	Flutey
Powell	9	Hodgson
Windo	1	Hatley
Van Niekerk	2	Russell
Taumoepeau	3	Skuse
Murphy	4	Casey (c)
Gillies	5	Roche
Vaili	6	Danaher
Sanderson (c)	7	Magne
Horstmann	8	Murphy

Replacements

Trueman	22	Penney
Gomarsall	21	Edwards
Whatling	20	Leguizamon
Harding	19	Dawson
Blaze	18	Strudwick
MacDonald	17	Paice
Hickie	16	Rautenbach

Event Line

TC	Try Converted			P	Penalty
T	Try			DG	Drop Goal

Min	Score Progress		Event	Players
3	0	5	T	O Roche
10	7	5	TC	O Delport / Drahm
15	7	5	▪	O Delport
27	7	5	⇄	O MacDonald > Taumoepeau
27	7	5	⇄	O Hickie > Van Niekerk
37	7	12	TC	O Geraghty / Flutey
Half time 7-12				
41	7	12	⇄	O Rautenbach > Skuse
41	7	12	⇄	O Leguizamon > Murphy
41	7	12	⇄	O Taumoepeau > Windo
48	7	12	⇄	O Paice > Russell
52	7	12	⇄	O Harding > Taumoepeau
53	7	12	⇄	O Dawson > Hatley
54	7	12	⇄	O Trueman > Tucker
55	7	12	▪	O Flutey
55	7	12	▪	O Delport
55	7	12	▪	O Delport
60	7	12	⇄	O Strudwick > Leguizamon
63	10	12	P	O Drahm
68	10	12	⇄	O Edwards > Hodgson
72	10	12	⇄	O Blaze > Vaili
72	10	12	⇄	O Gomarsall > Powell
Full time 10-12				

Match Stats

	Worcester	London Irish
Tackles	83	112
Missed Tackles	19	20
Ball Carries	117	112
Metres	393	452
Defenders Beaten	18	20
Passes	103	155
Clean Breaks	10	13
Pens Conceded	9	8
Turnovers	10	20
Breakdowns Won	82	62
% Scrums Won	92%	100%
% Line-Outs Won	83%	87%

Scoring Statistics

O Worcester Warriors

by Situation		by Half	
TC:	7	first:	70%
T:	0	second:	30%
P:	3		
DG:	0		

O London Irish

by Situation		by Half	
TC:	7	first:	100%
T:	5	second:	0%
P:	0		
DG:	0		

Premiership Table

Team	P	W	D	L	F	A	BP	Pts
7 Saracens	19	7	1	11	390	428	11	41
8 Worcester Warriors	19	8	1	10	378	415	6	40
9 Bath Rugby	19	7	1	11	373	418	7	37

Gloucester Rugby 27
Worcester Warriors 16

Premiership Away Record vs Gloucester Rugby					
Played	Won	Drawn	Lost	For	Against
2	**0**	**0**	**2**	**32**	**55**

The game started at a pace when Gloucester's Anthony Allen found a gap and started a move which resulted in Olly Morgan crossing the line.

Player of the Match

13 | **Dale Rasmussen**
Centre/Wing

Luckily for the Warriors, referee Dave Rose had seen a forward pass and the try didn't stand. Worcester replied by pressurising on the hosts, winning a penalty which Shane Drahm booted over from halfway. Drahm and Ryan Lamb then exchanged some punches and were sin-binned. Gloucester were awarded a penalty and Mike Tindall saw his simple 15 metre shot sail through the posts.

Gloucester finally penetrated the Worcester defence when a run down the right by Buxton took him to the corner. He passed to James Simpson-Daniel who managed to scramble it over. Ryan Lamb, back from the bin just before the break, extended Gloucester's lead a few minutes into the second half with a penalty from 30 metres. Drahm kicked a simple penalty under the posts. The Warriors began fighting back and another mistake from the home side brought Worcester to within five points at 14-9.

The introduction of Andy Gomarsall appeared at first to have swung the match in Worcester's favour and he dived over. Worcester were unable to protect their lead as Lamb scored a penalty and then with just a few minutes left on the clock, a sweeping move across the back line saw Mike Tindall put Mark Foster in on the right. Two minutes into injury time Foster got his second.

Venue:	Kingsholm		Referee:	David Rose - Season 05/06
Attendance:	12,500		Matches:	11
Capacity:	13,000		Yellow Cards:	16
Occupancy:	96%		Red Cards:	0

Gloucester Rugby
Worcester Warriors

Starting Line-Ups

○ Gloucester Rugby		Worcester Warriors ○
Morgan	15	Delport
Simpson-Daniel	14	Oduoza
Tindall	13	Rasmussen
Allen	12	Lombard
Foster	11	Trueman
Lamb	10	Drahm
Richards	9	Powell
Collazo	1	Windo
Davies	2	C Fortey
Forster	3	Taumoepeau
Eustace	4	Murphy
Brown	5	O'Donoghue
Buxton (c)	6	Sanderson (c)
Hazell	7	Harding
Forrester	8	Horstmann

Replacements

Bailey	22	Whatling
Mercier	21	Gomarsall
Thomas	20	Vaili
Narraway	19	L Fortey
Pendlebury	18	Blaze
Sigley	17	MacDonald
Elloway	16	Hickie

Match Stats

Tackles	117	85
Missed Tackles	5	16
Ball Carries	83	91
Metres	515	272
Defenders Beaten	11	3
Passes	125	103
Clean Breaks	8	2
Pens Conceded	10	10
Turnovers	12	13
Breakdowns Won	58	81
% Scrums Won	78%	88%
% Line-Outs Won	85%	81%

Premiership Table

Team	P	W	D	L	F	A	BP	Pts
9 Bristol Rugby	20	8	1	11	374	394	6	40
10 Worcester Warriors	20	8	1	11	394	442	6	40
11 Newcastle Falcons	19	7	1	11	303	358	6	36

Event Line

TC	Try Converted		P	Penalty
T	Try		DG	Drop Goal

Min	Score Progress	Event	Players
26	0 — 3	P	○ Drahm
30	0 — 3	■	○ Lamb
30	0 — 3	■	○ Drahm
31	3 — 3	P	○ Tindall
36	6 — 3	P	○ Tindall
38	11 — 3	T	○ Simpson-Daniel
	Half time 11-3		
48	14 — 3	P	○ Lamb
54	14 — 3	⇄	○ Whatling > Delport
55	14 — 3	⇄	○ Pendlebury > Eustace
55	14 — 3	⇄	○ Mercier > Morgan
55	14 — 6	P	○ Drahm
56	14 — 6	⇄	○ Gomarsall > Powell
60	14 — 6	⇄	○ Narraway > Buxton
60	14 — 6	⇄	○ Hickie > Fortey
60	14 — 9	P	○ Drahm
64	14 — 9	⇄	○ Sigley > Collazo
64	14 — 16	TC	○ Gomarsall / Drahm
65	14 — 16	⇄	○ Vaili > Harding
67	14 — 16	⇄	○ MacDonald > Windo
67	17 — 16	P	○ Lamb
73	22 — 16	T	○ Foster
76	22 — 16	⇄	○ Blaze > Drahm
77	22 — 16	⇄	○ Fortey > Taumoepeau
79	27 — 16	T	○ Foster
	Full time 27-16		

Scoring Statistics

○ Gloucester Rugby		○ Worcester Warriors	
by Situation	by Half	by Situation	by Half

Gloucester Rugby
- TC: 0
- T: 15
- P: 12
- DG: 0
- first: 41%
- second: 59%

Worcester Warriors
- TC: 7
- T: 0
- P: 9
- DG: 0
- first: 19%
- second: 81%

Gloucester Rugby 31
Worcester Warriors 23

Player of the Match

8 | **Kai Horstmann**
| Back row

Chris Fortey set the tone for the Warriors when he ploughed into Mefin Davies, his opposite number, at the first ruck and the visitors started the game on the front foot.

Phil Murphy charged into the Gloucester 22 on three minutes but the move came to an end when Shane Drahm knocked on. It was Gloucester who opened the scoring with a Ryan Lamb penalty after seven minutes but Worcester hit straight back with a three-pointer from Drahm. The Warriors continued to enjoy the better of both possession and territory but were punished twice for turning the ball over by a Gloucester side who was impressive on the counter attack.

On 14 minutes, a break from Ryan Lamb led to James Simpson-Daniel speeding over the right-hand corner, and eight minutes later Allen collected a pass from Lamb, cut inside Dale Rasmussen to score under the posts. Lamb added the conversion to put Gloucester in the driving seat at 15-3. But Worcester fought back superbly. After winning a ten-metre scrum, Matt Powell found Drahm and the Australian side-stepped his way under the posts. Worcester's leading points scorer was also at the heart of the move that led to Pat Sanderson muscling his way over in first-half injury time.

Leading 17-15 at the break, Worcester made the dream start to the second half when Drahm landed a drop goal and a penalty to extend their lead to eight points. However the Cherry & Whites came storming back. Ryan Lamb kicked his second penalty on 56 minutes, saw Ludovic Mercier land another from long-range ten minutes later and then created the match-clinching score for Mark Foster with a sailing crossfield kick. Ryan Lamb then landed an 80th minute penalty in front of the posts.

Attendance: 8,609
Capacity: 13,000
Occupancy: 66%

Starting Line-Ups

○ Gloucester Rugby		Worcester Warriors ○
Morgan	15	Le Roux
Simpson-Daniel	14	Oduoza
Tindall	13	Rasmussen
Allen	12	Lombard
Foster	11	Trueman
Lamb	10	Drahm
Richards	9	Powell
Collazo	1	Windo
Davies	2	C Fortey
Powell	3	Taumoepeau
Eustace	4	Murphy
Brown	5	Gillies
Buxton (c)	6	Sanderson (c)
Hazell	7	Harding
Forrester	8	Horstmann

Replacements

Bailey	22	Whatling
Mercier	21	Brown
Thomas	20	Runciman
Narraway	19	Vaili
Pendlebury	18	O'Donoghue
Forster	17	MacDonald
Elloway	16	L Fortey

Event Line

TC	Try Converted		P	Penalty
T	Try		DG	Drop Goal

Min	Score Progress		Event	Players
7	3	0	P	○ Lamb
8	3	3	P	○ Drahm
14	8	3	T	○ Simpson-Daniel
18	8	3	⇄	○ Bailey > Foster
20	8	3	⇄	○ Foster > Bailey
22	15	3	TC	○ Allen / Lamb
30	15	10	TC	○ Drahm / Drahm
39	15	10	⇄	○ Fortey > Taumoepeau
40	15	17	TC	○ Sanderson / Drahm
Half time 15-17				
41	15	17	⇄	○ Taumoepeau > Fortey
41	15	17	⇄	○ Narraway > Buxton
41	15	17	⇄	○ Bailey > Simpson-Daniel
41	15	17	⇄	○ Mercier > Morgan
42	15	20	DG	○ Drahm
51	15	23	P	○ Drahm
56	18	23	P	○ Lamb
65	18	23	⇄	○ Pendlebury > Hazell
66	18	23	⇄	○ Forster > Powell
66	21	23	P	○ Mercier
68	21	23	⇄	○ Vaili > Harding
69	21	23	⇄	○ Hazell > Pendlebury
70	21	23	⇄	○ Pendlebury > Eustace
73	28	23	TC	○ Foster / Lamb
74	28	23	⇄	○ O'Donoghue > Murphy
79	31	23	P	○ Lamb
80	31	23	⇄	○ Fortey > Taumoepeau
Full time 31-23				

Scoring Statistics

○ Gloucester Rugby		
by Situation	by Half	
▶ TC:	14	▶ first: 48%
▶ T:	5	▶ second: 52%
▶ P:	12	
▶ DG:	0	

○ Worcester Warriors		
by Situation	by Half	
▶ TC:	14	▶ first: 74%
▶ T:	0	▶ second: 26%
▶ P:	6	
▶ DG:	3	

Premiership Home Record vs Newcastle Falcons					
Played	Won	Drawn	Lost	For	Against
2	**1**	**0**	**1**	**44**	**57**

In the bright sunshine, the Warriors made the dream start when Shane Drahm passed a long ball out wide to Kai Horstmann who took it over the line in the corner.

The Warriors extended their lead two minutes later when wing Gary Trueman fended off a couple of Newcastle tackles before sprinting from 35 metres to the line to bag a glorious try. This time Drahm's conversion sailed over and Worcester found themselves 12-0 ahead. The Aussie fly-half added to the scoring thanks to a superb penalty to the delight of the home crowd.

Newcastle attempted to get back into the game with a try by Toby Flood, however this was short lived when Matthew Tait was sin binned for killing the ball. Worcester replied with a stunning move that saw skipper Pat Sanderson ploughing over. Drahm added the conversion to send Worcester into the half-time break with a 25-7 lead.

Player of the Match

11 | **Gary Trueman**
Centre

Jonny Wilkinson's entry in the second half gave the visitors a lift and Matt Burke burrowed over the line for their second try. However Worcester secured the bonus point thanks to an impressive Nick Runciman try to cap his Worcester league debut. James Brown came on to replace Shane Drahm and added the conversion before flanker Mike McCarthy had ploughed over for Newcastle's fourth. Brown then added a convincing penalty. The North East side added another try but it was a case of too little too late as Worcester cruised to a well deserved victory.

Venue:	Sixways	Referee:	Ashley Rowden - Season 05/06	**Worcester Warriors**
Attendance:	9,726	Matches:	10	**Newcastle Falcons**
Capacity:	9,726	Yellow Cards:	12	
Occupancy:	100%	Red Cards:	1	

Starting Line-Ups

O Worcester Warriors		Newcastle Falcons O
Delport	15	Burke (c)
Oduoza	14	May
Rasmussen	13	Tait
Lombard	12	Noon
Trueman	11	Phillips
Drahm	10	Flood
Runciman	9	Charlton
Windo	1	Williams
C Fortey	2	Thompson
L Fortey	3	Morris
Murphy	4	Perry
Gillies	5	Parling
Sanderson (c)	6	McCarthy
Harding	7	Harris
Horstmann	8	Woods

Replacements

Whatling	22	Wilkinson
Brown	21	Grindal
Hallam	20	Shaw
Hickey	19	Buist
O'Donoghue	18	Gross
Van Niekerk	17	Long
MacDonald	16	Ward

Match Stats

	Worcester	Newcastle
Tackles	77	83
Missed Tackles	8	9
Ball Carries	102	94
Metres	553	421
Defenders Beaten	9	8
Passes	93	135
Clean Breaks	8	7
Pens Conceded	12	12
Turnovers	13	8
Breakdowns Won	80	61
% Scrums Won	78%	100%
% Line-Outs Won	75%	80%

Premiership Table

Team	P	W	D	L	F	A	BP	Pts
7 Saracens	21	8	1	12	415	453	12	46
8 Worcester Warriors	21	9	1	11	429	469	7	45
9 Newcastle Falcons	21	8	1	12	362	414	8	42

Event Line

TC	Try Converted			P	Penalty
T	Try			DG	Drop Goal

Min	Score Progress		Event	Players
11	5	0	T	O Horstmann
13	12	0	TC	O Trueman / Drahm
18	12	0	▥	O Runciman
23	15	0	P	O Drahm
29	15	7	TC	O Flood / Burke
31	15	7	▥	O Tait
31	18	7	P	O Drahm
32	25	7	TC	O Sanderson / Drahm
Half time 25-7				
41	25	7	⇄	O Brown > Drahm
41	25	7	⇄	O Ward > Williams
41	25	7	⇄	O Wilkinson > Flood
42	25	12	T	O Burke
44	32	12	TC	O Runciman / Brown
50	32	12	⇄	O MacDonald > Windo
51	32	12	⇄	O Grindal > Charlton
51	32	12	⇄	O Long > Thompson
51	32	17	T	O McCarthy
55	32	17	⇄	O Hickey > Harding
55	32	17	▥	O Perry
56	35	17	P	O Brown
59	35	17	⇄	O Buist > McCarthy
59	35	22	T	O Burke
62	35	22	⇄	O Williams > Morris
64	35	22	⇄	O O'Donoghue > Gillies
64	35	27	T	O May
71	35	27	⇄	O Windo > Fortey
72	35	27	⇄	O Gross > Perry
72	35	27	⇄	O Van Niekerk > Fortey
77	35	27	⇄	O Whatling > Rasmussen
Full time 35-27				

Scoring Statistics

O Worcester Warriors

by Situation   by Half

► TC:	21	► first:	71%
► T:	5	► second:	29%
► P:	9		
► DG:	0		

O Newcastle Falcons

by Situation   by Half

► TC:	7	► first:	26%
► T:	20	► second:	74%
► P:	0		
► DG:	0		

Bath Rugby 25
Worcester Warriors 22

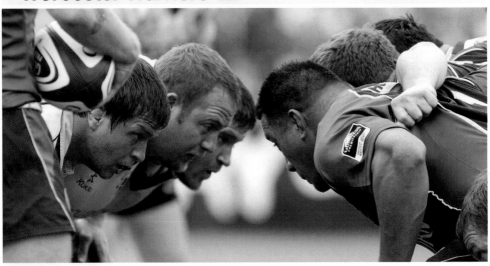

Premiership Away Record vs Bath Rugby					
Played	Won	Drawn	Lost	For	Against
2	**0**	**0**	**2**	**32**	**43**

It was all action from the kick-off and with two minutes on the clock a loose pass from Bath's Olly Barkley provided Worcester with the lineout throw from which they scored their first try.

Player of the Match

7 | **Tom Harding**
Flanker

Thomas Lombard, who was playing his last game in Worcester colours managed to ground the ball in the corner. James Brown failed to add the conversion.

It could have been the dream start for the Warriors but Tom Harding conceded a penalty for not releasing the ball, which Chris Malone kicked over. The hosts took the initiative when loosehead Taufa'ao Filise sprinted over the line. Bath missed the opportunity to extend their points tally when Malone missed the conversion.

Just before the break Worcester regained the ascendancy with a Dale Rasmussen try. James Brown failed to convert the try, however Worcester went into the break with a narrow 10-8 lead. This lead was short lived though as Bath captain Zak Feaunati peeled off a five metre scrum to score a try while centre Andy Higgins then sprinted through the gap to score two minutes later.

Bath's Joe Maddock then racked up the their third try of the match from a move started by Zak Feaunati, which Malone converted. It was Harding who sparked Worcester's recovery when he made a stunning 50 metre break from inside his own 22 before putting Lombard in for his second try while the New Zealander then scored a try of his own when he side stepped through a gap.

					Bath Rugby
Venue:	Recreation Ground		Referee:	David Rose - Season 05/06	**Worcester Warriors**
Attendance:	10,400		Matches:	12	
Capacity:	10,400		Yellow Cards:	18	
Occupancy:	100%		Red Cards:	0	

Starting Line-Ups

○ Bath Rugby		Worcester Warriors ●
Maddock	15	Delport
Stephenson	14	Oduoza
Higgins	13	Rasmussen
Barkley	12	Lombard
Bory	11	Trueman
Malone	10	Brown
Williams	9	Runciman
Filise	1	MacDonald
Mears	2	C Fortey
Bell	3	L Fortey
Hudson	4	Murphy
Short	5	Gillies
Feau'nati (c)	6	Sanderson (c)
Goodman	7	Harding
Beattie	8	Horstmann

Replacements

Davey	22	Hylton
Davis	21	Whatling
Walshe	20	Hallam
Fidler	19	Hickey
Fa'amatuainu	18	O'Donoghue
Barnes	17	Black
Hawkins	16	Van Niekerk

Match Stats

Tackles	116	101
Missed Tackles	11	7
Ball Carries	104	121
Metres	541	890
Defenders Beaten	3	7
Passes	140	156
Clean Breaks	7	6
Pens Conceded	5	9
Turnovers	20	16
Breakdowns Won	78	85
% Scrums Won	100%	75%
% Line-Outs Won	75%	54%

Premiership Table

Team	P	W	D	L	F	A	BP	Pts
7 Newcastle Falcons	22	9	1	12	416	433	9	47
8 Worcester Warriors	22	9	1	12	451	494	9	47
9 Saracens	22	8	1	13	433	483	12	46

Event Line

TC	Try Converted		P	Penalty
T	Try		DG	Drop Goal

Min	Score Progress		Event	Players
3	0	5	T	● Lombard
11	3	5	P	○ Malone
29	8	5	T	○ Filise
39	8	10	T	● Rasmussen
Half time 8-10				
49	8	10	⇄	● O'Donoghue > Gillies
49	13	10	T	○ Feau'nati
51	20	10	TC	○ Maddock / Malone
52	20	10	⇄	● Van Niekerk > Fortey
60	20	10	⇄	● Hickey > Horstmann
60	20	10	⇄	○ Barnes > Bell
60	20	10	⇄	○ Walshe > Williams
60	20	10	⇄	○ Fa'amatuainu > Goodman
60	20	10	⇄	● Hylton > Trueman
60	20	17	TC	● Lombard / Brown
62	20	22	T	● Harding
64	20	22	⇄	○ Davis > Malone
65	20	22	⇄	● Whatling > Lombard
66	25	22	T	○ Stephenson
69	25	22	⇄	○ Fidler > Feau'nati
69	25	22	⇄	● Hallam > Whatling
74	25	22	⇄	○ Bell > Filise
79	25	22	⇄	● Black > Fortey
Full time 25-22				

Scoring Statistics

○ Bath Rugby

by Situation   by Half

TC:	7	first:	32%
T:	15	second:	68%
P:	3		
DG:	0		

● Worcester Warriors

by Situation   by Half

TC:	7	first:	45%
T:	15	second:	55%
P:	0		
DG:	0		

▶ Left: Shane Drahm, Warriors top scorer. Above: Dale and Simon celebrate

Worcester Warriors have enjoyed a season full of action and excitement, finishing the 2005/2006 Guinness Premiership season in a credible eighth position. This is one place above last year's achievement, and with 47 points, it's five more than they accumulated the previous season leaving them plenty to be proud about.

Worcester won nine of their Premiership encounters, enjoying wins over Premiership play-off semi finalists London Wasps and Leicester Tigers, scoring an impressive 40 league tries throughout the season.

The Warriors European campaign saw them through to the semi-finals, winning five of their pool matches and putting in an impressive performance against Northampton Saints at Franklin's Gardens in the quarter finals, racking up 30 tries on their journey.

To add to the success, John Brain was voted Guinness Premiership's Director of Rugby and Shane Drahm picked up the Player of the month award, both in November.

Worcester look set to expand both on and off the pitch with the coaching team having already made seven key signings for next season including Lee Best from Bath,

► Warriors triumphant against Leicester in November

► Celebrations. Left: Aisea Havili; Right: Chris Fortey

Darren Morris from Tigers, Ben Gotting from Wasps, Ryan Powell from Cardiff Blues, Marcel Garvey from Gloucester, Gavin Quinnell from Llanelli Scarlets and Argentinian centre Miguel Avramovic, with John Brain and Anthony Eddy looking to recruit one or two further players.

In addition there has been major expansion work taking place over the summer and the club signed a new three-year, £1.5 million agreement with current sponsor - leading energy supplier - npower.

Work is already well advanced in the rebuilding of the East Stand, which will provide a Sixways Store, food outlets and bars all built in under the stand. It will also accommodate a VIP lounge with flat screen TVs, which will be unveiled in time for the coming season, increasing capacity to 10,200.

Over the next fifteen months, a staggering £23 million will be ploughed into Sixways making it one of the finest grounds in the Premiership. Overall capacity will be increased to over 13,200 with the development of a spectacular new North Stand. A joint venture with Worcestershire County Council and Esporta Health and Fitness Club will bring together a comprehensive sports and leisure complex and a public transport interchange at Sixways.

Premier Rugby Academy

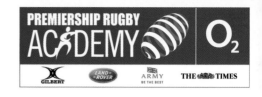

Worcester Warriors have a fantastic reputation for running very successful holiday training camps utilising their first team squad to inspire and share knowledge. As one of the twelve Premiership clubs able to deliver Premier Rugby Academy camps, Worcester Warriors provide the ideal environment for young player development. Last year we ran a record number of courses whilst maintaining a high coach/player ratio. Dan Zaltzman, Worcester Warriors Community Manager commented, "the success of the camps is largely due to the quality of coaching provided. Having Matt Sherratt on board to continually work with and develop our community coaches has given them a great opportunity to learn the coaching techniques used for the development of young players into Premiership first team players."

Premiership Rugby Academy Camps are where you can be your best by learning from the best. How to kick like Shane Drahm, how to beat a man like Craig Gillies and how to tackle like Pat Sanderson.

Our courses have been designed with the modern game in mind. They focus on all round player development, individual positional skills, unit skills and team strategy.

Every course is designed by Premiership Coaches. You'll learn all the latest techniques and skills from the very cutting edge of the game. All delivered by some of the countries leading development coaches.

Every course is visited by Premiership players, who'll pass on tips on how to take the game to the next level. Previously Pat Sanderson and Shane Drahm have been on hand to help deliver tips from the top.

Worcester Warriors with the support from npower now provide training camps for beginners to elite performers, with the Be Your Best residential camp offering the ultimate development opportunity for talented young players.

Book a Camp now
www.rugbycamps.com

Or to discuss email
community@wrfc.co.uk

James Brown
Fly Half

Date of Birth: 25.05.1978
Place of Birth: Solihull
Nationality: English
Height: 5'10"
Weight: 11st 2lb

Season Review 05/06

James Brown joined Worcester Warriors from London Irish in 2002, where he had spent three years. He made his debut for the Warriors against Coventry and was an integral part of the promotion winning team 2003/2004 team. He signed a new two year deal with the club this season that will keep him at Sixways until the end of the 2007/2008 season.

Throughout his four seasons at Sixways, James has made over 70 appearances and scored an impressive 359 points for the club.

Player Performance 05/06

Premiership Performance

Percentage of total possible time player was on pitch   ⊕ position in league table at end of month

Month:	Sep	Oct	Nov	Dec	Jan	Feb	Mar	Apr	May	Total
	29%	5 0%	5 0%	4 0%	55% 6	6 0%	7 0%	7 17%	100% 8	20%
League Pts:	10/20	4/5	12/20	0/5	6/15	2/15	5/10	6/15	2/5	47/110
Points F:	80	22	74	18	52	70	52	61	22	451
Points A:	88	15	71	36	59	97	37	66	25	494
Try Bonus:	0	0	0	0	0	0	1	1	1	3
Lose Bonus:	0	0	0	0	2	2	0	1	1	6
Total mins:	93	0	0	0	131	1	0	40	80	345
Starts (sub):	2	0	0	0	2	0 (1)	0	0 (1)	1	5 (2)
Points:	15	0	0	0	8	0	0	5	2	30
Tries:	0	0	0	0	0	0	0	0	0	0
Ball Carries:	1	0	0	0	4	1	1	0	0	7
Metres:	0	0	0	0	27	2	8	0	0	37
Tackles:	2	0	0	0	15	0	0	4	6	27

Prem. Performance Totals

Tries

- Brown: 0
- Team-mates: 36
- **Total: 36**
- Penalty Tries: 4

Points

- Brown: 30
- Team-mates: 401
- **Total: 431**
- Penalty Tries: 20

Cards

- Brown: 0
- Team-mates: 17
- **Total: 17**

Cup Games

	Apps	Pts
Euro Challenge Cup	4	4
Powergen Cup	1	5
Total	**5**	**9**

Prem. Career History

Premiership Career Milestones

Club Debut:
vs Newcastle (H), L, 9-30
▶ **05.09.04**
Time Spent at the Club:
▶ **2 Seasons**

First Try Scored for the Club:
vs Harlequins (H), W, 33-7
▶ **02.10.04**
Full International:
▶ **—**

Premiership Totals
97–06

Appearances	43
Points	148
Tries	1
Yellow Cards	0
Red Cards	0

Clubs

Year	Club	Apps	Pts
04-06	Worcester	23	143
98-02	London Irish	20	5

Off the Pitch

Age:
- Brown: 28 years
- Team: 27 years
- League: 26 years, 10 months

Height:
- Brown: 5'10"
- Team: 6'1"
- League: 6'1"

Weight:
- Brown: 11st 2lb
- Team: 15st 8lb
- League: 15st 10lb

Tim Collier
Lock

Date of Birth:	27.10.1977
Place of Birth:	Farnborough
Nationality:	English
Height:	6'6"
Weight:	21st 3lb

Season Review 05/06

At 6'6" and over 21 stone, Tim is one of the biggest players in the Premiership. Tim started his career at Harlequins but made only minimal appearances before deciding to move on.

He then had spells at Rugby Lions, Bridgend, London Welsh and time in South Africa before joining Worcester. Tim went on to be one of the star performers of Worcester's first season in the Premiership but made only five starts in all competitions last season after battling a hernia operation and a dislocated shoulder.

Player Performance 05/06

Premiership Performance
Percentage of total possible time player was on pitch   ⊙ position in league table at end of month

Month:	Sep	Oct	Nov	Dec	Jan	Feb	Mar	Apr	May	Total
Position	5	5	4	6	6	7	7	8	8	
Percentage	31%	11%	0%	14%	0%	0%	0%	0%	0%	7%
League Pts:	10/20	4/5	12/20	0/5	6/15	2/15	5/10	6/15	2/5	47/110
Points F:	80	22	74	18	52	70	52	61	22	451
Points A:	88	15	71	36	59	97	37	66	25	494
Try Bonus:	0	0	0	0	0	0	1	1	1	3
Lose Bonus:	0	0	0	0	2	2	0	1	1	6
Total mins:	100	9	0	11	0	0	0	0	0	120
Starts (sub):	1 (3)	0 (1)	0	0 (1)	0	0	0	0	0	1 (5)
Points:	0	0	0	0	0	0	0	0	0	0
Tries:	0	0	0	0	0	0	0	0	0	0
Ball Carries:	5	0	0	2	0	0	0	0	0	7
Metres:	14	0	0	5	0	0	0	0	0	19
Tackles:	5	0	0	0	0	0	0	0	0	5

Prem. Performance Totals

Tries
- Collier: 0
- Team-mates: 36
- **Total: 36**
- Penalty Tries: 4

Points
- Collier: 0
- Team-mates: 431
- **Total: 431**
- Penalty Tries: 20

Cards
- Collier: 0
- Team-mates: 17
- **Total: 17**

Cup Games

	Apps	Pts
Euro Challenge Cup	1	0
Powergen Cup	3	0
Total	**4**	**0**

Prem. Career History

Premiership Career Milestones

Club Debut:
vs Newcastle (H), L, 9-30
▶ **05.09.04**

Time Spent at the Club:
▶ **2 Seasons**

First Try Scored for the Club:
vs Wasps (H), W, 27-24
▶ **26.11.04**

Full International:
▶ **—**

Premiership Totals
97–06

Appearances	43
Points	5
Tries	1
Yellow Cards	3
Red Cards	0

Clubs

Year	Club	Apps	Pts
04-06	Worcester	25	5
98-99	W Hartlepool	3	0
97-00	Harlequins	15	0

Off the Pitch

Age:
- Collier: 28 years, 7 months
- Team: 27 years
- League: 26 years, 10 months

Height:
- Collier: 6'6"
- Team: 6'1"
- League: 6'1"

Weight:
- Collier: 21st 3lb
- Team: 15st 8lb
- League: 15st 10lb

Thinus Delport
Full Back

Date of Birth:	02.02.1975
Place of Birth:	Port Elizabeth, SA
Nationality:	South African
Height:	6'2"
Weight:	14st 6lb

Season Review 05/06

The 31 year-old South African international joined Worcester Warriors from Gloucester in 2004 and made his debut against Saracens at Vicarage Road. He signed a new two year deal with the club this season and has made over 50 appearances in the navy and gold, racking up 12 tries along the way.

Thinus played in the Tsunami Memorial game representing the southern hemisphere alongside some of the world's greatest players. He has played test rugby for the Springboks, with the highlight beating the All Blacks at Ellis Park.

Player Performance 05/06

Premiership Performance

Percentage of total possible time player was on pitch
⊙ position in league table at end of month

Month:	Sep	Oct	Nov	Dec	Jan	Feb	Mar	Apr	May	Total
	50%	100%	100%	100%	67%	33%	56%	75%	100%	70%
League Pts:	10/20	4/5	12/20	0/5	6/15	2/15	5/10	6/15	2/5	47/110
Points F:	80	22	74	18	52	70	52	61	22	451
Points A:	88	15	71	36	59	97	37	66	25	494
Try Bonus:	0	0	0	0	0	0	1	1	1	3
Lose Bonus:	0	0	0	0	2	2	0	1	1	6
Total mins:	161	80	320	80	160	80	90	179	80	1,230
Starts (sub):	2 (1)	1	4	1	2	1	1 (1)	3	1	16 (2)
Points:	0	5	5	0	0	0	5	5	0	20
Tries:	0	1	1	0	0	0	1	1	0	4
Ball Carries:	21	9	20	13	20	6	11	11	12	123
Metres:	171	105	135	107	185	58	80	74	142	1057
Tackles:	1	1	7	2	5	3	4	3	2	28

League table positions by month: 5, 5, 4, 6, 6, 7, 7, 8, 8

Prem. Performance Totals

Tries
- Delport: 4
- Team-mates: 32
- **Total: 36**
- Penalty Tries: 4

Points
- Delport: 20
- Team-mates: 411
- **Total: 431**
- Penalty Tries: 20

Cards
- Delport: 3
- Team-mates: 14
- **Total: 17**

Cup Games

	Apps	Pts
Euro Challenge Cup	5	5
Powergen Cup	1	0
Total	**6**	**5**

Prem. Career History

Premiership Career Milestones

Club Debut:
vs Newcastle (H), L, 9-30
 **05.09.04**

Time Spent at the Club:
➡ **2 Seasons**

First Try Scored for the Club:
vs Sale (H), W, 23-10
➡ **25.02.05**

Full International:
➡ **South Africa**

Premiership Totals
97–06

Appearances	64
Points	40
Tries	8
Yellow Cards	2
Red Cards	1

Clubs

Year	Club	Apps	Pts
04-06	Worcester	39	25
02-04	Gloucester	25	15

Off the Pitch

Age:
- Delport: 31 years, 3 months
- Team: 27 years
- League: 26 years, 10 months

Height:
- Delport: 6'2"
- Team: 6'1"
- League: 6'1"

Weight:
- Delport: 14st 6lb
- Team: 15st 8lb
- League: 15st 10lb

Shane Drahm
Fly Half

Date of Birth: 28.08.1977
Place of Birth: Brisbane
Nationality: English
Height: 5'9"
Weight: 12st 10lb

Season Review 05/06

Shane joined Worcester in the summer of 2005 from Northampton Saints and has been an integral part of the team playing 28 league and cup games. Shane has enjoyed a successful season, finishing top points scorer in the European Challenge Cup and third highest in the Guinness Premiership with 233 points.

He was voted the Guinness Premiership Play of the Month in November and his exceptional form was recognised at international level, being selected to play for England Saxons. Born in Australia, Shane qualifies to represent England due to residency.

Player Performance 05/06

Premiership Performance

Percentage of total possible time player was on pitch   ⊖ position in league table at end of month

Month:	Sep	Oct	Nov	Dec	Jan	Feb	Mar	Apr	May	Total
	71%	100%	100%	100%	45%	99%	100%	78%	0%	79%
League Pts:	10/20	4/5	12/20	0/5	6/15	2/15	5/10	6/15	2/5	47/110
Points F:	80	22	74	18	52	70	52	61	22	451
Points A:	88	15	71	36	59	97	37	66	25	494
Try Bonus:	0	0	0	0	0	0	1	1	1	3
Lose Bonus:	0	0	0	0	2	2	0	1	1	6
Total mins:	227	80	320	80	109	237	160	186	0	1,399
Starts (sub):	2 (2)	1	4	1	1 (1)	3	2	3	0	17 (3)
Points:	30	12	64	8	19	52	22	26	0	233
Tries:	0	0	2	0	0	1	0	0	0	3
Ball Carries:	14	2	29	9	6	25	14	15	0	114
Metres:	43	5	77	90	4	80	68	72	0	439
Tackles:	26	4	27	10	9	15	13	19	0	123

Prem. Performance Totals

Tries

▶ Drahm: 3
▷ Team-mates: 33
Total: 36
▶ Penalty Tries: 4

Points

▶ Drahm: 233
▷ Team-mates: 198
Total: 431
▶ Penalty Tries: 20

Cards

▶ Drahm: 1
▷ Team-mates: 16
Total: 17

Cup Games

	Apps	Pts
Euro Challenge Cup	8	102
Powergen Cup	2	13
Total	**10**	**115**

Prem. Career History

Premiership Career Milestones

Club Debut:
vs Gloucester (H), D, 15-15
▶ **04.09.05**

First Try Scored for the Club:
vs Sale (A), L, 13-24
▶ **11.11.05**

Time Spent at the Club:
▶ **1 Season**

Full International:
▶ —

Premiership Totals
97–06

Appearances	95
Points	911
Tries	12
Yellow Cards	1
Red Cards	0

Clubs

Year	Club	Apps	Pts
05-06	Worcester	20	233
03-05	Northampton	43	423
01-03	Bristol Rugby	32	255

Off the Pitch

Age:
▶ Drahm: 28 years, 9 months
▷ Team: 27 years
| League: 26 years, 10 months

Height:
▶ Drahm: 5'9"
▷ Team: 6'1"
| League: 6'1"

Weight:
▶ Drahm: 12st 10lb
▷ Team: 15st 8lb
| League: 15st 10lb

Chris Fortey
Hooker

Date of Birth:	25.08.1975
Place of Birth:	Gloucester
Nationality:	English
Height:	5'11"
Weight:	17st 8lb

Season Review 05/06

Gloucester born and bred, Chris Fortey joined up with Worcester Warriors in the summer of 2005 from the Cherry & Whites and made his debut for the Warriors ironically against Gloucester in the first match of the 2005/2006 season. Hooker Chris Fortey joined up with his twin Lee who was already a key member of the Warriors squad. They made history in the league game against Newcastle in April, being the first twins to run out together for the same side in the Premiership.

Chris has been an integral part of Worcester's front row this season making 23 starts for the club.

Player Performance 05/06

Premiership Performance

Percentage of total possible time player was on pitch   ⊖ position in league table at end of month

Month:	Sep	Oct	Nov	Dec	Jan	Feb	Mar	Apr	May	Total
	30%	88% 5	94%	81%	59% 6	54% 7	68% 7	55% 8	65% 8	62%
League Pts:	10/20	4/5	12/20	0/5	6/15	2/15	5/10	6/15	2/5	47/110
Points F:	80	22	74	18	52	70	52	61	22	451
Points A:	88	15	71	36	59	97	37	66	25	494
Try Bonus:	0	0	0	0	0	0	1	1	1	3
Lose Bonus:	0	0	0	0	2	2	0	1	1	6
Total mins:	95	70	300	65	142	129	109	132	52	1,094
Starts (sub):	0 (4)	1	4	1	2	2	2	2	1	15 (4)
Points:	0	0	0	0	0	0	0	0	0	0
Tries:	0	0	0	0	0	0	0	0	0	0
Ball Carries:	3	0	14	1	6	7	6	9	2	48
Metres:	0	0	23	0	18	16	8	12	1	78
Tackles:	5	0	8	5	15	6	7	4	3	53

Prem. Performance Totals

Tries

- ► Fortey: 0
- ⬛ Team-mates: 36
- **Total: 36**
- ► Penalty Tries: 4

Points

- ► Fortey: 0
- ⬛ Team-mates: 431
- **Total: 431**
- ► Penalty Tries: 20

Cards

- ► Fortey: 1
- ⬛ Team-mates: 16
- **Total: 17**

Cup Games

	Apps	Pts
Euro Challenge Cup	8	5
Powergen Cup	1	0
Total	**9**	**5**

Prem. Career History

Premiership Career Milestones

Club Debut:

vs Gloucester (H), D, 15-15

► **04.09.05**

Time Spent at the Club:

► **1 Season**

First Try Scored for the Club:

—

► **—**

Full International:

► **—**

Premiership Totals

97–06

Appearances	146
Points	20
Tries	4
Yellow Cards	5
Red Cards	2

Clubs

Year	Club	Apps	Pts
05-06	Worcester	19	0
97-05	Gloucester	127	20

Off the Pitch

Age:

- ► Fortey: 30 years, 9 months
- ⬛ Team: 27 years
- | League: 26 years, 10 months

Height:

- ► Fortey: 5'11"
- ⬛ Team: 6'1"
- | League: 6'1"

Weight:

- ► Fortey: 17st 8lb
- ⬛ Team: 15st 8lb
- | League: 15st 10lb

Lee Fortey
Prop

Date of Birth:	25.08.1975
Place of Birth:	Gloucester
Nationality:	English
Height:	5'10"
Weight:	16st 3lb

Season Review 05/06

Lee is fifteen minutes older than twin Chris and was a regular member of the team before Chris joined him at the beginning of last season.

Lee sustained a shoulder injury in the pre-season friendly against Benetton Treviso and spent much of the season on the sidelines. Lee made his league debut this season at home against Newcastle making history with his brother, being the first set of twins to start a Premiership game on the same side.

Player Performance 05/06

Premiership Performance

Percentage of total possible time player was on pitch
position in league table at end of month

Month:	Sep	Oct	Nov	Dec	Jan	Feb	Mar	Apr	May	Total
									99%	
	5	5	4	6	6	7	7	8	8	
	0%	0%	0%	0%	9%	5%	16%	31%		12%
League Pts:	10/20	4/5	12/20	0/5	6/15	2/15	5/10	6/15	2/5	47/110
Points F:	80	22	74	18	52	70	52	61	22	451
Points A:	88	15	71	36	59	97	37	66	25	494
Try Bonus:	0	0	0	0	0	0	1	1	1	3
Lose Bonus:	0	0	0	0	2	2	0	1	1	6
Total mins:	0	0	0	0	21	12	25	74	79	211
Starts (sub):	0	0	0	0	0 (2)	0 (1)	0 (2)	1 (1)	1	2 (6)
Points:	0	0	0	0	0	0	0	0	0	0
Tries:	0	0	0	0	0	0	0	0	0	0
Ball Carries:	0	3	0	0	1	0	2	3	1	10
Metres:	0	0	0	0	3	0	6	15	0	24
Tackles:	0	1	0	0	0	0	5	8	6	20

Prem. Performance Totals

Tries

▶ Fortey:	0
▷ Team-mates:	36
Total:	**36**
▶ Penalty Tries:	4

Points

▶ Fortey:	0
▷ Team-mates:	431
Total:	**431**
▶ Penalty Tries:	20

Cards

▶ Fortey:	0
▷ Team-mates:	17
Total:	**17**

Cup Games

	Apps	Pts
Euro Challenge Cup	7	0
Powergen Cup	0	0
Total	**7**	**0**

Prem. Career History

Premiership Career Milestones

Club Debut:
vs Newcastle (H), L, 9-30
▶ **05.09.04**

First Try Scored for the Club:
vs Harlequins (H), W, 33-7
▶ **02.10.04**

Time Spent at the Club:
▶ **2 Seasons**

Full International:
▶ **—**

Premiership Totals

97–06

Appearances	19
Points	5
Tries	1
Yellow Cards	0
Red Cards	0

Clubs

Year	Club	Apps	Pts
04-06	Worcester	19	5

Off the Pitch

Age:

▶ Fortey: 30 years, 9 months
▷ Team: 27 years
| League: 26 years, 10 months

Height:

▶ Fortey: 5'10"
▷ Team: 6'1"
| League: 6'1"

Weight:

▶ Fortey: 16st 3lb
▷ Team: 15st 8lb
| League: 15st 10lb

Andy Gomarsall
Scrum Half

Date of Birth:	24.07.1974
Place of Birth:	Durham
Nationality:	English
Height:	5'10"
Weight:	14st 4lb

Season Review 05/06

The England International, member of the winning World Cup squad joined Worcester on a three year deal in the summer of 2005 after four years with local rivals Gloucester. Prior to this, he enjoyed spells at Bedford and London Wasps.

He made his debut for the club in a pre-season friendly against Italian side Benetton Treviso, where he racked up two tries.

Andy formed the half back pairing with Shane Drahm and made 17 starts for the club this season.

Player Performance 05/06

Premiership Performance   Percentage of total possible time player was on pitch   ⊕ position in league table at end of month

Month:	Sep	Oct	Nov	Dec	Jan	Feb	Mar	Apr	May	Total
% time	58%	83%	81%	21%	40%	74%	91%	13%	0%	56%
League Pts:	10/20	4/5	12/20	0/5	6/15	2/15	5/10	6/15	2/5	47/110
Points F:	80	22	74	18	52	70	52	61	22	451
Points A:	88	15	71	36	59	97	37	66	25	494
Try Bonus:	0	0	0	0	0	0	1	1	1	3
Lose Bonus:	0	0	0	0	2	2	0	1	1	6
Total mins:	184	66	258	17	97	178	146	32		978
Starts (sub):	3	1	4	0 (1)	1 (1)	2 (1)	2	0 (2)	0	13 (5)
Points:	0	0	0	0	0	0	0	5	0	5
Tries:	0	0	0	0	0	0	0	1	0	1
Ball Carries:	11	4	12	1	4	12	15	16	0	75
Metres:	31	14	37	2	32	28	21	111	0	276
Tackles:	12	2	14	4	6	16	9	7	0	70

Prem. Performance Totals

Tries
- Gomarsall: 1
- Team-mates: 35

  Total: 36
- Penalty Tries: 4

Points
- Gomarsall: 5
- Team-mates: 426

  Total: 431
- Penalty Tries: 20

Cards
- Gomarsall: 0
- Team-mates: 17

  Total: 17

Cup Games

	Apps	Pts
Euro Challenge Cup	5	10
Powergen Cup	2	0
Total	7	10

Prem. Career History

Premiership Career Milestones

Club Debut:
vs L Irish (A), W, 20-15
▶ **11.09.05**

Time Spent at the Club:
▶ **1 Season**

First Try Scored for the Club:
vs Gloucester (A), L, 16-27
▶ **15.04.06**

Full International:
▶ **England**

Premiership Totals
97-06
Appearances	149
Points	153
Tries	15
Yellow Cards	1
Red Cards	0

Clubs
Year	Club	Apps	Pts
05-06	Worcester	18	5
00-05	Gloucester	83	73
99-00	Bedford Blues	20	70
98-99	Bath Rugby	2	0
97-99	London Wasps	26	5

Off the Pitch

Age:
- Gomarsall: 31 years, 10 months
- Team: 27 years
- League: 26 years, 10 months

Height:
- Gomarsall: 5'10"
- Team: 6'1"
- League: 6'1"

Weight:
- Gomarsall: 14st 4lb
- Team: 15st 8lb
- League: 15st 10lb

Craig Gillies
Lock

Date of Birth: 06.05.1976
Place of Birth: Glasgow
Nationality: English
Height: 6'7"
Weight: 17st 8lb

Season Review 05/06

Craig Gillies was born in Paisley and grew up in Tiverton, Devon. He joined Worcester in the summer of 2003 and his former clubs included Richmond and Llanelli. Craig has experienced both National One and the Premiership with Worcester and signed a new three year contract with the Club last year.

One of the best line-out takers in the Premiership, Craig has been one of Worcester's most consistent players this season making 29 starts for the club. He represented England A in 2000 but despite calls from rugby scribes he has yet to make his full England debut.

Player Performance 05/06

Premiership Performance

Percentage of total possible time player was on pitch — position in league table at end of month

Month:	Sep	Oct	Nov	Dec	Jan	Feb	Mar	Apr	May	Total
	100%	100%	75%	100%	100%	91%	100%	60%	61%	87%
position	5	5	4	6	6	7	7	8	8	
League Pts:	10/20	4/5	12/20	0/5	6/15	2/15	5/10	6/15	2/5	47/110
Points F:	80	22	74	18	52	70	52	61	22	451
Points A:	88	15	71	36	59	97	37	66	25	494
Try Bonus:	0	0	0	0	0	0	1	1	1	3
Lose Bonus:	0	0	0	0	2	2	0	1	1	6
Total mins:	320	80	240	80	240	218	160	144	49	1,531
Starts (sub):	4	1	3	1	3	3	2	2	1	20
Points:	0	0	0	0	0	0	0	0	0	0
Tries:	0	0	0	0	0	0	0	0	0	0
Ball Carries:	5	1	1	3	6	3	2	2	2	25
Metres:	9	1	0	6	17	4	2	0	0	39
Tackles:	8	2	7	5	25	13	2	7	1	70

Prem. Performance Totals

Tries
- Gillies: 0
- Team-mates: 36
- **Total: 36**
- Penalty Tries: 4

Points
- Gillies: 0
- Team-mates: 431
- **Total: 431**
- Penalty Tries: 20

Cards
- Gillies: 0
- Team-mates: 17
- **Total: 17**

Cup Games

	Apps	Pts
Euro Challenge Cup	8	0
Powergen Cup	1	0
Total	**9**	**0**

Prem. Career History

Premiership Career Milestones

Club Debut:
vs Newcastle (H), L, 9-30
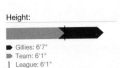
05.09.04

Time Spent at the Club:
2 Seasons

First Try Scored for the Club:
—
—

Full International:
—
—

Premiership Totals
97–06

Appearances	87
Points	5
Tries	1
Yellow Cards	0
Red Cards	0

Clubs

Year	Club	Apps	Pts
04-06	Worcester	41	0
97-99	Richmond	46	5

Off the Pitch

Age:
- Gillies: 30 years
- Team: 27 years
- League: 26 years, 10 months

Height:
- Gillies: 6'7"
- Team: 6'1"
- League: 6'1"

Weight:
- Gillies: 17st 8lb
- Team: 15st 8lb
- League: 15st 10lb

Tom Harding
Flanker

Date of Birth:	03.05.1982
Place of Birth:	Nelson
Nationality:	New Zealander
Height:	6'
Weight:	15st 4lb

Season Review 05/06

Tom Harding joined Worcester from New Zealand side North Harbour in October 2005 and previously played for Otago. He made his first start for the Warriors against Sale Sharks in the Guinness Premiership in February and has adapted well to the English game, putting in some impressive performances.

Born in Nelson, New Zealand, Tom has represented New Zealand at U 16's, U 19's and U 21's level, being part of the winning side in the U19 and U21 World Cups. His older brother Sam plays for Premiership side Northampton Saints.

Player Performance 05/06

Premiership Performance

Percentage of total possible time player was on pitch   ⊖ position in league table at end of month

Month:	Sep	Oct	Nov	Dec	Jan	Feb	Mar	Apr	May	Total
						100%			100%	
	5	5	4	6	6	7	50% 7	62% 8	8	34%
	0%	0%	0%	5%	22%					
League Pts:	10/20	4/5	12/20	0/5	8/15	2/15	5/10	6/15	2/5	47/110
Points F:	80	22	74	18	52	70	52	61	22	451
Points A:	88	15	71	36	59	97	37	66	25	494
Try Bonus:	0	0	0	0	0	0	1	1	1	3
Lose Bonus:	0	0	0	0	2	2	0	1	1	6
Total mins:	0	0	0	4	52	239	80	148	80	603
Starts (sub):	0	0	0	0 (1)	0 (2)	3	1	2 (1)	1	7 (4)
Points:	0	0	0	0	0	0	0	0	5	5
Tries:	0	0	0	0	0	0	0	0	1	1
Ball Carries:	0	0	0	0	6	13	4	10	13	46
Metres:	0	0	0	0	26	48	10	36	170	290
Tackles:	0	0	0	1	7	21	9	16	14	68

Prem. Performance Totals

Tries

- ▶ Harding: 1
- ▷ Team-mates: 35
- **Total:** 36
- ▶ Penalty Tries: 4

Points

- ▶ Harding: 5
- ▷ Team-mates: 426
- **Total:** 431
- ▶ Penalty Tries: 20

Cards

- ▶ Harding: 0
- ▷ Team-mates: 17
- **Total:** 17

Cup Games

	Apps	Pts
Euro Challenge Cup	1	0
Powergen Cup	1	0
Total	**2**	**0**

Prem. Career History

Premiership Career Milestones

Club Debut:
vs Bath (H), L, 18-36
▶ **26.12.05**

Time Spent at the Club:
▶ **1 Season**

First Try Scored for the Club:
vs Bath (A), L, 22-25
▶ **06.05.06**

Full International:
▶ **—**

Premiership Totals

97–06	
Appearances	11
Points	5
Tries	1
Yellow Cards	0
Red Cards	0

Clubs

Year	Club	Apps	Pts
05-06	Worcester	11	5

Off the Pitch

Age:
- ▶ Harding: 24 years
- ▷ Team: 27 years
- | League: 26 years, 10 months

Height:
- ▶ Harding: 6'
- ▷ Team: 6'1"
- | League: 6'1"

Weight:
- ▶ Harding: 15st 4lb
- ▷ Team: 15st 8lb
- | League: 15st 10lb

Aisea Havili
Wing

Date of Birth: 11.03.1977
Place of Birth: Tofoa, Tonga
Nationality: Tongan
Height: 5'7"
Weight: 15st 10lb

Season Review 05/06

Tongan born Aisea Havili made a real impact at Worcester since joining from Llanelli Scarlets in October 2005. The wing has displayed electric pace and a prolific try scoring record, being the top try scorer at Llanelli during his first year and has already racked up seven tries for the Warriors so far this season.

Aisea has five caps for Tonga although was forced to pull out of the 2003 World Cup due to personal reasons but hopes to be in the World Cup in 2007. Aisea Havili has signed a new two-year deal, which will see him at Sixways until the end of the 2007/8 season.

Player Performance 05/06

Premiership Performance

Percentage of total possible time player was on pitch   ⊖ position in league table at end of month

Month:	Sep	Oct	Nov	Dec	Jan	Feb	Mar	Apr	May	Total
League Pts:	10/20	4/5	12/20	0/5	6/15	2/15	5/10	6/15	2/5	47/110
Points F:	80	22	74	18	52	70	52	61	22	451
Points A:	88	15	71	36	59	97	37	66	25	494
Try Bonus:	0	0	0	0	0	0	1	1	1	3
Lose Bonus:	0	0	0	0	2	2	0	1	1	6
Total mins:	0	80	262	80	240	160	160	80	0	1,062
Starts (sub):	0	1	4	1	3	2	2	1	0	14
Points:	0	0	5	0	10	5	10	0	0	30
Tries:	0	0	1	0	2	1	2	0	0	6
Ball Carries:	0	8	21	8	16	13	19	11	0	96
Metres:	0	56	179	34	170	140	133	69	0	781
Tackles:	0	0	10	2	8	8	2	3	0	33

Graph percentages: Oct 100%, Nov 82%, Dec 100%, Jan 100%, Feb 67%, Mar 100%, Apr 33%, Total 60%

Prem. Performance Totals

Tries

► Havili:	6
▣ Team-mates:	30
Total:	**36**
► Penalty Tries:	4

Points

► Havili:	30
▣ Team-mates:	401
Total:	**431**
► Penalty Tries:	20

Cards

► Havili:	0
▣ Team-mates:	17
Total:	**17**

Cup Games

	Apps	Pts
Euro Challenge Cup	1	15
Powergen Cup	1	5
Total	**2**	**20**

Prem. Career History

Premiership Career Milestones

Club Debut:
vs LEED (H), W, 22-15

► **14.10.05**

Time Spent at the Club:

► **1 Season**

First Try Scored for the Club:
vs Bristol (H), W, 24-15

► **18.11.05**

Full International:

► **Tonga**

Premiership Totals
97–06

Appearances	14
Points	30
Tries	6
Yellow Cards	0
Red Cards	0

Clubs

Year	Club	Apps	Pts
05-06	Worcester	14	30

Off the Pitch

Age:

► Havili: 29 years, 2 months
▣ Team: 27 years
| League: 26 years, 10 months

Height:

► Havili: 5'7"
▣ Team: 6'1"
| League: 6'1"

Weight:

► Havili: 15st 10lb
▣ Team: 15st 8lb
| League: 15st 10lb

Drew Hickey
Back Row

Date of Birth:	16.05.1978
Place of Birth:	Melbourne
Nationality:	Australian
Height:	6'3"
Weight:	15st 12lb

Season Review 05/06

Drew Hickey played for the Sydney University XV team where he was coached by Anthony Eddy before signing for the Australian Super 12, NSW Waratahs. In 2002 Drew came over to England and signed on with National One side, Orrell before joining Worcester Warriors the following season.

Drew has played for the Australian Sevens side and also qualifies to play for Ireland thanks to an Irish father.

Player Performance 05/06

Premiership Performance

Percentage of total possible time player was on pitch ⊖ position in league table at end of month

Month:	Sep	Oct	Nov	Dec	Jan	Feb	Mar	Apr	May	Total
	75%	100%	97%	100%	100%	85%	89%	10%	25%	76%
	5	5	4	6	6	7	7	8	8	
League Pts:	10/20	4/5	12/20	0/5	6/15	2/15	5/10	6/15	2/5	47/110
Points F:	80	22	74	18	52	70	52	61	22	451
Points A:	88	15	71	36	59	97	37	66	25	494
Try Bonus:	0	0	0	0	0	0	1	1	1	3
Lose Bonus:	0	0	0	0	2	2	0	1	1	6
Total mins:	240	80	310	80	240	203	142	25	20	1,340
Starts (sub):	3	1	4	1	3	3	2	0 (1)	0 (1)	17 (2)
Points:	5	0	0	0	5	0	0	0	0	10
Tries:	1	0	0	0	1	0	0	0	0	2
Ball Carries:	23	8	34	6	29	34	21	1	5	161
Metres:	146	24	139	9	147	112	40	0	26	643
Tackles:	15	3	27	7	22	31	16	1	3	125

Prem. Performance Totals

Tries

▶ Hickey:	2
▶ Team-mates:	34
Total:	**36**
▶ Penalty Tries:	4

Points

▶ Hickey:	10
▶ Team-mates:	421
Total:	**431**
▶ Penalty Tries:	20

Cards

▶ Hickey:	1
▶ Team-mates:	16
Total:	**17**

Cup Games

	Apps	Pts
Euro Challenge Cup	6	10
Powergen Cup	2	0
Total	**8**	**10**

Prem. Career History

Premiership Career Milestones

Club Debut:
vs Newcastle (H), L, 9-30
▶ **05.09.04**

First Try Scored for the Club:
vs Saints (H), W, 21-19
▶ **30.04.05**

Time Spent at the Club:
▶ **2 Seasons**

Full International:
▶ —

Premiership Totals
97–06

Appearances	41
Points	15
Tries	3
Yellow Cards	1
Red Cards	0

Clubs

Year	Club	Apps	Pts
04-06	Worcester	41	15

Off the Pitch

Age:
▶ Hickey: 28 years
▶ Team: 27 years
| League: 26 years, 10 months

Height:
▶ Hickey: 6'3"
▶ Team: 6'1"
| League: 6'1"

Weight:
▶ Hickey: 15st 12lb
▶ Team: 15st 8lb
| League: 15st 10lb

Gavin Hickie
Hooker

Date of Birth:	**24.04.1980**
Place of Birth:	**Dublin**
Nationality:	**Irish**
Height:	**5'10"**
Weight:	**15st 10lb**

Season Review 05/06

Gavin Hickie signed for Worcester Warriors from Celtic League side Leinster in November 2005.

Irish born and bred, he made his first appearance in a Worcester shirt coming on as a replacement in the Guinness Premiership match against Northampton Saints at Franklin's Gardens at the end of November. He made his first start for the club against Leicester Tigers at Sixways.

Gavin has represented Ireland at under 19, 21 and 'A' level.

Player Performance 05/06

Premiership Performance

Percentage of total possible time player was on pitch   ⊖ position in league table at end of month

Month:	Sep	Oct	Nov	Dec	Jan	Feb	Mar	Apr	May	Total
	0%	0%	0%	19%	28%	26%	32%	30%	0%	16%
League Pts:	10/20	4/5	12/20	0/5	6/15	2/15	5/10	6/15	2/5	47/110
Points F:	80	22	74	18	52	70	52	61	22	451
Points A:	88	15	71	36	59	97	37	66	25	494
Try Bonus:	0	0	0	0	0	0	1	1	1	3
Lose Bonus:	0	0	0	0	2	2	0	1	1	6
Total mins:	0	0	20	15	66	62	51	73	0	287
Starts (sub):	0	0	0 (1)	0 (1)	0 (3)	1	0 (2)	0 (2)	0	1 (9)
Points:	0	0	0	0	0	0	0	0	0	0
Tries:	0	0	0	0	0	0	0	0	0	0
Ball Carries:	0	0	1	0	6	5	5	6	0	23
Metres:	0	0	3	0	8	15	10	19	0	55
Tackles:	0	0	3	1	2	3	3	2	0	14

Prem. Performance Totals

Tries

▶ Hickie:	0
▶ Team-mates:	36
Total:	**36**
▶ Penalty Tries:	4

Points

▶ Hickie:	0
▶ Team-mates:	431
Total:	**431**
▶ Penalty Tries:	20

Cards

▶ Hickie:	0
▶ Team-mates:	17
Total:	**17**

Cup Games

	Apps	Pts
Euro Challenge Cup	0	0
Powergen Cup	1	0
Total	**1**	**0**

Prem. Career History

Premiership Career Milestones

Club Debut:
vs Bristol (H), W, 24-15

▶ **18.11.05**

Time Spent at the Club:

▶ **1 Season**

First Try Scored for the Club:
—

▶ **—**

Full International:

▶ **—**

Premiership Totals

97–06

Appearances	10
Points	0
Tries	0
Yellow Cards	0
Red Cards	0

Clubs

Year	Club	Apps	Pts
05-06	Worcester	10	0

Off the Pitch

Age:

▶ Hickie:	26 years, 1 month
▶ Team:	27 years
	League: 26 years, 10 months

Height:

▶ Hickie:	5'10"
▶ Team:	6'1"
	League: 6'1"

Weight:

▶ Hickie:	15st 10lb
▶ Team:	15st 8lb
	League: 15st 10lb

Ben Hinshelwood
Centre

Date of Birth: 22.03.1977
Place of Birth: Melbourne
Nationality: Scottish
Height: 6'2"
Weight: 15st 10lb

Season Review 05/06

Ben Hinshelwood retired from professional rugby during the season after being plagued by a persistent back injury. His career with Worcester began in 2001 when he signed from Bedford. During his five years, Ben made over 80 appearances in the navy of Worcester Warriors and has scored over 40 tries, being an integral part of the team. With a successful Club record, Ben's international career is also an impressive one. Being part of the World Cup 2003, Ben took the decision to take time out from his international career earlier this season, after winning 19 Caps for Scotland.

Player Performance 05/06

Premiership Performance

Percentage of total possible time player was on pitch   G- position in league table at end of month

Month:	Sep	Oct	Nov	Dec	Jan	Feb	Mar	Apr	May	Total
	100%	100%								
				4	6	6	7	7	8	8
	5	5	50%							
										32%
			0%	0%	0%	0%	0%	0%	0%	
League Pts:	10/20	4/5	12/20	0/5	6/15	2/15	5/10	6/15	2/5	47/110
Points F:	80	22	74	18	52	70	52	61	22	451
Points A:	88	15	71	36	59	97	37	66	25	494
Try Bonus:	0	0	0	0	0	0	1	1	1	3
Lose Bonus:	0	0	0	0	2	2	0	1	1	6
Total mins:	320	80	160	0	0	0	0	0	0	560
Starts (sub):	4	1	2	0	0	0	0	0	0	7
Points:	0	0	0	0	0	0	0	0	0	0
Tries:	0	0	0	0	0	0	0	0	0	0
Ball Carries:	15	5	8	0	0	0	0	0	0	28
Metres:	65	10	11	0	0	0	0	0	0	86
Tackles:	10	1	11	0	0	0	0	0	0	22

Prem. Performance Totals

Tries

- Hinshelwood: 0
- Team-mates: 36

Total: 36
- Penalty Tries: 4

Points

- Hinshelwood: 0
- Team-mates: 431

Total: 431
- Penalty Tries: 20

Cards

- Hinshelwood: 0
- Team-mates: 17

Total: 17

Cup Games

	Apps	Pts
Euro Challenge Cup	1	0
Powergen Cup	1	5
Total	2	5

Prem. Career History

Premiership Career Milestones

Club Debut:
vs Bath (H), L, 22-26

▶ **18.09.04**

Time Spent at the Club:

▶ **2 Seasons**

First Try Scored for the Club:
vs Harlequins (H), W, 33-7

▶ **02.10.04**

Full International:

▶ **Scotland**

Premiership Totals

97–06

Appearances	21
Points	25
Tries	5
Yellow Cards	0
Red Cards	0

Clubs

Year	Club	Apps	Pts
04-06	Worcester	21	25

Off the Pitch

Age:

- Hinshelwood: 29 years, 2 months
- Team: 27 years
- League: 26 years, 10 months

Height:

- Hinshelwood: 6'2"
- Team: 6'1"
- League: 6'1"

Weight:

- Hinshelwood: 15st 10lb
- Team: 15st 8lb
- League: 15st 10lb

Chris Horsman
Prop

Date of Birth:	02.02.1977
Place of Birth:	Newport Pagnell
Nationality:	Welsh
Height:	6'2"
Weight:	17st 6lb

Season Review 05/06

Prop Chris Horsman signed for Worcester Warriors in July 2004 and has made 26 appearances in first team colours. An integral part of Worcester's front row, Chris has experienced a frustrating season undergoing an ankle operation in January which had been plaguing him all season. Chris signed a contract extension at the beginning of the year which will keep him at Sixways until the summer of 2010.

Although not Welsh born, Chris qualifies to represent Wales due to residency requirements and won three caps during the 2005 Autumn internationals.

Player Performance 05/06

Premiership Performance — Percentage of total possible time player was on pitch — ○ position in league table at end of month

Month:	Sep	Oct	Nov	Dec	Jan	Feb	Mar	Apr	May	Total
	89%	60%		50%						21%
League Pts:	10/20	4/5	12/20	0/5	6/15	2/15	5/10	6/15	2/5	47/110
Points F:	80	22	74	18	52	70	52	61	22	451
Points A:	88	15	71	36	59	97	37	66	25	494
Try Bonus:	0	0	0	0	0	0	1	1	1	3
Lose Bonus:	0	0	0	0	2	2	0	1	1	6
Total mins:	285	48	0	40	0	0	0	0	0	373
Starts (sub):	4	1	0	1	0	0	0	0	0	6
Points:	0	0	0	0	0	0	0	0	0	0
Tries:	0	0	0	0	0	0	0	0	0	0
Ball Carries:	9	4	0	0	0	0	0	0	0	13
Metres:	12	6	0	0	0	0	0	0	0	18
Tackles:	10	0	0	4	0	0	0	0	0	14

Prem. Performance Totals

Tries
- ▶ Horsman: 0
- ▷ Team-mates: 36
- **Total: 36**
- ▶ Penalty Tries: 4

Points
- ▶ Horsman: 0
- ▷ Team-mates: 431
- **Total: 431**
- ▶ Penalty Tries: 20

Cards
- ▶ Horsman: 1
- ▷ Team-mates: 16
- **Total: 17**

Cup Games

	Apps	Pts
Euro Challenge Cup	2	0
Powergen Cup	0	0
Total	**2**	**0**

Prem. Career History

Premiership Career Milestones

Club Debut:	First Try Scored for the Club:
vs Gloucester (H), L, 13-18	—

 **16.10.04**

Time Spent at the Club:

 **2 Seasons**

▶ —

Full International:

▶ **Wales**

Premiership Totals

97–06

Appearances	45
Points	0
Tries	0
Yellow Cards	3
Red Cards	0

Clubs

Year	Club	Apps	Pts
04-06	Worcester	18	0
97-01	Bath Rugby	27	0

Off the Pitch

Age:
- ▶ Horsman: 29 years, 3 months
- ▷ Team: 27 years
- ❙ League: 26 years, 10 months

Height:
- ▶ Horsman: 6'2"
- ▷ Team: 6'1"
- ❙ League: 6'1"

Weight:
- ▶ Horsman: 17st 6lb
- ▷ Team: 15st 8lb
- ❙ League: 15st 10lb

Kai Horstmann
Back Row

Date of Birth:	21.09.1981
Place of Birth:	Harare, Zimbabwe
Nationality:	English
Height:	6'3"
Weight:	16st 9lb

Season Review 05/06

Kai Horstmann joined Worcester Warriors from Harlequins in May 2005 on a two year deal and made his debut for the club against London Wasps in September. Kai has started all Guinness Premiership matches this season and has figured strongly within Worcester's European Challenge Cup campaign scoring his first try for the club against Amatori Catania in October. Kai picked up the Player's Player of the Year award which was voted for by members of the squad and acknowledged his team performances throughout the season. He was a member of the IRB World Sevens Series squad in 2003/2004 season.

Player Performance 05/06

Premiership Performance

Percentage of total possible time player was on pitch   position in league table at end of month

Month:	Sep	Oct	Nov	Dec	Jan	Feb	Mar	Apr	May	Total
	33%	64%	89%	100%	100%	93%	89%	100%	75%	81%
League Pts:	10/20	4/5	12/20	0/5	6/15	2/15	5/10	6/15	2/5	47/110
Points F:	80	22	74	18	52	70	52	61	22	451
Points A:	88	15	71	36	59	97	37	66	25	494
Try Bonus:	0	0	0	0	0	0	1	1	1	3
Lose Bonus:	0	0	0	0	2	2	0	1	1	6
Total mins:	105	51	286	80	240	222	142	240	60	1,426
Starts (sub):	1 (2)	1	4	1	3	3	2	3	1	19 (2)
Points:	0	0	0	5	5	0	0	5	0	15
Tries:	0	0	0	1	1	0	0	1	0	3
Ball Carries:	13	4	18	5	21	25	19	28	7	140
Metres:	22	6	87	27	129	95	39	56	29	490
Tackles:	12	3	15	9	34	19	11	25	7	135

Prem. Performance Totals

Tries

- Horstmann: 3
- Team-mates: 33
- **Total: 36**
- Penalty Tries: 4

Points

- Horstmann: 15
- Team-mates: 416
- **Total: 431**
- Penalty Tries: 20

Cards

- Horstmann: 2
- Team-mates: 15
- **Total: 17**

Cup Games

	Apps	Pts
Euro Challenge Cup	7	5
Powergen Cup	3	0
Total	10	5

Prem. Career History

Premiership Career Milestones

Club Debut:
vs Gloucester (H), D, 15-15
04.09.05

Time Spent at the Club:
1 Season

First Try Scored for the Club:
vs Bath (H), L, 18-36
26.12.05

Full International:
—

Premiership Totals

97–06	
Appearances	26
Points	15
Tries	3
Yellow Cards	1
Red Cards	1

Clubs

Year	Club	Apps	Pts
05-06	Worcester	21	15
02-05	Harlequins	5	0

Off the Pitch

Age:
- Horstmann: 24 years, 8 months
- Team: 27 years
- League: 26 years, 10 months

Height:
- Horstmann: 6'3"
- Team: 6'1"
- League: 6'1"

Weight:
- Horstmann: 16st 9lb
- Team: 15st 8lb
- League: 15st 10lb

Jonny Hylton
Wing

Date of Birth: 06.04.1981
Place of Birth: Epsom
Nationality: English
Height: 6'
Weight: 13st 5lb

Season Review 05/06

Jonny Hylton joined Worcester from London Wasps where he was unable to break into the team and made his 2005/06 Premiership debut for the Warriors in the opening match of the season against Gloucester.

Jonny has made seven starts for the club this season and played a key part in Worcester's A campaign.

Renowned for his outstanding pace, Jonny was part of the England 7's side which retained the Emirates Airline Dubai Sevens Cup back in December.

Prem. Career History

Premiership Career Milestones	First Try Scored for the Club:
Club Debut:	
vs Gloucester (H), D, 15-15	—
▶ 04.09.05	▶ —
Time Spent at the Club:	Full International:
▶ 1 Season	▶ —

Premiership Totals	
97–06	7
Appearances	7
Points	0
Tries	0
Yellow Cards	0
Red Cards	0

Clubs			
Year	Club	Apps	Pts
05-06	Worcester	7	0

Richard Blaze
Lock

Date of Birth: 19.04.1985
Place of Birth: Birmingham
Nationality: English
Height: 6'7"
Weight: 18st

Season Review 05/06

Richard Blaze was spotted by Moseley RFC whilst at school. He was nominated to the North Midlands Development Squad, where he was seen by Graham Smith, then Worcester Academy Assistant Manager, and pushed forward to the RFU U17 Development squad held at Loughborough. His mentor at the camp was Gary Meechan who went on to coach him at Midlands Division. Richard joined Worcester and became part of the full time system 3 years ago, since then he has played for England U18, U19 and 2 years at U21. He signed a 2 year full time playing contract with the 1st XV at the end of the 2004/2005 season.

Prem. Career History

Premiership Career Milestones	First Try Scored for the Club:
Club Debut:	
vs Newcastle (A), W, 21-16	—
▶ 10.04.05	▶ —
Time Spent at the Club:	Full International:
▶ 2 Seasons	▶ —

Premiership Totals	
97–06	4
Appearances	4
Points	0
Tries	0
Yellow Cards	0
Red Cards	0

Clubs			
Year	Club	Apps	Pts
04-06	Worcester	4	0

Thomas Lombard
Centre

Date of Birth: 05.06.1975
Place of Birth: Le Chesnay, France
Nationality: French
Height: 6'2"
Weight: 13st 5lb

Season Review 05/06

Thomas Lombard has enjoyed his second season with the Warriors. A versatile player who can cover wing and centre signed for Worcester in July 2004 from leading French side Stade Francais. He spent eight years with the French club winning four league titles.

During his two seasons, he has clocked up over 50 appearances for the Warriors scoring seven tries. The former French international has 16 caps which he won during his international career which spanned from 1998-2001, with the highlight of his career playing against Johah Lomu and the All Blacks in 2000.

Player Performance 05/06

Premiership Performance

Percentage of total possible time player was on pitch

G- position in league table at end of month

Month:	Sep	Oct	Nov	Dec	Jan	Feb	Mar	Apr	May	Total
	95%	100%	100%	50%	94%	98%	50%	100%	81%	90%
	5	5	4	6	6	7	7	8	8	
League Pts:	10/20	4/5	12/20	0/5	6/15	2/15	5/10	6/15	2/5	47/110
Points F:	80	22	74	18	52	70	52	61	22	451
Points A:	88	15	71	36	59	97	37	66	25	494
Try Bonus:	0	0	0	0	0	0	1	1	1	3
Lose Bonus:	0	0	0	0	2	2	0	1	1	6
Total mins:	303	80	320	40	226	234	80	240	65	1,588
Starts (sub):	4	1	4	1	3	3	1	3	1	21
Points:	0	0	0	0	0	0	0	0	10	10
Tries:	0	0	0	0	0	0	0	0	2	2
Ball Carries:	30	7	23	2	22	22	11	26	12	155
Metres:	86	13	94	13	46	76	20	101	75	524
Tackles:	19	6	29	4	17	22	13	28	5	143

Prem. Performance Totals

Tries
- Lombard: 2
- Team-mates: 34
- **Total: 36**
- Penalty Tries: 4

Points
- Lombard: 10
- Team-mates: 421
- **Total: 431**
- Penalty Tries: 20

Cards
- Lombard: 0
- Team-mates: 17
- **Total: 17**

Cup Games

	Apps	Pts
Euro Challenge Cup	6	12
Powergen Cup	2	0
Total	**8**	**12**

Prem. Career History

Premiership Career Milestones

Club Debut:
vs Newcastle (H), L, 9-30

 **05.09.04**

First Try Scored for the Club:
vs Bath (H), L, 22-26

▶ **18.09.04**

Time Spent at the Club:
▶ **2 Seasons**

Full International:
▶ **France**

Premiership Totals

97–06	
Appearances	40
Points	30
Tries	6
Yellow Cards	0
Red Cards	0

Clubs

Year	Club	Apps	Pts
04-06	Worcester	40	30

Off the Pitch

Age:
- Lombard: 30 years, 11 months
- Team: 27 years
- League: 26 years, 10 months

Height:
- Lombard: 6'2"
- Team: 6'1"
- League: 6'1"

Weight:
- Lombard: 13st 5lb
- Team: 15st 8lb
- League: 15st 10lb

Nicolas Le Roux
Full Back/Wing

Date of Birth: 01.10.1976
Place of Birth: Nantes-la-Jolie, France
Nationality: French
Height: 5'8"
Weight: 11st 13lb

Season Review 05/06

The French full back arrived at Sixways during the close season last year from French club Brive, bringing pace and flair to the side. Nicolas made his first start for the club against Saracens and racked up his first try against London Wasps at the Causeway at the end of September.

He made 17 starts for the club throughout the season, scoring three tries. Nicolas was part of the French Sevens squad this season. He left the Warriors to return to his former club Brive at the end of the 2005/2006 season.

Player Performance 05/06

Premiership Performance

Percentage of total possible time player was on pitch   ○- position in league table at end of month

Month:	Sep	Oct	Nov	Dec	Jan	Feb	Mar	Apr	May	Total
	52%	100%	100%	100%	33%	67%	82%	0%	0%	58%
League Pts:	10/20	4/5	12/20	0/5	6/15	2/15	5/10	6/15	2/5	47/110
Points F:	80	22	74	18	52	70	52	61	22	451
Points A:	88	15	71	36	59	97	37	66	25	494
Try Bonus:	0	0	0	0	0	0	1	1	1	3
Lose Bonus:	0	0	0	0	2	2	0	1	1	6
Total mins:	166	80	320	80	80	160	131	0	0	1,017
Starts (sub):	2 (1)	1	4	1	1	2	2	0	0	13 (1)
Points:	5	0	0	0	0	5	0	0	0	10
Tries:	1	0	0	0	0	1	0	0	0	2
Ball Carries:	18	8	35	12	6	19	12	0	0	110
Metres:	306	54	302	96	99	148	45	0	0	1050
Tackles:	6	0	8	1	2	5	6	0	0	28

Prem. Performance Totals

Tries

Le Roux:	2
Team-mates:	34
Total:	**36**
Penalty Tries:	4

Points

Le Roux:	10
Team-mates:	421
Total:	**431**
Penalty Tries:	20

Cards

Le Roux:	0
Team-mates:	17
Total:	**17**

Cup Games

	Apps	Pts
Euro Challenge Cup	5	5
Powergen Cup	1	0
Total	**6**	**5**

Prem. Career History

Premiership Career Milestones

Club Debut:
vs Gloucester (H), D, 15-15
▶ 04.09.05

First Try Scored for the Club:
vs Wasps (A), L, 20-34
▶ 25.09.05

Time Spent at the Club:
▶ 1 Season

Full International:
▶ —

Premiership Totals

97–06	
Appearances	14
Points	10
Tries	2
Yellow Cards	0
Red Cards	0

Clubs

Year	Club	Apps	Pts
05-06	Worcester	14	10

Off the Pitch

Age:

▶ Le Roux: 29 years, 7 months
▷ Team: 27 years
| League: 26 years, 10 months

Height:

▶ Le Roux: 5'8"
▷ Team: 6'1"
| League: 6'1"

Weight:

▶ Le Roux: 11st 13lb
▷ Team: 15st 8lb
| League: 15st 10lb

Mike MacDonald
Prop

Date of Birth: 27.11.1980
Place of Birth: Berkeley, USA
Nationality: American
Height: 6'1"
Weight: 20st 5lb

Season Review 05/06

American prop, Mike Macdonald joined Worcester during the early part of last season. An American international, he has played for the US Eagles during his career. Mike signed an initial one year contract with the Warriors but failed to secure a regular first team place although he was involved heavily in the A league fixtures.

He will play rugby next season for National One side Leeds Tykes.

Prem. Career History

Premiership Career Milestones		Premiership Totals		Clubs			
Club Debut:	First Try Scored for the Club:	97–06		Year	Club	Apps	Pts
vs L Irish (A), W, 20-15	—	Appearances	5	05-06	Worcester	5	0
▶ **11.09.05**	▶ **—**	Points	0				
Time Spent at the Club:	Full International:	Tries	0				
▶ **1 Season**	▶ **United States**	Yellow Cards	0				
		Red Cards	0				

Mike Maguire
Wing/Centre

Date of Birth: 17.01.1982
Place of Birth: Nelson
Nationality: New Zealander
Height: 6'1"
Weight: 14st 11lb

Season Review 05/06

Worcester Warriors signed 23 year-old New Zealand wing/centre Mike Maguire following the retirement of Ben Hinshelwood in November. Prior to joining Worcester, Mike played all his rugby in New Zealand, most recently for Otago's NPC squad. He holds an Irish passport and qualifies to play for Ireland.

Mike signed a contract to keep him at Sixways until the end of the season and made his debut against Newcastle on New Year's Day. He will play his rugby in Ireland next year, joining Celtic League side Ulster.

Prem. Career History

Premiership Career Milestones		Premiership Totals		Clubs			
Club Debut:	First Try Scored for the Club:	97–06		Year	Club	Apps	Pts
vs Newcastle (A), L, 15-21	—	Appearances	1	05-06	Worcester	1	0
▶ **01.01.06**	▶ **—**	Points	0				
Time Spent at the Club:	Full International:	Tries	0				
▶ **1 Season**	▶ **—**	Yellow Cards	0				
		Red Cards	0				

Phil Murphy
Lock

Date of Birth: 01.04.1980
Place of Birth: Beverley
Nationality: English
Height: 6'7"
Weight: 17st 6lb

Season Review 05/06

Born in Humberside, Phil Murphy spent a number of years playing for Leeds Tykes before signing for Worcester in 2004. Phil has proved to be a reliable member of Worcester's league and cup campaign despite battling achilles tendonitis for much of the season. He has made over 40 appearances for the Warriors during his time with the club and has signed a contract extension which will keep him at Sixways until the end of the 2007/2008 season.

Phil was voted 'most improved player' at Worcester's end of season awards ceremony.

Player Performance 05/06

Premiership Performance

Percentage of total possible time player was on pitch   ⊙ position in league table at end of month

Month:	Sep	Oct	Nov	Dec	Jan	Feb	Mar	Apr	May	Total
	69%	89%	94%	81%	91%	95%	87%	100%	100%	89%
	5	5	4	6	6	7	7	8	8	
League Pts:	10/20	4/5	12/20	0/5	6/15	2/15	5/10	6/15	2/5	47/110
Points F:	80	22	74	18	52	70	52	61	22	451
Points A:	88	15	71	36	59	97	37	66	25	494
Try Bonus:	0	0	0	0	0	0	1	1	1	3
Lose Bonus:	0	0	0	0	2	2	0	1	1	6
Total mins:	220	71	300	65	219	229	139	240	80	1,563
Starts (sub):	3 (1)	1	4	1	3	3	2	3	1	21 (1)
Points:	0	0	0	0	0	0	5	0	0	5
Tries:	0	0	0	0	0	0	1	0	0	1
Ball Carries:	7	3	8	1	15	15	12	16	7	84
Metres:	12	10	17	0	25	34	24	37	33	192
Tackles:	23	2	22	6	26	16	11	14	6	126

Prem. Performance Totals

Tries
- ▶ Murphy: 1
- ▶ Team-mates: 35
- **Total: 36**
- ▶ Penalty Tries: 4

Points
- ▶ Murphy: 5
- ▶ Team-mates: 426
- **Total: 431**
- ▶ Penalty Tries: 20

Cards
- ▶ Murphy: 0
- ▶ Team-mates: 17
- **Total: 17**

Cup Games

	Apps	Pts
Euro Challenge Cup	5	0
Powergen Cup	1	0
Total	**6**	**0**

Prem. Career History

Premiership Career Milestones

Club Debut:
vs Newcastle (H), L, 9-30
▶ **05.09.04**

Time Spent at the Club:
▶ **2 Seasons**

First Try Scored for the Club:
vs Wasps (H), W, 37-8
▶ **10.03.06**

Full International:
▶ **—**

Premiership Totals

97–06
Appearances	66
Points	5
Tries	1
Yellow Cards	0
Red Cards	0

Clubs

Year	Club	Apps	Pts
04-06	Worcester	35	5
01-04	Leeds Tykes	31	0

Off the Pitch

Age:
- ▶ Murphy: 26 years, 1 month
- ▍ Team: 27 years
- ▏ League: 26 years, 10 months

Height:
- ▶ Murphy: 6'7"
- ▍ Team: 6'1"
- ▏ League: 6'1"

Weight:
- ▶ Murphy: 17st 6lb
- ▍ Team: 15st 8lb
- ▏ League: 15st 10lb

Ed O'Donoghue
Lock

Date of Birth: 24.06.1982
Place of Birth: London
Nationality: Australian
Height: 6'6"
Weight: 17st 4lb

Season Review 05/06

Ed O'Donoghue signed from Northampton Saints in the summer of 2005. He made his first start in Worcester colours in the Powergen Cup game against Leicester Tigers. Although Ed was involved in Worcester's cup campaigns, he didn't make his first league start until April against Gloucester.

Ed's initial one year contract expired at the end of the 2005/2006 season and he will play his rugby next year in Australia for the Queensland Reds.

Player Performance 05/06

Premiership Performance Percentage of total possible time player was on pitch ⊙ position in league table at end of month

Month:	Sep	Oct	Nov	Dec	Jan	Feb	Mar	Apr	May	Total
	5	5	4	6	6	7	7	40% 8	39% 8	
	0%	0%	0%	0%	9%	14%	13%			13%
League Pts:	10/20	4/5	12/20	0/5	6/15	2/15	5/10	6/15	2/5	47/110
Points F:	80	22	74	18	52	70	52	61	22	451
Points A:	88	15	71	36	59	97	37	66	25	494
Try Bonus:	0	0	0	0	0	0	1	1	1	3
Lose Bonus:	0	0	0	0	2	2	0	1	1	6
Total mins:	0	0	20	0	21	33	21	96	31	222
Starts (sub):	0	0	0 (1)	0	0 (1)	0 (2)	0 (2)	1 (1)	0 (1)	1 (8)
Points:	0	0	0	0	0	0	0	0	0	0
Tries:	0	0	0	0	0	0	0	0	0	0
Ball Carries:	0	0	0	0	1	1	1	2	2	7
Metres:	0	0	0	0	7	2	0	2	4	15
Tackles:	0	0	3	0	4	2	2	8	5	24

Prem. Performance Totals

Tries
- O'Donoghue: 0
- Team-mates: 36
- **Total: 36**
- Penalty Tries: 4

Points
- O'Donoghue: 0
- Team-mates: 431
- **Total: 431**
- Penalty Tries: 20

Cards
- O'Donoghue: 0
- Team-mates: 17
- **Total: 17**

Cup Games

	Apps	Pts
Euro Challenge Cup	5	0
Powergen Cup	2	0
Total	**7**	**0**

Prem. Career History

Premiership Career Milestones

Club Debut:
vs Sale (A), L, 13-24
▶ **11.11.05**
Time Spent at the Club:
▶ **1 Season**

First Try Scored for the Club:
—
▶ **—**
Full International:
▶ **—**

Premiership Totals
97–06
Appearances	13
Points	0
Tries	0
Yellow Cards	0
Red Cards	0

Clubs

Year	Club	Apps	Pts
05-06	Worcester	9	0
04-05	Northampton	4	0

Off the Pitch

Age:
- O'Donoghue: 23 years, 11 months
- Team: 27 years
- League: 26 years, 10 months

Height:
- O'Donoghue: 6'6"
- Team: 6'1"
- League: 6'1"

Weight:
- O'Donoghue: 17st 4lb
- Team: 15st 8lb
- League: 15st 10lb

Uche Oduoza
Wing

Date of Birth: 15.10.1986
Place of Birth: Manchester
Nationality: English
Height: 6'3"
Weight: 14st 4lb

Season Review 05/06

Born in Manchester, Uche grew up in Exeter where he joined his local club side. He was spotted by Worcester's Academy Manager whilst representing England at Under 18s level. Uche joined the Worcester Warriors Academy side and was a regular in the A league. He made his senior side debut in the European Cup against Italian side Rovigo whilst he was still at school and his league debut against Gloucester in April. Uche made nine appearances in the European and Anglo Welsh Cup. Uche has represented his country at U18s, U19s and U21 level.

Player Performance 05/06

Premiership Performance

Percentage of total possible time player was on pitch   ☉ position in league table at end of month

Month:	Sep	Oct	Nov	Dec	Jan	Feb	Mar	Apr	May	Total
									100%	
	5	5	4	6	6	7	7	67%	8	
	0%	0%	0%	0%	0%	0%	0%	8		14%
League Pts:	10/20	4/5	12/20	0/5	6/15	2/15	5/10	6/15	2/5	47/110
Points F:	80	22	74	18	52	70	52	61	22	451
Points A:	88	15	71	36	59	97	37	66	25	494
Try Bonus:	0	0	0	0	0	0	1	1	1	3
Lose Bonus:	0	0	0	0	2	2	0	1	1	6
Total mins:	0	0	0	0	0	0	0	160	80	240
Starts (sub):	0	0	0	0	0	0	0	2	1	3
Points:	0	0	0	0	0	0	0	0	0	0
Tries:	0	0	0	0	0	0	0	0	0	0
Ball Carries:	0	0	0	0	0	0	0	19	9	28
Metres:	0	0	0	0	0	0	0	58	131	189
Tackles:	0	0	0	0	0	0	0	6	6	12

Prem. Performance Totals

Tries
- Oduoza: 0
- Team-mates: 36

Total: 36
- Penalty Tries: 4

Points
- Oduoza: 0
- Team-mates: 431

Total: 431
- Penalty Tries: 20

Cards
- Oduoza: 0
- Team-mates: 17

Total: 17

Cup Games

	Apps	Pts
Euro Challenge Cup	5	5
Powergen Cup	2	0
Total	7	5

Prem. Career History

Premiership Career Milestones

Club Debut:
vs Gloucester (A), L, 16-27

 **15.04.06**

Time Spent at the Club:

▶ **1 Season**

First Try Scored for the Club:
—

▶ —

Full International:

▶ —

Premiership Totals

97–06

Appearances	3
Points	0
Tries	0
Yellow Cards	0
Red Cards	0

Clubs

Year	Club	Apps	Pts
05-06	Worcester	3	0

Off the Pitch

Age:

- ▶ Oduoza: 19 years, 7 months
- ▶ Team: 27 years
- | League: 26 years, 10 months

Height:

- ▶ Oduoza: 6'3"
- ▶ Team: 6'1"
- | League: 6'1"

Weight:

- ▶ Oduoza: 14st 4lb
- ▶ Team: 15st 8lb
- | League: 15st 10lb

Matt Powell
Scrum Half

Date of Birth:	08.05.1978
Place of Birth:	Abergavenny
Nationality:	Welsh
Height:	5'10"
Weight:	13st 9lb

Season Review 05/06

Matt Powell spent this season battling with number nine former England international Andy Gomarsall for a starting spot at Sixways. They traded places throughout the season but Matt finished the campaign the favoured scrum-half making 14 starts for the club in all competitions.

He was involved in the Wales set-up for the last two games of the Six Nations and his consistent displays were rewarded with a late call-up to play for the Barbarians in their annual match at Leicester Tigers as a replacement for the former All Black, Justin Marshall.

Player Performance 05/06

Premiership Performance Percentage of total possible time player was on pitch   O- position in league table at end of month

Month:	Sep	Oct	Nov	Dec	Jan	Feb	Mar	Apr	May	Total
	43%	5	5	79%	60% 6	7	7	53% 8	8	35%
		18%	19%	4 6		26%	9%		0%	
League Pts:	10/20	4/5	12/20	0/5	6/15	2/15	5/10	6/15	2/5	47/110
Points F:	80	22	74	18	52	70	52	61	22	451
Points A:	88	15	71	36	59	97	37	66	25	494
Try Bonus:	0	0	0	0	0	0	1	1	1	3
Lose Bonus:	0	0	0	0	2	2	0	1	1	6
Total mins:	136	14	62	63	143	62	15	128	0	623
Starts (sub):	1 (3)	0 (1)	0 (3)	1	2	1 (1)	0 (2)	2	0	7 (10)
Points:	0	0	0	0	0	0	0	0	0	0
Tries:	0	0	0	0	0	0	0	0	0	0
Ball Carries:	7	1	3	2	7	4	5	20	0	49
Metres:	15	0	4	15	16	18	59	57	0	184
Tackles:	6	0	6	8	8	5	0	11	0	44

Prem. Performance Totals

Tries
- Powell: 0
- Team-mates: 36
- Total: 36
- Penalty Tries: 4

Points
- Powell: 0
- Team-mates: 431
- Total: 431
- Penalty Tries: 20

Cards
- Powell: 0
- Team-mates: 17
- Total: 17

Cup Games

	Apps	Pts
Euro Challenge Cup	6	0
Powergen Cup	3	0
Total	9	0

Prem. Career History

Premiership Career Milestones

Club Debut:	First Try Scored for the Club:
vs Saracens (A), L, 10-16	vs L Irish (H), W, 16-6
▶ 12.09.04	▶ 01.01.05
Time Spent at the Club:	Full International:
▶ 2 Seasons	▶ —

Premiership Totals

97–06	
Appearances	93
Points	30
Tries	6
Yellow Cards	0
Red Cards	0

Clubs

Year	Club	Apps	Pts
04-06	Worcester	34	15
00-03	Harlequins	40	5
97-00	Saracens	19	10

Off the Pitch

Age:
- Powell: 28 years
- Team: 27 years
- League: 26 years, 10 months

Height:
- Powell: 5'10"
- Team: 6'1"
- League: 6'1"

Weight:
- Powell: 13st 9lb
- Team: 15st 8lb
- League: 15st 10lb

Dale Rasmussen
Centre

Date of Birth:	05.07.1977
Place of Birth:	Auckland
Nationality:	Samoan
Height:	6'2"
Weight:	14st 12lb

Season Review 05/06

Dale has just completed his second successful season with the Warriors, after joining from Exeter two years ago. Dale cemented his place in the team straight away and has been a consistent player throughout the 2005/2006 season, playing 23 league and cup games throughout the campaign.

His performances and commitment was recognised by the Warriors coaching staff selecting him as the Player of the Year, which he picked up at the club's prestigious end of season awards event.

Player Performance 05/06

Premiership Performance — Percentage of total possible time player was on pitch — position in league table at end of month

Month:	Sep	Oct	Nov	Dec	Jan	Feb	Mar	Apr	May	Total
	98%				68%	100%	100%	99%	100%	79%
		5	5 50%	50%	6	7	7	8	8	
		0%	4	6						
League Pts:	10/20	4/5	12/20	0/5	6/15	2/15	5/10	6/15	2/5	47/110
Points F:	80	22	74	18	52	70	52	61	22	451
Points A:	88	15	71	36	59	97	37	66	25	494
Try Bonus:	0	0	0	0	0	0	1	1	1	3
Lose Bonus:	0	0	0	0	2	2	0	1	1	6
Total mins:	314	0	160	40	164	240	160	237	80	1,395
Starts (sub):	4	0	2	0 (1)	2 (1)	3	2	3	1	17 (2)
Points:	0	0	0	0	0	5	0	0	5	10
Tries:	0	0	0	0	0	1	0	0	1	2
Ball Carries:	19	0	9	4	5	14	12	28	12	103
Metres:	61	0	41	7	12	46	19	196	107	489
Tackles:	19	0	13	3	24	23	15	21	11	129

Prem. Performance Totals

Tries
- Rasmussen: 2
- Team-mates: 34
- **Total: 36**
- Penalty Tries: 4

Points
- Rasmussen: 10
- Team-mates: 421
- **Total: 431**
- Penalty Tries: 20

Cards
- Rasmussen: 1
- Team-mates: 16
- **Total: 17**

Cup Games

	Apps	Pts
Euro Challenge Cup	5	10
Powergen Cup	2	0
Total	**7**	**10**

Prem. Career History

Premiership Career Milestones

Club Debut:
vs Newcastle (H), L, 9-30
▶ 05.09.04
Time Spent at the Club:
▶ 2 Seasons

First Try Scored for the Club:
vs Wasps (H), W, 27-24
▶ 26.11.04
Full International:
▶ W Samoa

Premiership Totals
97–06

Appearances	37
Points	20
Tries	4
Yellow Cards	1
Red Cards	0

Clubs

Year	Club	Apps	Pts
04-06	Worcester	37	20

Off the Pitch

Age:
- Rasmussen: 28 years, 10 months
- Team: 27 years
- League: 26 years, 10 months

Height:
- Rasmussen: 6'2"
- Team: 6'1"
- League: 6'1"

Weight:
- Rasmussen: 14st 12lb
- Team: 15st 8lb
- League: 15st 10lb

Pat Sanderson
Back Row

Date of Birth: 06.09.1977
Place of Birth: Chester
Nationality: English
Height: 6'2"
Weight: 14st 8lb

Season Review 05/06

Pat Sanderson was given Captain duties for the 2005/06 season after displaying great leadership skills during his first year with the club, signing in 2004. He has made 17 league and cup appearances for the Warriors during the 2005/06 season, having missed periods of it due to injury. He won his first three senior England caps on the 1998 Southern Hemisphere tour, his next three on the North America tour in 2001 before playing in all three Investec Challenge matches in the Autumn of 2005. Pat also led England A to victory in the Churchill Cup in Edmonton, Canada in the summer of 2005 and was England Captain for the 2006 tour of Australia in June this year.

Player Performance 05/06

Premiership Performance
Percentage of total possible time player was on pitch   ⊖ position in league table at end of month

Month:	Sep	Oct	Nov	Dec	Jan	Feb	Mar	Apr	May	Total
	100%	100%						100%	100%	
	5	5	4	6	6	7	50% 7	8	8	48%
	0%	0%			17%	0%				
League Pts:	10/20	4/5	12/20	0/5	6/15	2/15	5/10	6/15	2/5	47/110
Points F:	80	22	74	18	52	70	52	61	22	451
Points A:	88	15	71	36	59	97	37	66	25	494
Try Bonus:	0	0	0	0	0	0	1	1	1	3
Lose Bonus:	0	0	0	0	2	2	0	1	1	6
Total mins:	320	80	0	0	40	0	80	240	80	840
Starts (sub):	4	1	0	0	1	0	1	3	1	11
Points:	5	0	0	0	0	0	0	5	0	10
Tries:	1	0	0	0	0	0	0	1	0	2
Ball Carries:	33	13	0	0	5	0	13	23	8	95
Metres:	129	51	0	0	16	0	16	70	10	292
Tackles:	27	7	0	0	7	0	8	14	5	68

Prem. Performance Totals

Tries
- Sanderson: 2
- Team-mates: 34
- **Total: 36**
- Penalty Tries: 4

Points
- Sanderson: 10
- Team-mates: 421
- **Total: 431**
- Penalty Tries: 20

Cards
- Sanderson: 1
- Team-mates: 16
- **Total: 17**

Cup Games

	Apps	Pts
Euro Challenge Cup	5	10
Powergen Cup	1	0
Total	**6**	**10**

Prem. Career History

Premiership Career Milestones

Club Debut:
vs Newcastle (H), L, 9-30
▶ **05.09.04**
Time Spent at the Club:
▶ **2 Seasons**

First Try Scored for the Club:
vs Harlequins (H), W, 33-7
▶ **02.10.04**
Full International:
▶ **England**

Premiership Totals
97–06

Appearances	135
Points	110
Tries	22
Yellow Cards	5
Red Cards	0

Clubs

Year	Club	Apps	Pts
04-06	Worcester	33	25
99-04	Harlequins	65	50
97-99	Sharks	37	35

Off the Pitch

Age:
- Sanderson: 28 years, 8 months
- Team: 27 years
- League: 26 years, 10 months

Height:
- Sanderson: 6'2"
- Team: 6'1"
- League: 6'1"

Weight:
- Sanderson: 14st 8lb
- Team: 15st 8lb
- League: 15st 10lb

Tevita Taumoepeau
Prop

Date of Birth:	16.05.1974
Place of Birth:	Hihifo, Haapai, Tonga
Nationality:	Tongan
Height:	6'
Weight:	18st

Season Review 05/06

The Tongan international joined Worcester during the close season last year from French side Bourgoin. The powerful prop made his debut in Worcester colours against Northampton Saints in the Powergen Cup and has been a consistent member of the squad throughout Worcester's league and cup campaigns.

Tevita scored his first and only try of the season against Amatori Catania in the European Challenge Cup.

Player Performance 05/06

Premiership Performance

Percentage of total possible time player was on pitch — position in league table at end of month

Month:	Sep	Oct	Nov	Dec	Jan	Feb	Mar	Apr	May	Total
	8%	40%	100%	50%	97%	95%	84%	48%	0%	64%
League Pts:	10/20	4/5	12/20	0/5	6/15	2/15	5/10	6/15	2/5	47/110
Points F:	80	22	74	18	52	70	52	61	22	451
Points A:	88	15	71	36	59	97	37	66	25	494
Try Bonus:	0	0	0	0	0	0	1	1	1	3
Lose Bonus:	0	0	0	0	2	2	0	1	1	6
Total mins:	25	32	320	40	233	228	135	115	0	1,128
Starts (sub):	0 (3)	0 (1)	4	0 (1)	3	3	2	2	0	14 (5)
Points:	0	0	0	0	0	0	0	0	0	0
Tries:	0	0	0	0	0	0	0	0	0	0
Ball Carries:	2	0	4	0	6	18	5	4	0	39
Metres:	4	0	13	0	13	36	5	2	0	73
Tackles:	4	1	9	0	23	10	5	2	0	54

Prem. Performance Totals

Tries

Tu'amoheloa:	0
Team-mates:	36
Total:	**36**
Penalty Tries:	4

Points

Taumoepeau:	0
Team-mates:	431
Total:	**431**
Penalty Tries:	20

Cards

Taumoepeau:	0
Team-mates:	17
Total:	**17**

Cup Games

	Apps	Pts
Euro Challenge Cup	6	5
Powergen Cup	2	0
Total	**8**	**5**

Prem. Career History

Premiership Career Milestones

Club Debut:
vs Gloucester (H), D, 15-15

▶ **04.09.05**

Time Spent at the Club:

▶ **1 Season**

First Try Scored for the Club:
—

▶ **—**

Full International:

▶ **Tonga**

Premiership Totals
97–06

Appearances	28
Points	0
Tries	0
Yellow Cards	1
Red Cards	0

Clubs

Year	Club	Apps	Pts
05-06	Worcester	19	0
03-04	Northampton	9	0

Off the Pitch

Age:

Taumoepeau:	32 years
Team:	27 years
League:	26 years, 10 months

Height:

Taumoepeau:	6'
Team:	6'1"
League:	6'1"

Weight:

Taumoepeau:	18st
Team:	15st 8lb
League:	15st 10lb

Steven Sparks
Prop

Date of Birth: 07.07.1974
Place of Birth: Blyth
Nationality: English
Height: 5'10"
Weight: 16st 9lb

Season Review 05/06

Steven Sparks joined Worcester from leading French side Stade Francais back in 2004 but the form of Tony Windo limited him to only 22 first team appearances.

He was released from the remainder of his contract in January 2006 to enable him to join French Top 14 side Pau.

His only appearances this season were against Leicester Tigers in the Powergen Cup and Amatori Catania in the European Challenge Cup.

Prem. Career History

Premiership Career Milestones

Club Debut:	First Try Scored for the Club:
vs Saracens (A), L, 10-16	vs Saracens (A), L, 10-16
▶ **12.09.04**	▶ **12.09.04**
Time Spent at the Club:	Full International:
▶ **1 Season**	▶ —

Premiership Totals
97–06

Appearances	52
Points	5
Tries	1
Yellow Cards	5
Red Cards	0

Clubs

Year	Club	Apps	Pts
04-05	Worcester	10	5
03-04	Saracens	17	0
98-99	W Hartlepool	25	0

Johnny Tuamoheloa
Back Row

Date of Birth: 20.08.1980
Place of Birth: Tofoa, Tonga
Nationality: Tongan
Height: 5'10"
Weight: 14st 6lb

Season Review 05/06

Johnny Tuamoheloa has been an integral member of Worcester's pack this season. He joined in the summer of 2005 from Newbury after helping the National Two side gain promotion. Previous to this Johnny was a member of the National Provincial Championship side North Harbour.

Johnny was born in Tonga and then moved to New Zealand aged 14. He has represented his country at international level and will return to Tonga this summer to take part in the Pacific Five Nations.

Prem. Career History

Premiership Career Milestones

Club Debut:	First Try Scored for the Club:
vs Wasps (A), L, 20-34	—
▶ **25.09.05**	▶ —
Time Spent at the Club:	Full International:
▶ **1 Season**	▶ **Tonga**

Premiership Totals
97–06

Appearances	7
Points	0
Tries	0
Yellow Cards	1
Red Cards	0

Clubs

Year	Club	Apps	Pts
05-06	Worcester	7	0

Gary Trueman
Centre

Date of Birth: 21.08.1980
Place of Birth: Wendover
Nationality: English
Height: 6'
Weight: 14st 2lb

Season Review 05/06

Since joining Worcester Warriors in 2001 Gary has made over 80 appearances, scoring 23 tries.

He made his first start of the season against Leicester Tigers at Sixways enjoying a memorable win over the East Midlands side. Gary cemented his place in the side in the last couple of months of the season and scored an impressive try against Newcastle in Worcester's last home game of the season. With his contract expiring at the end of the season, Gary penned a new two year deal which will keep him at Sixways until the summer of 2008.

Player Performance 05/06

Premiership Performance — Percentage of total possible time player was on pitch — ⊙ position in league table at end of month

Month:	Sep	Oct	Nov	Dec	Jan	Feb	Mar	Apr	May	Total
						33%	18%	78%	75%	21%
League Pts:	10/20	4/5	12/20	0/5	6/15	2/15	5/10	6/15	2/5	47/110
Points F:	80	22	74	18	52	70	52	61	22	451
Points A:	88	15	71	36	59	97	37	66	25	494
Try Bonus:	0	0	0	0	0	0	1	1	1	3
Lose Bonus:	0	0	0	0	2	2	0	1	1	6
Total mins:	17	0	0	0	0	80	29	186	60	372
Starts (sub):	0 (2)	0	0	0	0	1	0 (1)	2 (1)	1	4 (4)
Points:	0	0	0	0	0	0	0	5	0	5
Tries:	0	0	0	0	0	0	0	1	0	1
Ball Carries:	2	0	0	0	0	7	4	19	7	39
Metres:	10	0	0	0	0	23	9	112	77	231
Tackles:	2	0	0	0	0	3	0	11	4	20

Prem. Performance Totals

Tries
- Trueman: 1
- Team-mates: 35
- **Total: 36**
- Penalty Tries: 4

Points
- Trueman: 5
- Team-mates: 426
- **Total: 431**
- Penalty Tries: 20

Cards
- Trueman: 0
- Team-mates: 17
- **Total: 17**

Cup Games

	Apps	Pts
Euro Challenge Cup	4	0
Powergen Cup	1	0
Total	**5**	**0**

Prem. Career History

Premiership Career Milestones

Club Debut:
vs Newcastle (H), L, 9-30
▶ 05.09.04

First Try Scored for the Club:
vs Leicester (A), L, 7-50
▶ 27.12.04

Time Spent at the Club:
▶ 2 Seasons

Full International:
▶ —

Premiership Totals

97–06	
Appearances	19
Points	10
Tries	2
Yellow Cards	0
Red Cards	0

Clubs

Year	Club	Apps	Pts
04-06	Worcester	18	10
00-01	Saracens	1	0

Off the Pitch

Age:
- Trueman: 25 years, 9 months
- Team: 27 years
- League: 26 years, 10 months

Height:
- Trueman: 6'
- Team: 6'1"
- League: 6'1"

Weight:
- Trueman: 14st 2lb
- Team: 15st 8lb
- League: 15st 10lb

Mark Tucker
Centre/Wing

Date of Birth: 16.04.1980
Place of Birth: Johannesburg
Nationality: English
Height: 6'
Weight: 15st 10lb

Season Review 05/06

Mark signed from Northampton in the summer of 2005 after being with the Saints for seven seasons, where he graduated through the Academy. He made his first start for the club against his former team in the Powergen Cup in October and made his league debut again against them at Sixways in January. He has made 10 starts throughout the season and scored his only try against Amatori Catania in Worcester's 44–8 victory.

Born in South Africa, Mark holds a British passport after having spent over fourteen years in the UK and has represented England at U18,19 and 21 level.

Player Performance 05/06

Premiership Performance

Percentage of total possible time player was on pitch   Ⓖ position in league table at end of month

Month:	Sep	Oct	Nov	Dec	Jan	Feb	Mar	Apr	May	Total
					67%	91%	44%			
Ⓖ	5	5	4	6	6	7	7	8	8	
								23%		29%
	0%	0%	0%	0%					0%	
League Pts:	10/20	4/5	12/20	0/5	6/15	2/15	5/10	6/15	2/5	47/110
Points F:	80	22	74	18	52	70	52	61	22	451
Points A:	88	15	71	36	59	97	37	66	25	494
Try Bonus:	0	0	0	0	0	0	1	1	1	3
Lose Bonus:	0	0	0	0	2	2	0	1	1	6
Total mins:	0	0	0	0	160	218	70	54	0	502
Starts (sub):	0	0	0	0	2	3	1	1	0	7
Points:	0	0	0	0	0	0	0	0	0	0
Tries:	0	0	0	0	0	0	0	0	0	0
Ball Carries:	0	0	0	0	6	13	7	2	0	28
Metres:	0	0	0	0	33	111	26	17	0	187
Tackles:	0	0	0	0	3	6	1	5	0	15

Prem. Performance Totals

Tries
- Tucker: 0
- Team-mates: 36
- Total: 36
- Penalty Tries: 4

Points
- Tucker: 0
- Team-mates: 431
- Total: 431
- Penalty Tries: 20

Cards
- Tucker: 1
- Team-mates: 16
- Total: 17

Cup Games

	Apps	Pts
Euro Challenge Cup	4	10
Powergen Cup	3	0
Total	7	10

Prem. Career History

Premiership Career Milestones

Club Debut:
vs L Irish (A), W, 20-15
▶ **11.09.05**

First Try Scored for the Club:
—
▶ **—**

Time Spent at the Club:
▶ **1 Season**

Full International:
▶ **—**

Premiership Totals

97–06

Appearances	76
Points	93
Tries	13
Yellow Cards	2
Red Cards	0

Clubs

Year	Club	Apps	Pts
05-06	Worcester	7	0
99-05	Northampton	69	93

Off the Pitch

Age:
- Tucker: 26 years, 1 month
- Team: 27 years
- League: 26 years, 10 months

Height:
- Tucker: 6'
- Team: 6'1"
- League: 6'1"

Weight:
- Tucker: 15st 10lb
- Team: 15st 8lb
- League: 15st 10lb

Siaosi Vaili
Back Row

Date of Birth:	07.09.1977
Place of Birth:	Apia, Samoa
Nationality:	Samoan
Height:	6'4"
Weight:	17st 6lb

Season Review 05/06

The Samoan joined Worcester from Exeter two seasons ago on a two-year contract and made an impact during his first season. This season Saiosi made nine starts for the club and was mainly used as an impact player.

His contract expired at the end of the 2005/2006 season. He has signed for the Italian side, Viadana who Worcester will play in a pre-season friendly and then meet later in the season through their European Challenge Cup campaign.

Player Performance 05/06

Premiership Performance — Percentage of total possible time player was on pitch — ⊖ position in league table at end of month

Month:	Sep	Oct	Nov	Dec	Jan	Feb	Mar	Apr	May	Total
	88%	34%	14%	0%	3%	21%	23%	36%	0%	30%
position	5	5	4	6	6	7	7	8	8	
League Pts:	10/20	4/5	12/20	0/5	6/15	2/15	5/10	6/15	2/5	47/110
Points F:	80	22	74	18	52	70	52	61	22	451
Points A:	88	15	71	36	59	97	37	66	25	494
Try Bonus:	0	0	0	0	0	0	1	1	1	3
Lose Bonus:	0	0	0	0	2	2	0	1	1	6
Total mins:	280	27	44	0	8	51	36	87	0	533
Starts (sub):	4	0 (1)	0 (3)	0	0 (1)	0 (3)	0 (2)	1 (1)	0	5 (11)
Points:	0	5	0	0	0	0	5	0	0	10
Tries:	0	1	0	0	0	0	1	0	0	2
Ball Carries:	31	5	1	0	1	10	12	12	0	72
Metres:	90	18	6	0	0	50	39	37	0	240
Tackles:	13	1	4	0	2	5	3	6	0	34

Prem. Performance Totals

Tries
- ▶ Vaili: 2
- ▷ Team-mates: 34
- **Total: 36**
- ▶ Penalty Tries: 4

Points
- ▶ Vaili: 10
- ▷ Team-mates: 421
- **Total: 431**
- ▶ Penalty Tries: 20

Cards
- ▶ Vaili: 1
- ▷ Team-mates: 16
- **Total: 17**

Cup Games

	Apps	Pts
Euro Challenge Cup	6	5
Powergen Cup	1	0
Total	**7**	**5**

Prem. Career History

Premiership Career Milestones

Club Debut:
vs Harlequins (H), W, 33-7
▶ **02.10.04**

First Try Scored for the Club:
vs Harlequins (H), W, 33-7
▶ **02.10.04**

Time Spent at the Club:
▶ **2 Seasons**

Full International:
▶ **W Samoa**

Premiership Totals

97–06	
Appearances	27
Points	20
Tries	4
Yellow Cards	2
Red Cards	0

Clubs

Year	Club	Apps	Pts
04-06	Worcester	27	20

Off the Pitch

Age:
- ▶ Vaili: 28 years, 8 months
- ▷ Team: 27 years
- | League: 26 years, 10 months

Height:
- ▶ Vaili: 6'4"
- ▷ Team: 6'1"
- | League: 6'1"

Weight:
- ▶ Vaili: 17st 6lb
- ▷ Team: 15st 8lb
- | League: 15st 10lb

Andre Van Niekerk
Hooker

Date of Birth: 26.12.1976
Place of Birth: Harare, Zimbabwe
Nationality: South African
Height: 5'10"
Weight: 16st 12lb

Season Review 05/06

South African born, the influential hooker joined the Warriors back in 2004. Despite being sidelined for much of the season after suffering a dislocated shoulder against Northampton in the Powergen Cup in October last year. Andre has made an impressive 39 appearances for the club during his two seasons at Sixways. A fan's favourite, he made his comeback against Bristol at the Memorial Stadium in January of this year. Andre's working visa expired at the end of the 2005/2006 season and he has returned to his native South Africa where he will continue to play rugby at club level.

Player Performance 05/06

Premiership Performance

Percentage of total possible time player was on pitch   ⊖ position in league table at end of month

Month:	Sep	Oct	Nov	Dec	Jan	Feb	Mar	Apr	May	Total
	70% 5	5	4	6	6	7	7	8	35% 8	21%
		0%	0%	0%	13%	20%	0%	15%		
League Pts:	10/20	4/5	12/20	0/5	6/15	2/15	5/10	6/15	2/5	47/110
Points F:	80	22	74	18	52	70	52	61	22	451
Points A:	88	15	71	36	59	97	37	66	25	494
Try Bonus:	0	0	0	0	0	0	1	1	1	3
Lose Bonus:	0	0	0	0	2	2	0	1	1	6
Total mins:	223	0	0	0	32	49	0	35	28	367
Starts (sub):	4	0	0	0	1	0 (2)	0	1 (1)	0 (1)	6 (4)
Points:	0	0	0	0	0	0	0	0	0	0
Tries:	0	0	0	0	0	0	0	0	0	0
Ball Carries:	12	0	0	0	1	8	0	1	2	24
Metres:	32	0	0	0	1	14	0	7	5	59
Tackles:	6	0	0	0	1	6	0	4	1	18

Prem. Performance Totals

Tries

- Van Niekerk: 0
- Team-mates: 36
- **Total:** 36
- Penalty Tries: 4

Points

- Van Niekerk: 0
- Team-mates: 431
- **Total:** 431
- Penalty Tries: 20

Cards

- Van Niekerk: 1
- Team-mates: 16
- **Total:** 17

Cup Games

	Apps	Pts
Euro Challenge Cup	1	0
Powergen Cup	1	0
Total	2	0

Prem. Career History

Premiership Career Milestones

Club Debut:

vs Saracens (A), L, 10-16

▶ **12.09.04**

First Try Scored for the Club:

—

▶ —

Time Spent at the Club:

▶ **2 Seasons**

Full International:

▶ —

Premiership Totals

97–06

Appearances	30
Points	0
Tries	0
Yellow Cards	2
Red Cards	0

Clubs

Year	Club	Apps	Pts
04-06	Worcester	30	0

Off the Pitch

Age:

- Van Niekerk: 29 years, 5 months
- Team: 27 years
- League: 26 years, 10 months

Height:

- Van Niekerk: 5'10"
- Team: 6'1"
- League: 6'1"

Weight:

- Van Niekerk: 16st 12lb
- Team: 15st 8lb
- League: 15st 10lb

Tony Windo
Prop

Date of Birth: 30.04.1969
Place of Birth: Gloucester
Nationality: English
Height: 6'
Weight: 16st 12lb

Season Review 05/06

Tony Windo signed for Worcester Warriors in 1999 and made his debut against Manchester. One of the longest serving players in the Premiership, Tony has made over 189 league and cup appearances for the Warriors, racking up 33 tries.

This season Tony has undertaken the Captain's duties whilst Pat Sanderson was sidelined with injury.

Tony has signed a contract extension this season which will see him at Sixways until June 2007.

Player Performance 05/06

Premiership Performance

Percentage of total possible time player was on pitch   ⊖ position in league table at end of month

Month:	Sep	Oct	Nov	Dec	Jan	Feb	Mar	Apr	May	Total
	100%	100%	100%	100%	94%	100%	100%	70%	0%	91%
position	5	5	4	6	6	7	7	8	8	
League Pts:	10/20	4/5	12/20	0/5	6/15	2/15	5/10	6/15	2/5	47/110
Points F:	80	22	74	18	52	70	52	61	22	451
Points A:	88	15	71	36	59	97	37	66	25	494
Try Bonus:	0	0	0	0	0	0	1	1	1	3
Lose Bonus:	0	0	0	0	2	2	0	1	1	6
Total mins:	320	80	320	80	226	240	160	167	0	1,593
Starts (sub):	4	1	4	1	3	3	2	3	0	21
Points:	10	0	0	0	5	0	0	0	0	15
Tries:	2	0	0	0	1	0	0	0	0	3
Ball Carries:	21	0	5	2	5	8	6	2	0	49
Metres:	39	0	20	7	10	18	6	4	0	104
Tackles:	11	3	8	3	21	11	8	7	0	72

Prem. Performance Totals

Tries
- Windo: 3
- Team-mates: 33
- **Total: 36**
- Penalty Tries: 4

Points
- Windo: 15
- Team-mates: 416
- **Total: 431**
- Penalty Tries: 20

Cards
- Windo: 0
- Team-mates: 17
- **Total: 17**

Cup Games

	Apps	Pts
Euro Challenge Cup	7	0
Powergen Cup	1	0
Total	**8**	**0**

Prem. Career History

Premiership Career Milestones

Club Debut:
vs Newcastle (H), L, 9-30
▶ **05.09.04**

Time Spent at the Club:
▶ **2 Seasons**

First Try Scored for the Club:
vs Gloucester (H), L, 13-18
▶ **16.10.04**

Full International:
▶ **—**

Premiership Totals

97–06
Appearances	77
Points	35
Tries	7
Yellow Cards	0
Red Cards	0

Clubs

Year	Club	Apps	Pts
04-06	Worcester	43	25
97-99	Gloucester	34	10

Off the Pitch

Age:
- Windo: 37 years, 1 month
- Team: 27 years
- League: 26 years, 10 months

Height:
- Windo: 6'
- Team: 6'1"
- League: 6'1"

Weight:
- Windo: 16st 12lb
- Team: 15st 8lb
- League: 15st 10lb

RUGBY PREMIERSHIP
KICK OFF
2006/07

Premiership Roll of Honour

Season	Champions	Relegated	Promoted
2005/06 Premiership	**Sale Sharks**	Leeds Tykes	NEC Harlequins
2004/05 Premiership	**London Wasps**	NEC Harlequins	Bristol Rugby
2003/04 Premiership	**London Wasps**	Rotherham Titans	Worcester Warriors
2002/03 Premiership	**London Wasps**	Bristol Rugby	Rotherham Titans
2001/02 Premiership	**Leicester Tigers**	N/A	N/A
2000/01 Premiership	**Leicester Tigers**	Rotherham Titans	Leeds Tykes
1999/00 Premiership	**Leicester Tigers**	Bedford Blues	RotherhamTitans
1998/99 Premiership	**Leicester Tigers**	West Hartlepool	Bristol Rugby
1997/98 Premiership	**Newcastle Falcons**	Bristol Rugby	Bedford
			West Hartlepool
			London Scottish

RUGBY PREMIERSHIP
KICK OFF
2006/07

Season Statistics 2005/06

Final Premiership Table 2005/06

Team	RECORD			POINTS			ATTACK					DEFENCE					PD
	W	D	L	TB	LB	Tot	T	C	PG	DG	For	T	C	PG	DG	Agst	PD
1 Sale Sharks (C)	16	1	5	6	2	74	52	38	73	6	573	42	27	56	4	444	129
2 Leicester Tigers	14	3	5	5	1	68	51	34	64	1	518	24	20	78	7	415	103
3 London Irish	14	0	8	6	4	66	54	32	47	6	493	44	30	56	2	454	39
4 London Wasps	12	3	7	7	3	64	53	41	58	2	527	42	30	57	2	447	80
5 Gloucester Rugby	11	1	10	4	9	59	46	32	61	2	483	33	26	53	3	385	98
6 Northampton Saints	10	1	11	4	7	53	53	35	41	2	464	50	32	54	4	488	-24
7 Newcastle Falcons	9	1	12	3	6	47	42	25	45	7	416	44	30	50	1	433	-17
8 Worcester Warriors	9	1	12	3	6	47	40	28	61	4	451	56	32	48	2	494	-43
9 Bath Rugby	9	1	12	3	5	46	38	25	61	6	441	49	33	58	3	494	-53
10 Saracens	8	1	13	5	7	46	42	32	51	2	433	48	30	56	5	483	-50
11 Bristol Rugby	8	1	13	0	7	41	28	23	69	0	393	41	30	55	5	445	-52
12 Leeds Tykes (R)	5	0	17	1	7	28	36	24	42	3	363	62	49	52	3	573	-210

▨ = Premiership Semi-Finalists ▨ = Qualified for European Cup ▨ = Relegated

Premiership Play-Off SF
14 May 2006 **Sale Sharks** **22-12** **London Wasps** **Edgeley Park**

Scoring sequence: 1' Hodgson (PG) 3-0, 5' Van Gisbergen (PG) 3-3, 16' Hodgson (PG) 6-3, 20' Hodgson (PG) 9-3, 31' Robinson (T) 14-3, Hodgson (C) 16-3, 43' Van Gisbergen (PG) 16-6, 45' Hodgson (PG) 19-6, 51' Van Gisbergen (PG) 19-9, 65' Van Gisbergen (PG) 19-12, 78' Hodgson (PG) 22-12.

Referee: Chris White (England)
Attendance: 10,641

Premiership Play-Off SF
14 May 2006 **Leicester Tigers** **40-8** **London Irish** **Welford Road**

Scoring sequence: 7' Goode (PG) 3-0, 15' Alesana Tuilagi (T) 8-0, Goode (C) 10-0, 25' Magne (T) 10-5, 32' Ellis (T) 15-5, Goode (C) 17-5, 40' Goode (PG) 20-5, 51' Catt (PG) 20-8, 56' Goode (PG) 23-8, 60' Lloyd (T) 28-8, 67' Murphy (T) 33-8, Goode (C) 35-8, 73' Lloyd (T) 40-8.

Referee: Dave Pearson (England)
Attendance: 14,069

Premiership Play-Off Final
27 May 2006 **Sale Sharks** **45-20** **Leicester Tigers** **Twickenham**

Scoring sequence: 3' Hodgson (PG) 3-0, 8' Cueto (T) 8-0, 9' Moody (T) 8-5, Goode (C) 8-7, 17' Lund (T) 13-7, 31' Hodgson (PG) 16-7, 36' Goode (PG) 16-10, 40' Ripol (T) 21-10, Hodgson (C) 23-10, 43' Goode (PG) 23-13, 45' Hodgson (PG) 26-13, 48' Hodgson (PG) 29-13, 63' Hodgson (PG) 32-13, 70' Hodgson (DG) 35-13, 74' Hamilton (T) 35-18, Goode (C) 35-20, 78' Hodgson (PG) 38-20, 80' Mayor (T) 43-20, Courrent (C) 45-20.

Referee: Dave Pearson (England)
Attendance: 58,000

Tries and Points

[includes play-off data]

Top Try Scorer

	Player	Team	Tries
1	**Tom Varndell**	**Leicester Tigers**	**14**
2	Tom Voyce	London Wasps	10
3	Delon Armitage	London Irish	8
4	Tom Biggs	Leeds Tykes	8
5	Matthew Burke	Newcastle Falcons	8
6	Anthony Elliott	Newcastle Falcons	8
7	David Lemi	Bristol Rugby	8
8	Paul Sackey	London Wasps	8

Top Points Scorer

	Player	Team	Points
1	**Charlie Hodgson**	**Sale Sharks**	**248**
2	Jason Strange	Bristol Rugby	244
3	Glen Jackson	Saracens	238
4	Shane Drahm	Worcester Warriors	233
5	Andy Goode	Leicester Tigers	225
6	Ludovic Mercier	Gloucester Rugby	213
7	Mark Van Gisbergen	London Wasps	211
8	Bruce Reihana	Northampton Saints	206

Statistics

Premiership Records

Individual Game Records

	All Time	Best in 2005/06
Most points	32 – Niall Woods (Irish v Harlequins, 25 Apr 98) 32 – Dave Walder (Falcons v Saracens, 26 Nov 00) 32 – Tim Stimpson (Tigers v Falcons, 21 Sep 02)	27 – Andy Goode (Tigers v Sharks, 28 Jan)
Most tries	6 – Ryan Constable (Saracens at Bedford, 16 Apr 00)	4 – Sean Lamont (Saints v Saracens, 18 Feb)
Most conversions	13 – Richie Butland (Richmond at Bedford, 16 May 99)	6 – Valentin Courrent (Sharks at Warriors, 11 Feb) 6 – Bruce Reihana (Saints v Saracens, 18 Feb) 6 – Jonny Wilkinson (Falcons v Tykes, 6 May)
Most penalty goals	9 – Simon Mannix (Gloucester v Quins, 23 Sep 00) 9 – Luke Smith (Saracens v Gloucester, 8 Sep 01) 9 – Braam van Straaten (Tykes v Irish, 8 Sep 02) 9 – Alex King (Wasps v Falcons, 11 Nov 01)	8 – Andy Goode (Tigers v Sharks, 28 Jan)
Most drop goals	3 – Ludovic Mercier (Gloucester at Sharks, 22 Sep 01) 3 – Mark Mapletoft (Irish vs Saints, 27 Dec 04)	2 – Shane Drahm (Warriors at Irish, 11 Sep) 2 – Dave Walder (Falcons at Saints, 17 Sep) 2 – Barry Everitt (Irish v Tigers, 8 Jan)
Fastest try	9.63 secs – Tom Voyce (Wasps v Harlequins, 5 Nov 04)	28 secs – Tom Varndell (Tigers v Bath, 17 Sep)
Quickest bonus point try	14 mins – Mike Worsley (Quins v Saracens, 12 Nov 04)	20 mins – Sailosi Tagicakibau (Irish at Wasps, 30 Apr)

Team Records

	All Time	Best in 2005/06
Most points in a home game	77-19 – Bath v Harlequins (The Rec, 29 Apr 00)	58-17 – Saints v Saracens (Franklin's Gardens, 18 Feb)
Most points in an away game	106-12 – Richmond at Bedford (Goldington Road, 16 May 99)	56-37 – Irish at Wasps (Causeway Stadium, 30 Apr)
Highest aggregate of points in game	118pts – Bedford 12, Richmond 106 (Goldington Road, 16 May 99)	93pts – Wasps 37, Irish 56 (Causeway Stadium, 30 Apr)
Biggest home win	76pts – Sale 76, Bristol 0 (Heywood Road, 9 Nov 97)	41pts – Saints 58, Saracens 17 (Franklin's Gardens, 18 Feb)
Biggest away win	94pts – Bedford 12, Richmond 106 (Goldington Road, 16 May 99)	32pts – Bristol 9, Gloucester 41 (Memorial Stadium, 18 Sep)
Highest attendance (non-Twickenham)	20,840 – Irish v Bath (Madejski Stadium, 21 Mar 04)	19,884 – Irish v Sharks (Madejski Stadium, 25 Mar)

Bath Rugby

Season Summary 2005/06

Position	Won	Drawn	Lost	For	Against		Bonus Points	Total Points
9	**9**	**1**	**12**	**441**	**494**		**8**	**46**

Despite pre-season optimism, this was another disappointing Premiership campaign for the West Country side. Three consecutive defeats in the opening games left John Connolly's side playing catch up. Connolly's departure opened the way for the return of Rec favourite Brian Ashton and performances improved. However, despite reaching the semi-finals of both the Heineken and Powergen Cups, ninth in the league was ultimately disappointing for a club that sets such high standards. The season ended with the club looking to appoint a new coaching set-up following the summer departures of Ashton, Michael Foley and Richard Graham.

Forwards Coach: Mark Bakewell
Backs Coach: Steve Meehan

Club Honours
Courage League / Zurich Premiership: 1988-89, 1990-91, 1991-92, 1992-93, 1993-94, 1995-96, 2003-04 (lost play-offs)

John Player Cup / Pilkington Cup: 1984, 1985, 1986, 1987 1989, 1990, 1992, 1994, 1995, 1996
Heineken Cup: 1997-1998

Season Squad

Stats 2005-06

Position	Player	Height	Weight	Apps	Rep	Tries	Points	Position	Player	Height	Weight	Apps	Rep	Tries	Points
FB/W	N.Abendanon	5'10"	13st 0lb	1	3	-	-	P	D.Flatman	6'1"	18st 12lb	6	3	-	-
FH/C	O.Barkley	5'10"	14st 6lb	12	-	-	118	FH	E.Fuimaono-Sapolu	6'1"	16st 0lb	3	1	1	5
P	D.Barnes	6'0"	17st 10lb	11	1	-	-	BR	C.Goodman	6'2"	16st 5lb	1	1	-	-
SH	M.Baxter	5'10"	13st 10lb	-	1	-	-	L	D.Grewcock	6'6"	18st 10lb	14	-	-	-
BR	A.Beattie	6'5"	18st 8lb	20	-	2	10	H	R.Hawkins	6'0"	16st 4lb	-	3	-	-
P	D.Bell	6'2"	19st 8lb	17	4	1	5	C	A.Higgins	5'11"	13st 12lb	15	2	1	5
FB/W	L.Best	6'3"	15st 2lb	4	2	1	5	L	J.Hudson	6'7"	17st 10lb	6	-	2	10
L	S.Borthwick	6'6"	17st 5lb	13	-	-	-	BR	M.Lipman	6'1"	15st 7lb	11	2	2	10
W	D.Bory	5'11"	14st 9lb	14	-	2	10	P	C.Loader	5'10"	18st 6lb	-	3	-	-
C	T.Cheeseman	6'0"	14st 2lb	2	1	-	-	FB/W	J.Maddock	5'8"	13st 5lb	16	1	3	15
C	A.Crockett	5'11"	14st 9lb	14	-	2	10	FH	C.Malone	6'0"	14st 9lb	17	-	4	130
C	S.Davey	6'1"	15st 2lb	-	1	-	-	H	L.Mears	5'9"	15st 8lb	14	1	2	10
FB/FH/C	R.Davis	5'6"	13st 12lb	1	7	-	-	FB	M.Perry	6'1"	13st 12lb	7	-	-	-
BR	G.Delve	6'3"	18st 0lb	7	10	3	15	BR	J.Scaysbrook	6'3"	15st 6lb	8	4	1	5
H	P.Dixon	5'11"	16st 7lb	8	5	-	-	BR/L	P.Short	6'5"	18st 8lb	8	5	-	-
FH	A.Dunne	5'8"	12st 8lb	4	1	-	20	W	M.Stephenson	6'0"	13st 0lb	9	4	1	8
L	J.Fa'amatuainu	6'4"	16st 4lb	1	1	-	-	P	M.Stevens	6'0"	19st 0lb	6	3	1	5
8	Z.Feau'nati	6'2"	18st 8lb	17	3	3	15	SH	N.Walshe	5'10"	13st 6lb	11	2	-	-
L	R.Fidler	6'5"	18st 4lb	4	7	-	-	W/C	F.Welsh	6'1"	15st 6lb	7	1	2	10
P	T.Filise	6'2"	19st 7lb	4	3	1	5	SH	A.Williams	5'11"	13st 12lb	6	8	-	-
W	S.Finau	6'0"	16st 0lb	6	2	2	10	SH	M.Wood	5'10"	14st 11lb	5	-	1	5

Bath Rugby

Last Season Form 2005/06

Season Progression

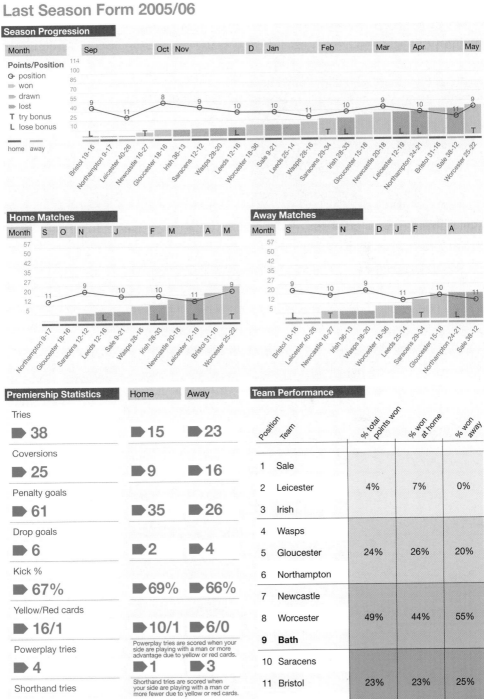

| Month | Sep | Oct | Nov | D | Jan | Feb | Mar | Apr | May |

Points/Position
- position
- won
- drawn
- lost
- T try bonus
- L lose bonus

home away

Bristol 19-16, Northampton 9-17, Leicester 40-26, Newcastle 16-27, Gloucester 18-16, Irish 36-13, Saracens 12-12, Wasps 28-20, Leeds 12-16, Worcester 18-36, Sale 9-21, Leeds 25-14, Wasps 28-16, Saracens 29-34, Irish 28-33, Gloucester 15-18, Newcastle 20-18, Leicester 12-19, Northampton 24-21, Bristol 31-16, Sale 38-12, Worcester 25-22

Home Matches

| Month | S | O | N | J | F | M | A | M |

Northampton 9-17, Gloucester 18-16, Saracens 12-12, Leeds 12-16, Sale 9-21, Wasps 28-16, Irish 28-33, Newcastle 20-18, Leicester 12-19, Bristol 31-16, Worcester 25-22

Away Matches

| Month | S | | N | | D | J | F | | A | |

Bristol 19-16, Leicester 40-26, Newcastle 16-27, Irish 36-13, Wasps 28-20, Worcester 18-36, Leeds 25-14, Saracens 29-34, Gloucester 15-18, Northampton 24-21, Sale 38-12

Premiership Statistics

		Home	Away
Tries	38	15	23
Coversions	25	9	16
Penalty goals	61	35	26
Drop goals	6	2	4
Kick %	67%	69%	66%
Yellow/Red cards	16/1	10/1	6/0
Powerplay tries	4	1	3
Shorthand tries	1	1	0

Powerplay tries are scored when your side are playing with a man or more advantage due to yellow or red cards.

Shorthand tries are scored when your side are playing with a man or more fewer due to yellow or red cards.

Team Performance

Position	Team	% total points won	% won at home	% won away
1	Sale			
2	Leicester	4%	7%	0%
3	Irish			
4	Wasps			
5	Gloucester	24%	26%	20%
6	Northampton			
7	Newcastle			
8	Worcester	49%	44%	55%
9	**Bath**			
10	Saracens			
11	Bristol	23%	23%	25%
12	Leeds			

Bath Rugby

Top Scorer – Chris Malone

Total points	% team points	Home	Away
▶130	▶29	▶73	▶57

Points by Time Period

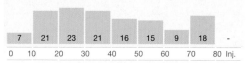

7	21	23	21	16	15	9	18	-
0	10	20	30	40	50	60	70	80 Inj.

Team Tries and Points

Tries by Time Period

- scored
- conceded

3	5	3	8	6	5	3	4	1
0	10min	20min	30min	40min	50min	60min	70min	80 Injury time
5	1	5	7	4	8	5	14	0

Tries by Halves

- scored
- conceded

	Total	1st half	2nd half	1st half %	2nd half %
scored	▶38	▶19	▶19	▶50%	▶50%
conceded	▶49	▶18	▶31	▶37%	▶63%

How Points were Scored

- tries: 190
- conversions: 50
- pen goals: 183
- drop goals: 18

How Points were Conceded

- tries: 245
- conversions: 66
- pen goals: 174
- drop goals: 9

Tries Scored by Player

- backs: 20
- forwards: 18

Tries Conceded by Player

- backs: 36
- forwards: 10

Bath Rugby

Eight-Season Form 1998-2006

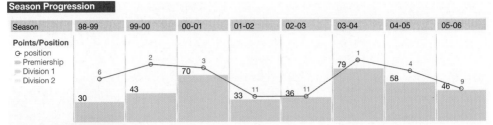

Season Progression

Season	98-99	99-00	00-01	01-02	02-03	03-04	04-05	05-06

Points/Position
- ○ position
- ▬ Premiership
- ▬ Division 1
- ▬ Division 2

	98-99	99-00	00-01	01-02	02-03	03-04	04-05	05-06
position	6	2	3	11	11	1	4	9
points	30	43	70	33	36	79	58	46

Games

	98-99	99-00	00-01	01-02	02-03	03-04	04-05	05-06
won	15	15	14	7	7	18	12	9
drawn		2			2		2	1
lost	11	5	8	15	13	4	8	12

Points

	98-99	99-00	00-01	01-02	02-03	03-04	04-05	05-06
scored	698	690	680	311	385	508	407	441
conceded	574	425	430	524	490	311	366	494

Points Difference

	98-99	99-00	00-01	01-02	02-03	03-04	04-05	05-06
points	+124	+265	+250	-213	-105	+197	+41	-53

Total Premiership Record

Largest win

▶ **76-13**
vs London Scottish (H)
15.05.99

Largest defeat

▶ **12-68**
vs Gloucester (A)
04.05.02

Most tries scored in a game

▶ **12**
vs London Scottish (H)
15.05.99

Most tries conceded in a game

▶ **9**
vs Gloucester (A)
04.05.02

Top points scorer

▶ O.Barkley 750

Top try scorer

▶ I.Balshaw 36

Top drop goal scorer

▶ C.Malone 22

Most appearances

▶ S.Borthwick 139

Longest winning sequence

▶ **10 wins** from 22.01.00 to 06.05.00

Longest losing sequence

▶ **6 defeats** from 31.10.98 to 02.01.99

Guinness Premiership 2006-07 | **Premiership History**

Legend: ■ won ■ drawn ■ lost □ not played

Date	Team	H/A	05-06	Played	Total Points F	A	Outcome after a half-time lead No.	W	D	L	Close games No.	W
02.09.06	Gloucester	A	15-18	9	164	230	6►3	-	3		4	3
09.09.06	Leicester	H	12-19	9	125	135	5►3	-	2		2	-
16.09.06	Northampton	A	24-21	9	113	212	2►1	-	1		3	1
23.09.06	Worcester	H	25-22	2	43	32	1►1	-	-		1	1
15.10.06	Saracens	A	29-34	9	202	229	5►5	-	-		1	1
04.11.06	Irish	H	28-33	9	239	163	7►6	1	-		5	3
12.11.06	Wasps	A	28-20	9	167	202	3►3	-	-		3	2
17.11.06	Bristol	H	31-16	6	167	99	4►4	-	-		2	2
25.11.06	Newcastle	H	20-18	9	199	137	5►5	-	-		2	2
22.12.06	Sale	H	9-21	9	212	151	7►6	-	1		4	4
27.12.06	Bristol	A	19-16	6	115	143	3►1	1	1		3	1
01.01.07	Wasps	H	28-16	9	221	179	4►4	-	-		5	1
06.01.07	Harlequins	A	N/A	8	167	165	3►1	-	2		2	-
27.01.07	Harlequins	H	N/A	8	241	116	8►6	-	2		2	-
17.02.07	Irish	A	36-13	9	287	239	3►3	-	-		3	3
24.02.07	Saracens	H	12-12	9	178	172	5►3	-	2		1	-
03.03.07	Worcester	A	18-36	2	62	40	1►1	-	-		1	1
10.03.07	Northampton	H	9-17	9	188	135	4►4	-	-		1	-
17.03.07	Leicester	A	40-26	9	163	277	5►1	1	3		3	1
07.04.07	Gloucester	H	18-16	9	272	122	7►7	-	-		4	3
13.04.07	Sale	A	38-12	9	167	224	3►1	-	2		6	3
28.04.07	Newcastle	A	16-27	9	161	175	3►2	-	1		7	3

Club Information

Useful Information

Founded
1865
Address
The Recreation Ground
Bath
BA2 6PW
Capacity
10,600 (5,740 seated)
Main switchboard
01225 325200
Website
www.bathrugby.com

Travel Information

Car
(Lambridge Park & Ride):
Leave the M4 at Junction 18 and follow the A46 to Bath. Follow the signs for the town centre. The Park & Ride is at Bath Rugby's training ground on your left after the first set of traffic lights.
The Park & Ride is open for all 1st XV weekend fixtures. To go direct to the stadium, carry on past the training ground until you reach the junction on London Road with Bathwick Street. Turn left and then right down Sydney Place. Go straight on at the roundabout then turn left down North Parade. The ground is on your right.

Train
Bath has direct links to London, Bristol, Cardiff, Salisbury and Southampton. From Birmingham and the Midlands, there are con-necting services at Bristol Temple Meads. National Rail enquiries: 08457 48 49 50.

Coach
National Express services operate between most major towns and cities in Britain.
For further information contact Bath Bus Station on 01225 464446 or National Express direct on 08705 80 80 80 or visit www.nationalexpress.com

Bath Rugby

Maps

Area Map

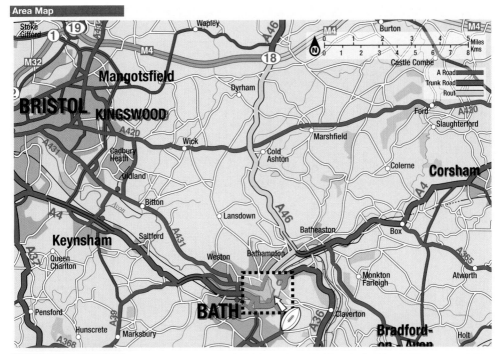

Local Map

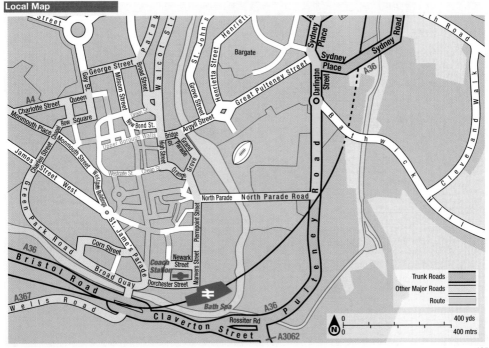

Bristol Rugby

Season Summary 2005/06

Position	Won	Drawn	Lost	For	Against	Bonus Points	Total Points
11	8	1	13	393	445	7	41

As with Worcester the previous year, there are few that would have wanted to see Bristol fall at the first hurdle. Head coach Richard Hill made a series of shrewd signings to ensure his side was no easy proposition and they proved to be a hard team to beat, enjoying victories against Tigers, Sale and Saracens. Fly half Jason Strange formed a successful pairing with newcomer Shaun Perry, with Strange finishing the season as the Premiership's top points scorer. The West Country side finished the season in 11th place with 41 points.

Head Coach: Richard Hill

Club Honours
John Player Cup: 1983

Season Squad

Stats 2005-06

Position	Player	Height	Weight	Apps	Rep	Tries	Points	Position	Player	Height	Weight	Apps	Rep	Tries	Points
BR	N.Budgett	6'5"	17st 0lb	8	-	-	-	L	G.Llewellyn	6'6"	17st 7lb	19	-	-	-
H	N.Clark	5'11"	16st 0lb	-	6	-	-	BR	R.Martin-Redman	6'3"	17st 0lb	-	1	-	-
P	A.Clarke	5'11"	17st 0lb	-	8	-	-	FL	C.Morgan	6'2"	16st 4lb	-	2	-	-
C	M.Contepomi	6'2"	14st 2lb	4	2	-	-	H	S.Nelson	5'10"	14st 9lb	4	4	-	-
C	S.Cox	6'0"	13st 10lb	16	-	1	5	SH	G.Nicholls	5'8"	12st 0lb	1	1	-	-
P	D.Crompton	6'2"	18st 0lb	22	-	1	5	SH	S.Perry	5'10"	15st 0lb	19	-	4	20
C	M.Denney	6'0"	17st 4lb	-	5	-	-	SH	J.Rauluni	5'11"	14st 6lb	2	2	-	-
FL	J.El Abd	6'2"	16st 0lb	14	-	2	10	H	M.Regan	5'10"	15st 2lb	18	-	1	5
FB	V.Going	5'11"	14st 2lb	14	1	-	-	W	L.Robinson	6'2"	17st 1lb	17	-	3	15
FH	D.Gray	5'10"	13st 0lb	-	5	-	-	BR	M.Salter	6'4"	16st 4lb	21	-	-	-
FH	T.Hayes	6'0"	14st 4lb	1	5	1	19	L	M.Sambucetti	6'5"	17st 1lb	6	6	-	-
C	R.Higgitt	6'2"	14st 7lb	17	1	-	-	BR	C.Short	6'2"	16st 0lb	8	1	-	-
P	D.Hilton	5'11"	16st 10lb	21	-	-	-	W	M.Stanojevic	5'11"	12st 7lb	5	1	2	10
L	O.Hodge	6'8"	16st 10lb	-	1	-	-	FB	B.Stortoni	6'1"	14st 4lb	14	-	-	-
P	M.Irish	6'0"	16st 0lb	1	4	-	-	FH	J.Strange	5'10"	13st 3lb	21	1	1	244
W	D.Lemi	5'9"	11st 11lb	12	-	8	40	8	D.Ward-Smith	6'4"	17st 8lb	10	8	-	-
BR	G.Lewis	6'3"	15st 8lb	13	6	1	5	L	R.Winters	6'4"	17st 10lb	11	5	1	5
W	B.Lima	6'0"	15st 4lb	11	2	2	10								

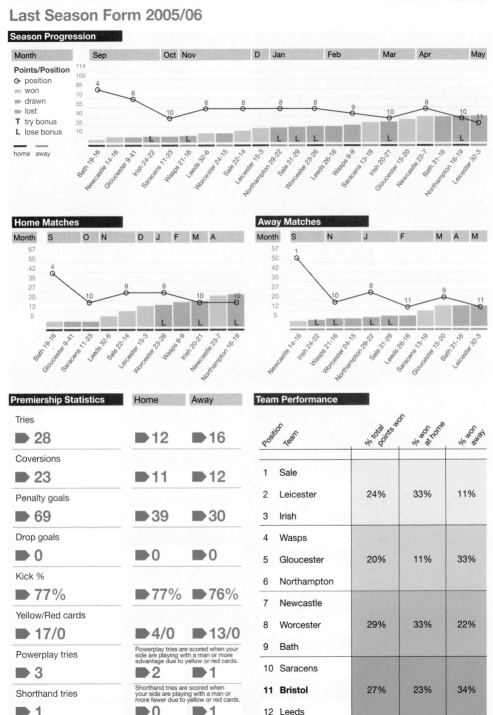

Bristol Rugby

Top Scorer – Jason Strange

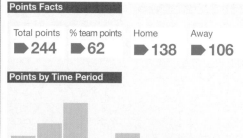

Points Facts

Total points	% team points	Home	Away
➤244	➤62	➤138	➤106

Points by Time Period

33	41	54	19	35	27	19	16	-
0	10	20	30	40	50	60	70	80 Inj.

Team Tries and Points

Tries by Time Period

- scored
- conceded

7	0	3		2		4		2		4		6		0
0	10min	20min	30min	40min	50min	60min	70min	80 Injury time
3	3	8		7		2		6		7		4		1

Tries by Halves

- scored
- conceded

➤ 28	➤ 12	➤ 16	➤ 43%	➤ 57%
Total	1st half	2nd half	1st half %	2nd half %
➤ 41	➤ 21	➤ 20	➤ 51%	➤ 49%

How Points were Scored

- tries: 140
- conversions: 46
- pen goals: 207
- drop goals: 0

How Points were Conceded

- tries: 205
- conversions: 60
- pen goals: 165
- drop goals: 15

Tries Scored by Player

- backs: 22
- forwards: 6

Tries Conceded by Player

- backs: 25
- forwards: 16

Bristol Rugby

Eight-Season Form 1998-2006

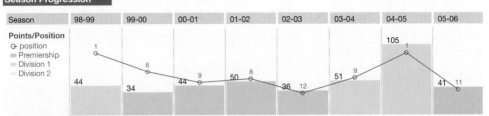

Season Progression

Season	98-99	99-00	00-01	01-02	02-03	03-04	04-05	05-06
Points/Position ○ position ▬ Premiership ▬ Division 1 ▬ Division 2	44 (1)	34 (6)	44 (9)	50 (8)	36 (12)	51 (9)	105 (1)	41 (11)

Games

Season	98-99	99-00	00-01	01-02	02-03	03-04	04-05	05-06
won	22	12	9	9	7	10	22	8
drawn		1	1	1	1			1
lost	4	9	12	12	14	16	4	13

Points

Season	98-99	99-00	00-01	01-02	02-03	03-04	04-05	05-06
scored	848	632	443	591	504	547	940	393
conceded	418	602	492	632	633	650	355	445

Points Difference

Season	98-99	99-00	00-01	01-02	02-03	03-04	04-05	05-06
points	+430	+30	-49	-41	-129	-103	+585	-52

Total Premiership Record

Largest win	Largest defeat	Most tries scored in a game	Most tries conceded in a game
▶ **57-19** vs Bedford Blues (A) 29.04.00	▶ **0-76** vs Sale Sharks (A) 09.11.97	▶ **9** vs Bedford Blues (A) 29.04.00	▶ **12** vs Sale Sharks (A) 09.11.97

Top points scorer	Top try scorer	Top drop goal scorer	Most appearances
▶ F.Contepomi 573	▶ F.Contepomi 19	▶ F.Contepomi 3	▶ C.Short 85

Longest winning sequence	Longest losing sequence
▶ **4 wins** from 19.04.00 to 10.05.00	▶ **13 defeats** from 18.01.98 to 10.05.98

Bristol Rugby EFL

ENHANCED FIXTURE LIST
[does not include play-off data]

Guinness Premiership 2006-07 — Premiership History

Date	Team	H/A	05-06	Played	98-99	99-00	00-01	01-02	02-03	03-04	04-05	05-06	F	A	No.	W	D	L	No.	W
					won		drawn		lost		not played		(Total Points)		(Outcome after a half-time lead)				(Close games)	
02.09.06	Worcester	A	24-15	1									15	24	-	-	-	-	-	-
10.09.06	Saracens	H	11-23	6									151	186	2	-	-	2	1	-
16.09.06	Irish	A	24-22	6									126	188	-	-	-	-	2	-
24.09.06	Wasps	H	9-9	6									124	140	3	2	-	1	1	-
15.10.06	Harlequins	H	N/A	5									165	142	5	4	-	1	2	2
03.11.06	Newcastle	A	14-16	6									126	161	3	3	-	-	2	2
10.11.06	Sale	H	22-14	6									128	132	3	3	-	-	-	-
17.11.06	Bath	A	31-16	6									99	167	1	1	-	-	2	-
24.11.06	Gloucester	H	9-41	6									126	181	1	-	-	1	2	-
22.12.06	Leicester	A	32-3	6									82	185	1	-	-	1	-	-
27.12.06	Bath	H	19-16	6									143	115	2	2	-	-	3	1
01.01.07	Sale	A	31-29	6									156	228	1	1	-	-	3	1
07.01.07	Northampton	H	16-19	6									158	152	2	-	-	2	1	-
27.01.07	Northampton	A	29-22	6									99	170	2	1	-	1	2	2
18.02.07	Newcastle	H	23-7	6									159	109	5	5	-	-	-	-
24.02.07	Harlequins	A	N/A	5									140	163	2	1	-	1	3	2
04.03.07	Wasps	A	21-16	6									133	173	3	1	-	2	4	1
10.03.07	Irish	H	20-21	6									130	145	2	-	-	2	5	1
18.03.07	Saracens	A	13-19	6									95	148	1	1	-	-	3	2
08.04.07	Worcester	H	23-26	1									23	26	-	-	-	-	1	-
15.04.07	Leicester	H	15-3	6									149	121	4	4	-	-	3	2
28.04.07	Gloucester	A	15-20	6									107	213	3	-	-	3	2	1

Club Information

Useful Information

Founded
1888
Address
The Memorial Stadium
Filton Avenue
Horfield
Bristol
BS7 0AQ
Stadium capacity
12,000 (3,000 seated)
Main switchboard
0117 952 0500
Website
www.bristolrugby.co.uk

Travel Information

Car

From the M4: Exit at junction 19 and follow signs onto the M32. Leave the M32 at junction 2 and at the roundabout turn right towards Horfield and the B4469. Continue for 1.4 miles, then after passing the bus garage (on your right) turn left at the second set of traffic lights into Filton Avenue. Take the first left into the club car park.

From the M5: Exit at junction 16 and join the A38 towards Bristol City Centre. After 5 miles turn left at traffic lights onto B4469. Turn right at the next traffic lights into Filton Avenue and then first left into car park.

Train

Nearest mainline rail stations are Bristol Parkway or Bristol Temple Meads.

Bristol Rugby

Maps

Area Map

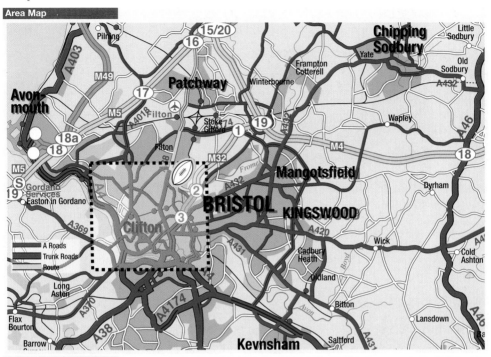

Local Map

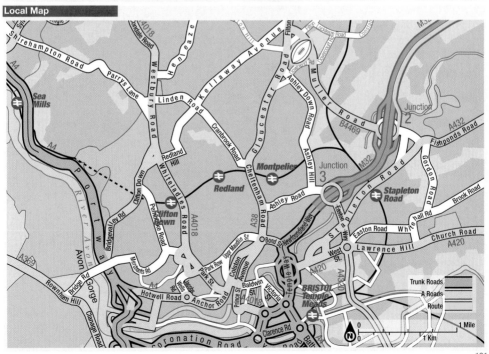

Gloucester Rugby

Season Summary 2005/06

Position	Won	Drawn	Lost	For	Against	Bonus Points	Total Points
5	**11**	**1**	**10**	**483**	**385**	**13**	**59**

The Kingsholm faithful had high expectations at the start of the season and welcomed new boy Mike Tindall from Bath. However, it was the young fly half Ryan Lamb who really stole the show throughout the season, especially for his performance against Worcester in the semi-final of the European Challenge Cup. Despite a positive start to their league campaign – winning four out of their first six matches – Dean Ryan's side failed to display that kind of consistency throughout the season. They did enjoy success in the European Challenge Cup, beating London Irish in the final thanks to a moment of inspirational attacking instinct from James Forrester to score what proved to be the winning try.

Head Coach: Dean Ryan

Club Honours
Zurich Premiership: 2002-03 (playoffs won by Wasps)
John Player Cup: 1972, 1978, 1982, 2003
European Challenge Cup: 2006

Season Squad

Stats 2005-06

Position	Player	Height	Weight	Apps	Rep	Tries	Points	Position	Player	Height	Weight	Apps	Rep	Tries	Points
C	J.Adams	6'0"	16st 5lb	-	2	-	-	FB	J.Goodridge	6'1"	13st 8lb	9	1	1	5
C	A.Allen	5'11"	14st 2lb	8	1	4	20	FL	A.Hazell	6'0"	14st 9lb	17	1	1	5
FH/SH	S.Amor	5'7"	12st 0lb	1	3	-	-	C	R.Keil	6'1"	13st 5lb	3	1	-	-
H	O.Azam	6'0"	18st 0lb	3	3	1	5	FH	R.Lamb	5'10"	12st 10lb	4	1	1	49
W	J.Bailey	5'11"	13st 0lb	10	2	5	25	FH/FB	D.McRae	5'7"	12st 10lb	-	2	-	-
8	A.Balding	6'2"	17st 7lb	8	5	-	-	FH	L.Mercier	5'10"	14st 2lb	18	4	2	213
FL	J.Boer	6'1"	16st 8lb	9	3	1	5	FL	J.Merriman	6'0"	14st 7lb	1	-	-	-
L	A.Brown	6'7"	17st 5lb	18	-	-	-	FB	O.Morgan	6'2"	14st 0lb	12	-	1	5
BR	P.Buxton	6'3"	17st 9lb	16	3	-	-	BR	L.Narraway	6'3"	15st 10lb	2	8	-	-
P	P.Collazo	6'1"	17st 4lb	19	-	-	-	H	J.Parkes	5'10"	15st 6lb	2	4	-	-
L	M.Cornwell	6'7"	18st 2lb	1	2	-	-	C	H.Paul	5'11"	14st 10lb	5	-	-	-
L	Q.Davids	6'6"	19st 4lb	2	1	-	-	L	J.Pendlebury	6'7"	16st 5lb	8	3	-	-
FH	B.Davies	5'9"	14st 1lb	1	4	-	-	P	G.Powell	6'0"	17st 9lb	7	5	-	-
H	M.Davies	5'10"	15st 0lb	13	3	-	-	SH	P.Richards	5'9"	14st 10lb	14	4	6	30
H	R.Elloway	6'0"	15st 6lb	4	2	-	-	P	T.Sigley	6'2"	19st 4lb	3	8	-	-
L	A.Eustace	6'4"	17st 0lb	14	8	-	-	W/C	J.Simpson-Daniel	6'0"	12st 7lb	16	-	6	30
C	T.Fanolua	6'0"	14st 10lb	5	5	1	5	W	R.Thirlby	6'1"	14st 0lb	7	3	1	5
8	J.Forrester	6'5"	15st 9lb	14	2	3	15	SH	H.Thomas	5'8"	12st 4lb	7	7	1	5
P	J.Forster	6'1"	17st 11lb	4	3	-	-	C	M.Tindall	6'2"	16st 8lb	13	1	1	11
W	M.Foster	6'0"	14st 4lb	19	-	5	25	P	P.Vickery	6'3"	18st 4lb	8	-	-	-
W	M.Garvey	5'8"	13st 7lb	2	1	-	-	P	N.Wood	6'1"	17st 0lb	3	4	-	-

Gloucester Rugby

Last Season Form 2005/06

Season Progression

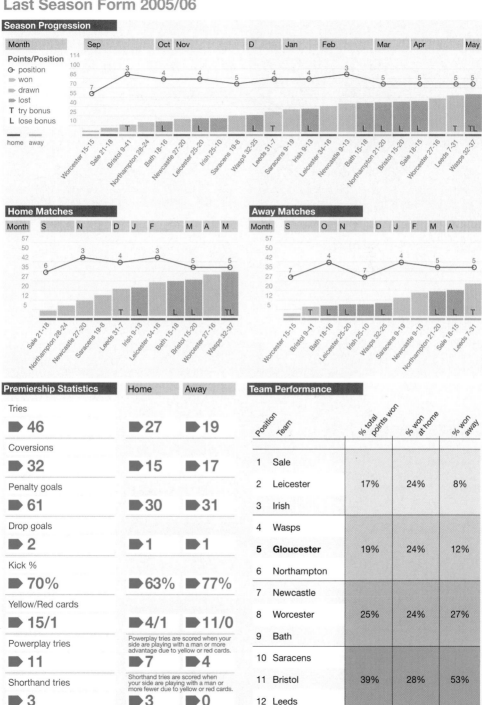

Month	Sep	Oct	Nov	D	Jan	Feb	Mar	Apr	May

Points/Position
- ⊙ position
- won
- drawn
- lost
- T try bonus
- L lose bonus

home / away

Positions: 7, 3, 4, 4, 5, 4, 4, 3, 5, 5, 5, 5

Matches: Worcester 15-15, Sale 21-18, Bristol 9-41, Northampton 28-24, Bath 18-16, Newcastle 27-20, Leicester 25-20, Irish 25-10, Saracens 19-8, Wasps 32-25, Leeds 31-7, Saracens 9-19, Irish 9-13, Leicester 34-16, Newcastle 9-13, Bath 15-18, Northampton 21-20, Bristol 15-20, Sale 18-15, Worcester 27-16, Leeds 7-31, Wasps 32-37

Home Matches

Month	S	N	D	J	F	M	A	M

Positions: 6, 3, 4, 3, 5, 5

Matches: Sale 21-18, Northampton 28-24, Newcastle 27-20, Saracens 19-8, Leeds 31-7, Irish 9-13, Leicester 34-16, Bath 15-18, Bristol 15-20, Worcester 27-16, Wasps 32-37

Away Matches

Month	S	O	N	D	J	F	M	A

Positions: 7, 4, 7, 4, 5, 5

Matches: Worcester 15-15, Bristol 9-41, Bath 18-16, Leicester 25-20, Irish 25-10, Wasps 32-25, Saracens 9-19, Newcastle 9-13, Northampton 21-20, Sale 18-15, Leeds 7-31

Premiership Statistics

		Home	Away
Tries	46	27	19
Coversions	32	15	17
Penalty goals	61	30	31
Drop goals	2	1	1
Kick %	70%	63%	77%
Yellow/Red cards	15/1	4/1	11/0
Powerplay tries	11	7	4
Shorthand tries	3	3	0

Powerplay tries are scored when your side are playing with a man or more advantage due to yellow or red cards.

Shorthand tries are scored when your side are playing with a man or more fewer due to yellow or red cards.

Team Performance

Position	Team	% total points won	% won at home	% won away
1	Sale			
2	Leicester	17%	24%	8%
3	Irish			
4	Wasps			
5	**Gloucester**	19%	24%	12%
6	Northampton			
7	Newcastle			
8	Worcester	25%	24%	27%
9	Bath			
10	Saracens			
11	Bristol	39%	28%	53%
12	Leeds			

Gloucester Rugby

Top Scorer – Ludovic Mercier

Points Facts

Total points	% team points	Home	Away
▶213	▶47	▶104	▶109

Points by Time Period

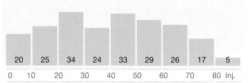

| 20 | 25 | 34 | 24 | 33 | 29 | 26 | 17 | 5 |
| 0 | 10 | 20 | 30 | 40 | 50 | 60 | 70 | 80 Inj. |

Team Tries and Points

Tries by Time Period

▪ scored
▪ conceded

2	5	7	5	4	9	4	9	1
0	10min	20min	30min	40min	50min	60min	70min	80 Injury time
3	4	4	8	3	2	5	4	0

Tries by Halves

▪ scored
▪ conceded

	Total	1st half	2nd half	1st half %	2nd half %
scored	▶46	▶19	▶27	▶41%	▶59%
conceded	▶33	▶19	▶14	▶58%	▶42%

How Points were Scored

- tries: 230
- conversions: 64
- pen goals: 183
- drop goals: 6

How Points were Conceded

- tries: 165
- conversions: 52
- pen goals: 159
- drop goals: 9

Tries Scored by Player

- backs: 35
- forwards: 6

Tries Conceded by Player

- backs: 14
- forwards: 18

Gloucester Rugby

Eight-Season Form 1998-2006

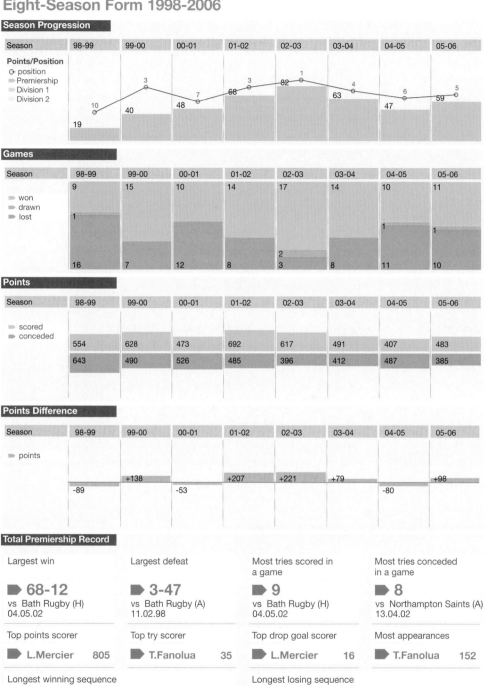

Season Progression

Season	98-99	99-00	00-01	01-02	02-03	03-04	04-05	05-06

Points/Position
- ⊙ position
- ▬ Premiership
- ▬ Division 1
- ▬ Division 2

Position: 10, 3, 7, 68→3, 82→1, 4, 6, 5
Points: 19, 40, 48, 68, 82, 63, 47, 59

Games

Season	98-99	99-00	00-01	01-02	02-03	03-04	04-05	05-06
won	9	15	10	14	17	14	10	11
drawn	1				2		1	1
lost	16	7	12	8	3	8	11	10

Points

Season	98-99	99-00	00-01	01-02	02-03	03-04	04-05	05-06
scored	554	628	473	692	617	491	407	483
conceded	643	490	526	485	396	412	487	385

Points Difference

Season	98-99	99-00	00-01	01-02	02-03	03-04	04-05	05-06
points	-89	+138	-53	+207	+221	+79	-80	+98

Total Premiership Record

Largest win
▶ 68-12
vs Bath Rugby (H)
04.05.02

Largest defeat
▶ 3-47
vs Bath Rugby (A)
11.02.98

Most tries scored in a game
▶ 9
vs Bath Rugby (H)
04.05.02

Most tries conceded in a game
▶ 8
vs Northampton Saints (A)
13.04.02

Top points scorer
▶ L.Mercier 805

Top try scorer
▶ T.Fanolua 35

Top drop goal scorer
▶ L.Mercier 16

Most appearances
▶ T.Fanolua 152

Longest winning sequence
▶ 8 wins from 24.11.02 to 12.04.03

Longest losing sequence
▶ 8 defeats from 23.01.99 to 07.05.99

Gloucester Rugby EFL

ENHANCED FIXTURE LIST
[does not include play-off data]

Guinness Premiership 2006-07 | **Premiership History**

Legend: ■ won   ■ drawn   ■ lost   □ not played

Date	Team	H/A	05-06	Played	98-99	99-00	00-01	01-02	02-03	03-04	04-05	05-06	Total Points		Outcome after a half-time lead				Close games	
													F	A	No.	W	D	L	No.	W
02.09.06	Bath	H	15-18	9									230	164	3	2	-	1	4	1
09.09.06	Harlequins	A	N/A	8									148	183	5	4	-	1	2	1
16.09.06	Leicester	A	25-20	9									159	229	3	1	-	2	3	-
23.09.06	Northampton	H	28-24	9									200	184	3	3	-	-	3	2
13.10.06	Worcester	A	15-15	2									33	28	-	-	-	-	2	1
04.11.06	Saracens	H	19-8	9									246	132	6	6	-	-	4	3
10.11.06	Irish	A	25-10	9									179	231	1	-	-	1	5	2
18.11.06	Wasps	H	32-37	9									207	187	6	5	-	1	3	1
24.11.06	Bristol	A	9-41	6									181	126	5	4	-	1	2	2
22.12.06	Newcastle	H	27-20	9									275	187	6	6	-	-	3	2
26.12.06	Wasps	A	32-25	9									160	274	1	-	-	1	2	-
01.01.07	Irish	H	9-13	9									238	134	5	5	-	-	2	1
06.01.07	Sale	A	18-15	9									215	221	3	2	-	1	3	-
27.01.07	Sale	H	21-18	9									277	152	7	6	-	1	2	1
18.02.07	Saracens	A	9-19	9									178	240	3	3	-	-	2	-
24.02.07	Worcester	H	27-16	2									55	32	2	2	-	-	-	-
03.03.07	Northampton	A	21-20	9									164	221	4	4	-	-	4	3
10.03.07	Leicester	H	34-16	9									226	167	6	5	-	1	1	-
17.03.07	Harlequins	H	N/A	8									196	152	5	4	-	1	5	4
07.04.07	Bath	A	18-16	9									122	272	1	-	1	-	4	-
13.04.07	Newcastle	A	9-13	9									189	245	4	2	1	1	5	3
28.04.07	Bristol	H	15-20	6									213	107	3	2	-	1	2	1

Club Information

Useful Information

Founded
1873
Address
Kingsholm
Kingsholm Road
Gloucester
GL1 3AX
Capacity
13,000 (1,498 seated)
Main switchboard
01452 381087
Website
www.gloucesterrugbyclub.com

Travel Information

Car
From Midlands: From the M5 southbound, exit at junction 11 (Cheltenham south and Gloucester north). Follow A40 to Gloucester/ Ross and Northern Bypass. Turn left at Longford roundabout (where A40 crosses A38) towards the City Centre. Go straight over the Tewkesbury Road roundabout and the ground is on your right after a quarter of a mile.
From South: From the M4 westbound, exit at junction 15 (Swindon) and follow the A419/417 to Gloucester. At Zoons Court roundabout follow the signs A40 to Ross and continue along Northern Bypass until you reach Longford roundabout. The as route for Midlands.
From West Country: Exit the M5 northbound at junction 11A (Gloucester) until you reach Zoons Court round-about. Then as above.
Parking is available approx 5 minutes from the ground. Turn right at the Tewkesbury Road roundabout and follow the signs for the Park and Ride Car Park.
Train
Gloucester station is a 5 minute walk from the ground, and is well sign-posted. Virgin Trains, Great Western and Central Trains all serve Gloucester from the Midlands, and there are direct services from all regions.

Gloucester Rugby

Maps

Area Map

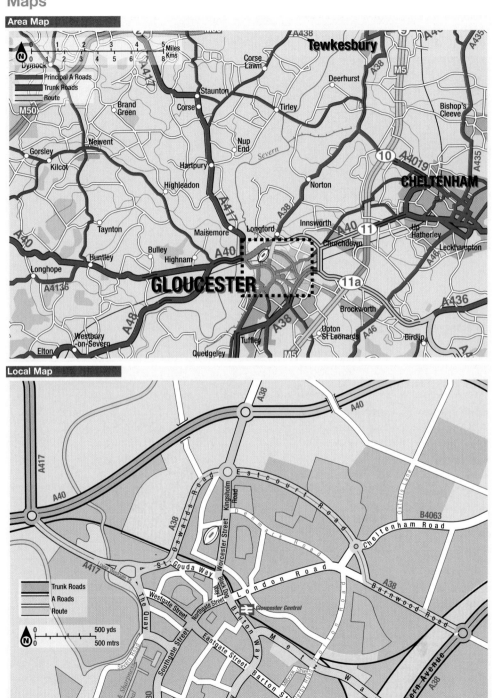

Local Map

Leicester Tigers

Season Summary 2005/06

Position	Won	Drawn	Lost	For	Against	Bonus Points	Total Points
2	**14**	**3**	**5**	**518**	**415**	**6**	**68**

Despite being out-classed in the Premiership final, Pat Howard will reflect on the 2005/06 season with a great deal of satisfaction. After an indifferent start, Tigers ended the season as the competition's form side. The Heineken Cup quarter-final defeat to Bath Rugby at the Walkers Stadium was a watershed, as Leicester went on an unbeaten run that resulted in them cruising into the Premiership semi-finals where they defeated London Irish. Much had been made of the recent retirement of influential players, but Tigers remain a force in the domestic game. Welford Road is still one of the toughest places to earn a win, while the Midlands team will be looking to appease fans by winning some silverware.

Head Coach: Pat Howard

Club Honours

Courage League / Allied Dunbar Premiership / Zurich Premiership: 1987-88, 1994-95, 1998-99 1999-2000, 2000-01, 2001-02, 2004-05 (lost in play-offs)

John Player Cup / Pilkington Cup: 1979, 1980, 1981, 1993, 1997
Heineken Cup: 2000-01 2001-02

Season Squad

Stats 2005-06

Position	Player	Height	Weight	Apps	Rep	Tries	Points
FL/H	L.Abraham	6'2"	16st 5lb	5	6	-	-
SH	S.Bemand	5'11"	13st 5lb	4	4	-	-
FH	R.Broadfoot	5'11"	13st 2lb	4	4	-	28
H	J.Buckland	5'11"	16st 11lb	6	9	1	5
H	G.Chuter	5'10"	15st 12lb	17	2	3	15
SH	N.Cole	5'11"	12st 6lb	1	2	-	-
C/FB	M.Cornwell	6'1"	15st 0lb	3	3	3	15
FL	M.Corry	6'5"	17st 10lb	13	1	-	-
L	T.Croft	6'5"	16st 4lb	2	-	-	-
L	L.Cullen	6'6"	17st 5lb	14	6	-	-
FL	B.Deacon	6'4"	17st 0lb	10	-	-	-
L	L.Deacon	6'5"	17st 10lb	14	4	1	5
C	A.Dodge	6'2"	15st 0lb	-	2	-	-
SH	H.Ellis	5'10"	13st 4lb	10	2	2	10
C	D.Gibson	5'11"	15st 6lb	8	2	-	-
FH	A.Goode	5'11"	13st 9lb	15	4	-	225
L	J.Hamilton	6'8"	19st 4lb	7	10	3	15
UB	A.Healey	5'10"	13st 9lb	14	8	1	5
C	D.Hipkiss	5'10"	14st 2lb	12	1	1	5
P	M.Holford	5'11"	16st 1lb	8	11	4	20

Position	Player	Height	Weight	Apps	Rep	Tries	Points
FH	I.Humphreys	5'11"	13st 1lb	2	1	-	15
FL	S.Jennings	6'0"	16st 1lb	16	3	1	5
BR	W.Johnson	6'4"	17st 0lb	10	4	1	5
L	B.Kay	6'6"	17st 9lb	18	2	1	5
W/C	L.Lloyd	6'4"	15st 2lb	16	5	4	20
FL	L.Moody	6'3"	16st 8lb	8	-	1	5
P	A.Moreno	6'1"	17st 5lb	6	1	-	-
P	D.Morris	6'1"	19st 10lb	8	6	1	5
FB/W	G.Murphy	6'1"	13st 3lb	13	-	2	13
C/W	S.Rabeni	6'2"	15st 0lb	2	1	-	-
P	G.Rowntree	6'0"	17st 3lb	13	-	-	-
FL	W.Skinner	5'11"	14st 2lb	3	6	2	10
C/W	O.Smith	6'1"	14st 7lb	17	4	2	10
H	E.Taukafa	5'11"	17st 0lb	1	6	1	5
W/C	A.Tuilagi	6'1"	17st 7lb	14	4	5	25
BR	H.Tuilagi	6'1"	18st 10lb	-	2	1	5
W	T.Varndell	6'3"	14st 13lb	18	3	14	70
FH/FB	S.Vesty	6'0"	14st 2lb	15	5	2	27
P	J.White	6'1"	18st 0lb	13	2	-	-

Leicester Tigers

Last Season Form 2005/06

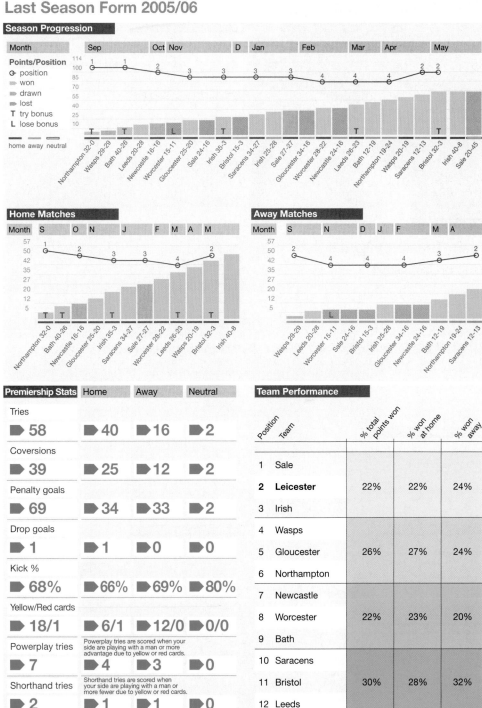

Season Progression

| Month | Sep | | Oct | Nov | | D | Jan | | Feb | | Mar | | Apr | | May |

Points/Position
- ⊙ position
- ▶ won
- ▶ drawn
- ▶ lost
- T try bonus
- L lose bonus

home away neutral

Positions: 1, 1, 2, 3, 3, 3, 3, 4, 4, 4, 2, 2

Matches: Northampton 32-0, Wasps 29-29, Bath 40-26, Leeds 20-28, Newcastle 16-16, Worcester 15-11, Gloucester 25-20, Sale 24-16, Irish 35-3, Bristol 15-3, Saracens 34-27, Irish 25-28, Sale 27-27, Gloucester 34-16, Worcester 28-22, Newcastle 24-16, Leeds 26-23, Bath 12-19, Northampton 19-24, Wasps 20-19, Saracens 12-13, Bristol 32-3, Irish 40-8, Sale 20-45

Home Matches

| Month | S | O | N | J | F | M | A | M |

Positions: 1, 2, 3, 3, 4, 2

Matches: Northampton 32-0, Bath 40-26, Newcastle 16-16, Gloucester 25-20, Irish 35-3, Saracens 34-27, Sale 27-27, Worcester 28-22, Leeds 26-23, Wasps 20-19, Bristol 32-3, Irish 40-8

Away Matches

| Month | S | N | | D | J | F | | M | A |

Positions: 2, 4, 4, 4, 3, 2

Matches: Wasps 29-29, Leeds 20-28, Worcester 15-11, Sale 24-16, Bristol 15-3, Irish 25-28, Gloucester 34-16, Newcastle 24-16, Bath 12-19, Northampton 19-24, Saracens 12-13

Premiership Stats

	Home	Away	Neutral
Tries			
58	40	16	2
Coversions			
39	25	12	2
Penalty goals			
69	34	33	2
Drop goals			
1	1	0	0
Kick %			
68%	66%	69%	80%
Yellow/Red cards			
18/1	6/1	12/0	0/0
Powerplay tries			
7	4	3	0
Shorthand tries			
2	1	1	0

Powerplay tries are scored when your side are playing with a man or more advantage due to yellow or red cards.

Shorthand tries are scored when your side are playing with a man or more fewer due to yellow or red cards.

Team Performance

Position	Team	% total points won	% won at home	% won away
1	Sale			
2	Leicester	22%	22%	24%
3	Irish			
4	Wasps			
5	Gloucester	26%	27%	24%
6	Northampton			
7	Newcastle			
8	Worcester	22%	23%	20%
9	Bath			
10	Saracens			
11	Bristol	30%	28%	32%
12	Leeds			

Leicester Tigers

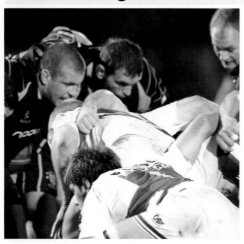

Top Scorer – Andy Goode

Points Facts

Total points	% team points	Home	Away	Neutral
▶225	▶39	▶144	▶71	▶10

Points by Time Period

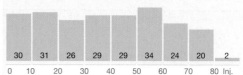

30	31	26	29	29	34	24	20	2
0	10	20	30	40	50	60	70	80 Inj.

Team Tries and Points

Tries by Time Period

- scored
- conceded

9	6	9	9	6	4	4	10	1
0	10min	20min	30min	40min	50min	60min	70min	80 Injury time
2	5	4	6	2	3	1	6	0

Tries by Halves

- scored
- conceded

	Total	1st half	2nd half	1st half %	2nd half %
scored	▶58	▶33	▶25	▶57%	▶43%
conceded	▶29	▶17	▶12	▶59%	▶41%

How Points were Scored

- tries: 290
- conversions: 78
- pen goals: 207
- drop goals: 3

How Points were Conceded

- tries: 145
- conversions: 44
- pen goals: 255
- drop goals: 24

Tries Scored by Player

- backs: 35
- forwards: 21

Tries Conceded by Player

- backs: 17
- forwards: 11

Leicester Tigers

Eight-Season Form 1998-2006

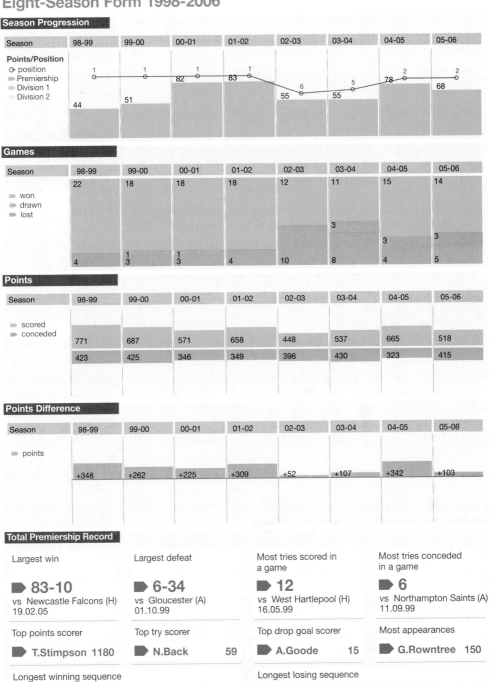

Season Progression

Season	98-99	99-00	00-01	01-02	02-03	03-04	04-05	05-06
Points/Position ⊙ position ➡ Premiership ➡ Division 1 ➡ Division 2	1 44	1 51	1 82	1 83	6 55	5 55	2 78	2 68

Games

Season	98-99	99-00	00-01	01-02	02-03	03-04	04-05	05-06
➡ won	22	18	18	18	12	11	15	14
➡ drawn						3	3	3
➡ lost	4	3	3	4	10	8	4	5

Points

Season	98-99	99-00	00-01	01-02	02-03	03-04	04-05	05-06
➡ scored	771	687	571	658	448	537	665	518
➡ conceded	423	425	346	349	396	430	323	415

Points Difference

Season	98-99	99-00	00-01	01-02	02-03	03-04	04-05	05-06
➡ points	+348	+262	+225	+309	+52	+107	+342	+103

Total Premiership Record

Largest win

➡ **83-10**
vs Newcastle Falcons (H)
19.02.05

Largest defeat

➡ **6-34**
vs Gloucester (A)
01.10.99

Most tries scored in a game

➡ **12**
vs West Hartlepool (H)
16.05.99

Most tries conceded in a game

➡ **6**
vs Northampton Saints (A)
11.09.99

Top points scorer

➡ T.Stimpson 1180

Top try scorer

➡ N.Back 59

Top drop goal scorer

➡ A.Goode 15

Most appearances

➡ G.Rowntree 150

Longest winning sequence

➡ **17 wins** from 26.12.99 to 06.09.00

Longest losing sequence

➡ **5 defeats** from 04.10.03 to 01.11.03

ENHANCED FIXTURE LIST

[does not include play-off data]

Guinness Premiership 2006-07 — Premiership History

Date	Team	H/A	05-06	Played	98-99	99-00	00-01	01-02	02-03	03-04	04-05	05-06	F	A	No.	W	D	L	No.	W
					won		drawn		lost		not played		F	A						
03.09.06	Sale	H	27-27	9									282	139	6►6		-	-	2	-
09.09.06	Bath	A	12-19	9									135	125	2►2		-	-	2	1
16.09.06	Gloucester	H	25-20	9									229	159	6►6		-	-	3	3
23.09.06	Harlequins	A	N/A	8									212	108	6►5		-	1	3	3
14.10.06	Northampton	A	19-24	9									136	168	3►3		-	-	2	2
04.11.06	Worcester	H	28-22	2									78	29	1►1		-	-	1	1
12.11.06	Saracens	A	12-13	9									184	171	5►2		-	3	4	2
18.11.06	Irish	H	35-3	9									271	129	6►6		-	-	1	-
26.11.06	Wasps	A	29-29	9									214	229	5►3		-	2	4	1
22.12.06	Bristol	H	32-3	6									185	82	4►4		-	-	-	-
26.12.06	Irish	A	25-28	9									263	177	8►6		-	2	3	2
01.01.07	Saracens	H	34-27	9									291	137	8►7	1	-		2	1
07.01.07	Newcastle	A	24-16	9									191	180	5►2	2	1		5	1
27.01.07	Newcastle	H	16-16	9									334	144	7►6		-	1	2	-
17.02.07	Worcester	A	15-11	2									49	26	1►1		-	-	1	-
24.02.07	Northampton	H	32-0	9									217	156	7►6	1	-		2	1
03.03.07	Harlequins	H	N/A	8									257	102	8►8		-	-	1	1
10.03.07	Gloucester	A	34-16	9									167	226	3►2		-	1	1	1
17.03.07	Bath	H	40-26	9									277	163	4►4		-	-	3	3
06.04.07	Sale	A	24-16	9									218	167	4►3		-	1	2	-
15.04.07	Bristol	A	15-3	6									121	149	2►2		-	-	3	1
28.04.07	Wasps	H	20-19	9									268	121	6►6		-	-	2	2

Column headers: Total Points (F, A) · Outcome after a half-time lead (No. W D L) · Close games (No. W)

Club Information

Useful Information

Founded
1888
Address
Welford Road Stadium
Aylestone Road
Leicester LE2 7TR
Capacity
16,815 (12,411 seated)
Main switchboard
08701 283 430
Website
www.leicestertigers.com

Travel Information

Car
From M1 (North and South) and M69 (East): Exit the motorway at Junction 21 (M1). Follow the signs for the city centre via Narborough Road (A5460). After 3 miles, at the crossroad junction with Upperton Road, turn right. The stadium is 1/2 mile ahead (past Leicester City Football ground on the right).
From A6 (South): Follow the signs for the city centre, coming in via London Road. At the main set of lights opposite the entrance to the railway station (on the right), turn left onto the Waterloo Way. The stadium is 1/2 mile further on.
From A47 (East): Follow the signs for the city centre, coming in via Uppingham Road. At the St Georges Retail Park roundabout, take the second exit into St Georges Way (A594). Carry on past the Leicester Mercury offices on the right, and then filter off right into Waterloo Way just before the Railway Station. The stadium is 1/2 mile further on.

Train
Leicester Station is a ten minute walk away, along Waterloo Way.

Maps

Area Map

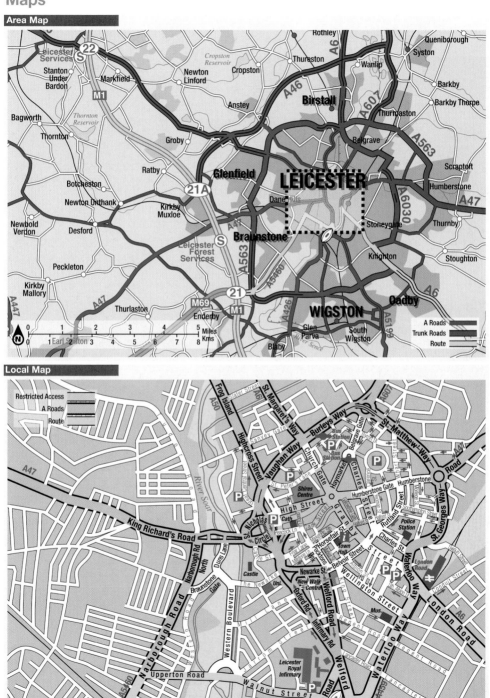

Local Map

London Irish

Season Summary 2005/06

Position	Won	Drawn	Lost	For	Against	Bonus Points	Total Points
3	14	0	8	493	454	10	66

If the Premiership title was decided by a style of play, London Irish would have been worthy champions in 2005/06. In a remarkable close season turn around, Brian Smith's side went from the lowest try-scoring Premiership side to the competition's most prolific. Key to that success was an ambition to play open, attacking rugby which suited the Exiles' talented and pacey back line. While players such as Tipsy Ojo and Delon Armitage set the Premiership alight, it was Mike Catt who was to prove most influential for Irish. The veteran World Cup winner enjoyed an Indian summer of a season, winning an England recall and sparking everything that was good about Irish.

Director of Rugby: Brian Smith

Club Honours
Powergen Cup: 2002

Season Squad

Stats 2005-06

Position	Player	Height	Weight	Apps	Rep	Tries	Points	Position	Player	Height	Weight	Apps	Rep	Tries	Points
W/FB	D.Armitage	6'1"	12st 8lb	21	1	8	40	FH	R.Laidlaw	5'10"	13st 2lb	1	1	-	17
W/C	J.Bishop	6'1"	13st 10lb	9	2	1	5	BR	J.Leguizamon	6'2"	16st 1lb	10	6	1	5
L	B.Casey	6'7"	19st 3lb	21	1	2	10	FL	O.Magne	6'2"	15st 0lb	11	-	2	10
C/FH	M.Catt	5'10"	13st 8lb	19	1	2	33	C	N.Mordt	6'1"	14st 12lb	6	1	1	5
H	D.Coetzee	6'1"	17st 5lb	8	2	-	-	8	P.Murphy	6'5"	17st 3lb	12	8	2	10
P	M.Collins	5'10"	17st 9lb	2	11	-	-	W	T.Ojo	5'11"	13st 1lb	8	3	7	35
BR	D.Danaher	6'4"	16st 3lb	13	1	1	5	H	D.Paice	6'1"	15st 12lb	4	9	2	10
FL	K.Dawson	6'1"	15st 3lb	11	4	1	5	C	R.Penney	6'0"	14st 7lb	12	-	1	5
SH	D.Edwards	5'8"	12st 9lb	1	3	-	-	P	F.Rautenbach	6'2"	18st 0lb	13	2	-	-
FH	B.Everitt	5'9"	12st 13lb	9	4	-	109	L/BR	K.Roche	6'7"	18st 2lb	20	1	1	5
W	D.Feau'nati	6'1"	17st 5lb	5	-	2	10	H	R.Russell	5'10"	15st 4lb	6	7	-	-
H	A.Flavin	5'10"	16st 7lb	5	3	-	-	P	R.Skuse	5'11"	18st 2lb	7	6	-	-
FH	R.Flutey	5'11"	13st 9lb	16	-	7	112	W/FB	S.Staniforth	6'2"	15st 11lb	7	-	3	15
C	P.Franze	6'1"	15st 6lb	2	1	-	-	C	J.Storey	6'3"	14st 5lb	-	1	-	-
FH	S.Geraghty	5'11"	13st 0lb	2	5	1	5	L	R.Strudwick	6'5"	17st 0lb	2	11	1	5
BR	P.Gustard	6'4"	17st 0lb	2	9	1	5	W/FB	S.Tagicakibau	6'3"	14st 12lb	9	1	4	20
P	R.Hardwick	5'11"	18st 10lb	3	1	-	-	FL	R.Thorpe	6'1"	15st 7lb	1	2	-	-
P	N.Hatley	6'1"	18st 11lb	21	2	-	-	C	G.Tiesi	6'1"	13st 12lb	2	4	1	5
SH	P.Hodgson	5'8"	12st 9lb	15	5	2	10	P	T.Warren	6'1"	17st 0lb	-	1	-	-
FB	M.Horak	6'3"	14st 6lb	10	2	1	5	P	D.Wheatley	6'2"	18st 12lb	-	2	-	-
L	N.Kennedy	6'8"	17st 10lb	12	3	-	-	SH	B.Willis	5'9"	13st 8lb	7	7	-	-

London Irish

Last Season Form 2005/06

Season Progression

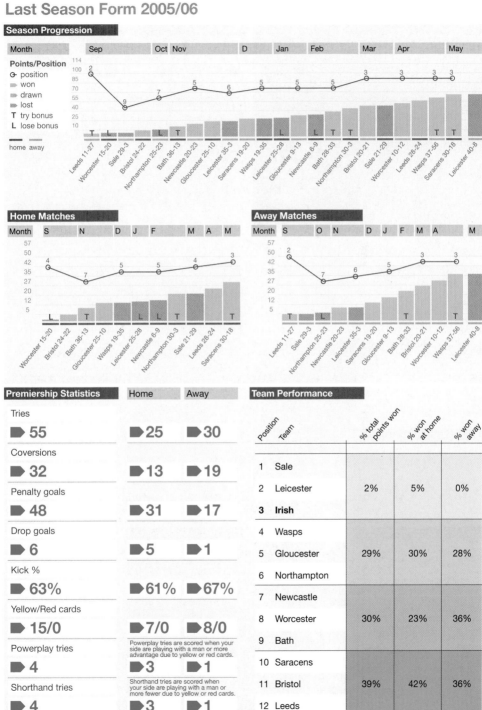

Month	Sep		Oct	Nov				D	Jan	Feb			Mar	Apr		May

Points/Position
- G position
- won
- drawn
- lost
- T try bonus
- L lose bonus

home away

Home Matches

Month	S	N		D	J	F		M	A		M

Away Matches

Month	S	O	N		D	J	F	M	A		M

Premiership Statistics

	Home	Away
Tries		
▶ 55	▶ 25	▶ 30
Coversions		
▶ 32	▶ 13	▶ 19
Penalty goals		
▶ 48	▶ 31	▶ 17
Drop goals		
▶ 6	▶ 5	▶ 1
Kick %		
▶ 63%	▶ 61%	▶ 67%
Yellow/Red cards		
▶ 15/0	▶ 7/0	▶ 8/0
Powerplay tries		
▶ 4	▶ 3	▶ 1
Shorthand tries		
▶ 4	▶ 3	▶ 1

Powerplay tries are scored when your side are playing with a man or more advantage due to yellow or red cards.

Shorthand tries are scored when your side are playing with a man or more fewer due to yellow or red cards.

Team Performance

Position	Team	% total points won	% won at home	% won away
1	Sale			
2	Leicester	2%	5%	0%
3	**Irish**			
4	Wasps			
5	Gloucester	29%	30%	28%
6	Northampton			
7	Newcastle			
8	Worcester	30%	23%	36%
9	Bath			
10	Saracens			
11	Bristol	39%	42%	36%
12	Leeds			

London Irish

Top Scorer – Riki Flutey

Points Facts

Total points	% team points	Home	Away
▶112	▶22	▶47	▶65

Points by Time Period

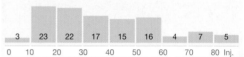

3	23	22	17	15	16	4	7	5

0 10 20 30 40 50 60 70 80 Inj.

Team Tries and Points

Tries by Time Period

▸ scored
▸ conceded

5	10	11	11	3	5	4	5	1

0   10min   20min   30min   40min   50min   60min   70min   80 Injury time

8	2	9	2	9	1	6	10	2

Tries by Halves

▸ scored
▸ conceded

	55	37	18	67%	33%
	Total	1st half	2nd half	1st half %	2nd half %
	49	21	28	43%	57%

How Points were Scored

▸ tries:	275	
▸ conversions:	64	
▸ pen goals:	144	
drop goals:	18	

How Points were Conceded

▸ tries:	245	
▸ conversions:	66	
▸ pen goals:	177	
drop goals:	6	

Tries Scored by Player

▸ backs:	41
▸ forwards:	14

Tries Conceded by Player

▸ backs:	31
▸ forwards:	16

London Irish

Eight-Season Form 1998-2006

Season Progression

Season	98-99	99-00	00-01	01-02	02-03	03-04	04-05	05-06

Points/Position
- ⊖ position
- ➡ Premiership
- ➡ Division 1
- ➡ Division 2

Position line: 5, 8, 8, 4, 9, 8, 10, 3
Points bars: 30, 25, 45, 57, 40, 49, 40, 66

Games

Season	98-99	99-00	00-01	01-02	02-03	03-04	04-05	05-06
won	15	9	10	11	8	10	8	14
drawn		1	1	3	1	1		
lost	11	12	11	8	13	11	14	8

Points

Season	98-99	99-00	00-01	01-02	02-03	03-04	04-05	05-06
scored	703	613	476	574	432	427	378	493
conceded	607	616	576	465	485	454	421	454

Points Difference

Season	98-99	99-00	00-01	01-02	02-03	03-04	04-05	05-06
points	+96	-3	-100	+109	-53	-27	-43	+39

Total Premiership Record

Largest win
➡ **56-8**
vs Newcastle Falcons (H) 03.10.99

Largest defeat
➡ **16-64**
vs Bath Rugby (H) 11.03.00

Most tries scored in a game
➡ **9**
vs London Wasps (A) 30.04.06

Most tries conceded in a game
➡ **9**
vs Bath Rugby (H) 11.03.00

Top points scorer
➡ B.Everitt 1162

Top try scorer
➡ J.Bishop 30

Top drop goal scorer
➡ B.Everitt 25

Most appearances
➡ N.Hatley 162

Longest winning sequence
➡ **7 wins** from 19.12.98 to 07.02.99

Longest losing sequence
➡ **8 defeats** from 01.11.97 to 14.02.98

London Irish `EFL`

ENHANCED FIXTURE LIST
[does not include play-off data]

Guinness Premiership 2006-07 | Premiership History

Date	Team	H/A	05-06	Played	98-99	99-00	00-01	01-02	02-03	03-04	04-05	05-06	Total Points F	A	Outcome after a half-time lead No.	W	D	L	Close games No.	W
					won		drawn		lost		not played		F	A	No.	W	D	L	No.	W
02.09.06	Harlequins	H	N/A	8									176	124	6▶3		2	1	6	3
08.09.06	Wasps	A	37-56	9									229	273	4▶2		-	2	1	1
16.09.06	Bristol	H	24-22	6									188	126	6▶5		1	-	2	1
22.09.06	Newcastle	A	20-23	9									201	244	2▶1		-	1	5	3
15.10.06	Sale	H	21-29	9									178	173	6▶3		-	3	5	1
04.11.06	Bath	A	28-33	9									163	239	2▶1		-	1	5	1
10.11.06	Gloucester	H	25-10	9									231	179	6▶4		-	2	5	3
18.11.06	Leicester	A	35-3	9									129	271	2▶1		-	1	1	1
26.11.06	Northampton	H	30-3	9									179	218	4▶3		-	1	3	1
22.12.06	Worcester	A	10-12	2									18	26	1▶1		-	-	1	1
26.12.06	Leicester	H	25-28	9									177	263	1▶-		-	1	3	1
01.01.07	Gloucester	A	9-13	9									134	238	3▶1		-	2	2	1
07.01.07	Saracens	H	30-18	9									211	188	6▶4		-	2	3	1
28.01.07	Saracens	A	19-20	9									250	214	4▶3		-	1	4	4
17.02.07	Bath	H	36-13	9									239	287	4▶3		-	1	3	-
23.02.07	Sale	A	29-3	9									173	264	6▶3		1	2	4	2
03.03.07	Newcastle	H	6-9	9									190	139	5▶4		-	1	6	3
10.03.07	Bristol	A	20-21	6									145	130	4▶1		2	1	5	2
18.03.07	Wasps	H	19-35	9									214	240	3▶3		-	-	2	2
07.04.07	Harlequins	A	N/A	8									193	158	5▶4		-	1	5	3
15.04.07	Worcester	H	15-20	2									40	35	2▶1		-	1	1	-
28.04.07	Northampton	A	25-23	9									190	195	8▶4		-	4	4	2

Club Information

Useful Information

Founded
1898
Address
Madejski Stadium
Reading
Berkshire
RG2 OFL
Capacity
24,105 (all seated)
Main switchboard
0118 987 9730
Website
www.london-irish.com

Travel Information

Car
Approaching on the M4, exit at junction 11 onto the A33 towards Reading. When you reach a roundabout, take the 2nd exit onto the Reading Relief Road, the stadium is on your left.
For parking, carry on past the stadium and turn left onto Northern Way and follow the signs for the car parks.

Train
Trains run from London Paddington and London Waterloo to Reading station. A shuttle bus runs from Reading station to the ground on matchdays, costing £2 for adults and £1 for children.

Coach
National Express coaches run from London Victoria station approx every half hour.
Visit www.nationalexpress.com for further information.

London Irish

Maps

Area Map

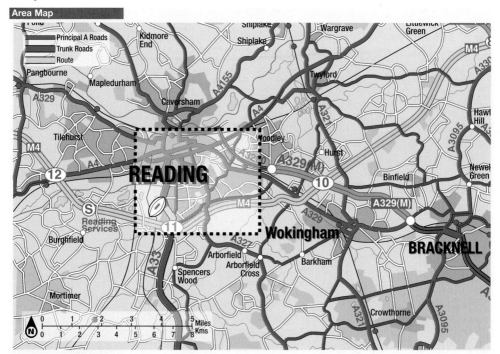

Local Map

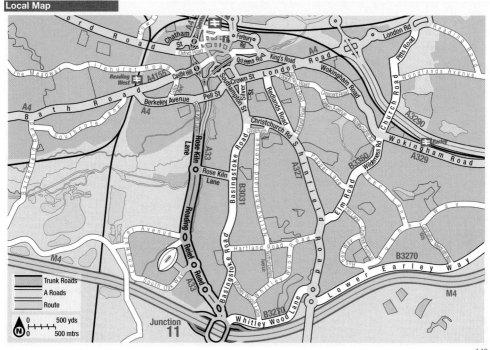

London Wasps

Season Summary 2005/06

Position	Won	Drawn	Lost	For	Against	Bonus Points	Total Points
4	12	3	7	527	447	10	64

Director of Rugby: Ian McGeechan

London Wasps' vice-like grip on the Premiership ended with Sale Sharks' first Premiership league title. For a club whose name has become a byword for winning, the 2005/06 Premiership campaign was ultimately a disappointment. In previous victorious Premiership campaigns, Wasps were the masters of peaking for the season's climax, but captain Lawrence Dallaglio and his side looked tired this term, eventually having to settle for fourth place. Winning the Powergen Cup in a rather one-sided game against Llanelli Scarlets ensured that Ian McGeechan's side did at least add some silverware, but even the celebrations at Twickenham couldn't mask what was a far from satisfactory Premiership campaign.

Club Honours

Courage League / Zurich Premiership: 1989-90, 1996-97, 2002-03, 2003-04, 2004-05
Tetley's Bitter Cup: 1998-99, 1999-2000

Heineken Cup: 2003-04
Parker Pen Shield: 2002-03
Powergen Cup: 2005-06

Season Squad

Stats 2005-06

Position	Player	Height	Weight	Apps	Rep	Tries	Points
C	S.Abbott	6'0"	14st 2lb	20	1	-	-
H	J.Barrett	5'10"	16st 4lb	3	3	-	-
W	N.Baxter	6'2"	13st 12lb	1	1	2	10
SH	H.Biljon	5'11"	13st 2lb	-	1	-	-
L	R.Birkett	6'3"	17st 1lb	17	2	1	5
P	P.Bracken	6'2"	18st 7lb	11	5	-	-
FH	J.Brooks	5'9"	13st 9lb	1	5	-	-
FL	G.Chamberlain	6'2"	14st 2lb	-	1	-	-
L	M.Corker	6'6"	17st 6lb	-	1	-	-
8	L.Dallaglio	6'3"	17st 8lb	16	2	-	-
P	J.Dawson	5'10"	18st 7lb	8	3	-	-
SH	M.Dawson	5'10"	14st 2lb	6	8	1	5
C	A.Erinle	6'3"	17st 4lb	12	7	2	10
W	T.Evans	6'1"	14st 8lb	1	-	-	-
SH	W.Fury	6'0"	13st 7lb	-	1	-	-
H	B.Gotting	6'0"	16st 7lb	2	7	-	-
BR	J.Hart	6'4"	17st 10lb	11	2	2	10
BR	J.Haskell	6'3"	17st 6lb	1	4	-	-
C	R.Hoadley	6'0"	13st 13lb	7	5	2	10
SH	J.Honeyben	6'0"	14st 4lb	2	1	-	-
H	R.Ibanez	6'0"	15st 10lb	10	5	4	20
FH	A.King	6'0"	14st 6lb	11	4	-	55
FB	R.Laird	6'0"	14st 2lb	-	1	-	-
L/BR	D.Leo	6'6"	17st 8lb	8	2	-	-
W	J.Lewsey	5'10"	13st 9lb	9	1	3	15
BR	M.Lock	6'2"	16st 2lb	6	4	-	-
P	A.McKenzie	6'3"	18st 12lb	5	4	-	-
FL	J.O'Connor	5'10"	15st 10lb	7	3	-	-
P	T.Payne	6'0"	18st 3lb	21	-	1	5
L	M.Purdy	6'6"	17st 8lb	3	2	-	-
SH	E.Reddan	5'7"	12st 8lb	15	3	1	5
FL	T.Rees	5'11"	15st 10lb	10	3	4	20
W	P.Sackey	6'1"	14st 4lb	23	-	8	40
L	S.Shaw	6'7"	19st 0lb	12	3	1	5
L	G.Skivington	6'6"	17st 6lb	12	-	1	5
FH/FB	J.Staunton	6'0"	15st 1lb	12	3	2	33
P	J.Va'a	6'0"	21st 3lb	1	8	-	-
FB	M.Van Gisbergen	5'10"	13st 13lb	19	-	3	211
W	T.Voyce	6'0"	14st 13lb	18	1	10	50
H	J.Ward	6'0"	17st 8lb	8	4	-	-
C	F.Waters	6'0"	14st 10lb	4	7	1	5
FL	J.Worsley	6'5"	17st 6lb	12	1	4	20

London Wasps

Last Season Form 2005/06

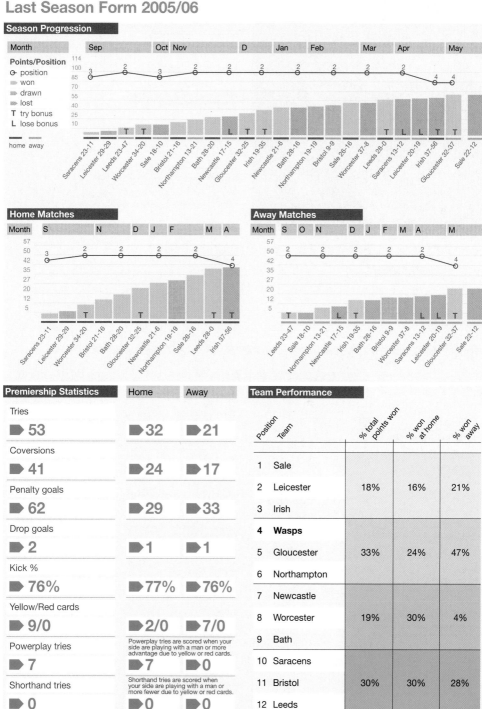

Season Progression

| Month | Sep | Oct Nov | D | Jan | Feb | Mar | Apr | May |

Points/Position
- ○ position
- ⇒ won
- ⇒ drawn
- ⇒ lost
- T try bonus
- L lose bonus

home away

Saracens 23-11, Leicester 29-29, Leeds 23-47, Worcester 34-20, Sale 18-10, Bristol 21-16, Northampton 13-21, Bath 28-20, Newcastle 17-15, Gloucester 32-25, Irish 19-35, Newcastle 21-6, Bath 28-16, Northampton 19-19, Bristol 9-9, Sale 26-16, Worcester 37-8, Leeds 28-0, Saracens 13-12, Leicester 20-19, Irish 37-56, Gloucester 32-37, Sale 22-12

Home Matches

| Month | S | N | D J | F | M A |

Saracens 23-11, Leicester 29-29, Worcester 34-20, Bristol 21-16, Bath 28-20, Gloucester 32-25, Newcastle 21-6, Northampton 19-19, Sale 26-16, Leeds 28-0, Irish 37-56

Away Matches

| Month | S | O | N | D J | F | M A | M |

Leeds 23-47, Sale 18-10, Northampton 13-21, Newcastle 17-15, Irish 19-35, Bath 28-16, Bristol 9-9, Worcester 37-8, Saracens 13-12, Leicester 20-19, Gloucester 32-37, Sale 22-12

Premiership Statistics

		Home	Away
Tries	53	32	21
Coversions	41	24	17
Penalty goals	62	29	33
Drop goals	2	1	1
Kick %	76%	77%	76%
Yellow/Red cards	9/0	2/0	7/0
Powerplay tries	7	7	0
Shorthand tries	0	0	0

Powerplay tries are scored when your side are playing with a man or more advantage due to yellow or red cards.

Shorthand tries are scored when your side are playing with a man or more fewer due to yellow or red cards.

Team Performance

Position	Team	% total points won	% won at home	% won away
1	Sale			
2	Leicester	18%	16%	21%
3	Irish			
4	**Wasps**			
5	Gloucester	33%	24%	47%
6	Northampton			
7	Newcastle			
8	Worcester	19%	30%	4%
9	Bath			
10	Saracens			
11	Bristol	30%	30%	28%
12	Leeds			

London Wasps

Points Facts

Total points	% team points	Home	Away
➥211	➥39	➥101	➥110

Points by Time Period

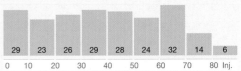

29	23	26	29	28	24	32	14	6
0	10	20	30	40	50	60	70	80 Inj.

Team Tries and Points

Tries by Time Period

- scored
- conceded

10	3	5	5	6	10	4	7	3
0	10min	20min	30min	40min	50min	60min	70min	80 Injury time
11	4	3	5	7	6	0	7	0

Tries by Halves

- scored
- conceded

	Total	1st half	2nd half	1st half %	2nd half %
scored	➥53	➥23	➥30	➥43%	➥57%
conceded	➥43	➥23	➥20	➥53%	➥47%

How Points were Scored

- tries: 265
- conversions: 82
- pen goals: 186
- drop goals: 6

How Points were Conceded

- tries: 215
- conversions: 62
- pen goals: 186
- drop goals: 6

Tries Scored by Player

- backs: 35
- forwards: 18

Tries Conceded by Player

- backs: 31
- forwards: 10

Eight-Season Form 1998-2006

Season Progression

Season	98-99	99-00	00-01	01-02	02-03	03-04	04-05	05-06
Points/Position								

Points/Position
- ○ position
- Premiership
- Division 1
- Division 2

Positions: 5, 7, 2, 7, 2, 2, 2, 4

Points: 31, 31, 74, 54, 67, 73, 73, 64

Games

Season	98-99	99-00	00-01	01-02	02-03	03-04	04-05	05-06
won	15	11	16	12	13	16	15	12
drawn	1	1			2		1	3
lost	10	10	6	10	7	6	6	7

Points

Season	98-99	99-00	00-01	01-02	02-03	03-04	04-05	05-06
scored	717	640	663	519	553	575	561	527
conceded	506	461	428	507	460	406	442	447

Points Difference

Season	98-99	99-00	00-01	01-02	02-03	03-04	04-05	05-06
points	+211	+179	+235	+12	+93	+169	+119	+80

Total Premiership Record

Largest win

▶ **71-14**
vs West Hartlepool (H)
27.09.98

Largest defeat

▶ **21-59**
vs Newcastle Falcons (A)
23.09.00

Most tries scored in a game

▶ **10**
vs West Hartlepool (H)
27.09.98

Most tries conceded in a game

▶ **9**
vs London Irish (H)
30.04.06

Top points scorer

▶ A.King　937

Top try scorer

▶ J.Lewsey　41

Top drop goal scorer

▶ A.King　32

Most appearances

▶ S.Shaw　171

Longest winning sequence

▶ **11 wins** from 21.11.03 to 18.04.04

Longest losing sequence

▶ **6 defeats** from 08.09.01 to 11.11.01

Guinness Premiership 2006-07 | **Premiership History**

Date	Team	H/A	05-06	Played	98-99	99-00	00-01	01-02	02-03	03-04	04-05	05-06	Total Points F	A	Outcome after a half-time lead No.	W	D	L	Close games No.	W
					won		drawn		lost		not played		F	A	No.	W	D	L	No.	W
02.09.06	Saracens	A	13-12	9									241	175	7▶4		-	3	6	2
08.09.06	Irish	H	37-56	9									273	229	4▶4		-	-	1	-
17.09.06	Harlequins	H	N/A	8									201	167	5▶4		-	1	6	4
24.09.06	Bristol	A	9-9	6									140	124	3▶2		1	-	1	-
15.10.06	Newcastle	H	21-6	9									252	182	6▶6		-	-	6	4
03.11.06	Sale	A	18-10	9									234	198	8▶5		1	2	4	2
12.11.06	Bath	H	28-20	9									202	167	4▶4		-	-	3	1
18.11.06	Gloucester	A	32-37	9									187	207	2▶2		-	-	3	2
26.11.06	Leicester	H	29-29	9									229	214	3▶2		1	-	4	1
22.12.06	Northampton	A	13-21	9									184	180	1▶1		-	-	3	3
26.12.06	Gloucester	H	32-25	9									274	160	6▶6		-	-	2	2
01.01.07	Bath	A	28-16	9									179	221	5▶3		1	1	5	3
07.01.07	Worcester	H	34-20	2									66	37	1▶1		-	-	-	-
26.01.07	Worcester	A	37-8	2									32	64	-▶-		-	-	1	-
18.02.07	Sale	H	26-16	9									273	217	5▶4		-	1	1	-
23.02.07	Newcastle	A	17-15	9									193	226	2▶2		-	-	4	2
04.03.07	Bristol	H	21-16	6									173	133	3▶3		-	-	4	3
10.03.07	Harlequins	A	N/A	8									201	222	5▶3		-	2	1	-
18.03.07	Irish	A	19-35	9									240	214	6▶5		-	1	2	-
08.04.07	Saracens	H	23-11	9									268	123	7▶5		1	1	3	1
15.04.07	Northampton	H	19-19	9									236	125	6▶6		-	-	2	-
28.04.07	Leicester	A	20-19	9									121	268	2▶-		-	2	2	-

Club Information

Useful Information

Founded
1867

Address
Adam's Park
Hillbottom Road
Sands
High Wycombe
Buckinghamshire
HP12 4HJ

Capacity
10,200 (all seated)

Main switchboard
0208 993 8298

Website
www.wasps.co.uk

Travel Information

Car
From North
Approaching on the M1, exit onto the M25 at junction 6a (anti-clockwise). Continue on the M25 until junction 16 (M40), then head to junction 4 for the A404 High Wycombe. When you reach the junction take the slip road and turn right, taking the exit for the A4010 John Hall Way. Continue on this road, which becomes New Road, until you reach a mini roundabout with a left turn on to Lane End Road. Take this left turning and continue straight ahead onto Hillbottom Road, which leads to Causeway Stadium.

Train
Train services run from London Marylebone to High Wycombe.

London Wasps

Maps

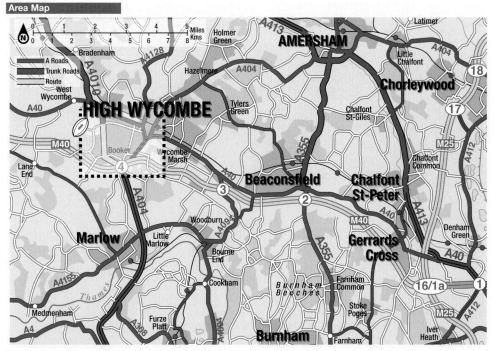

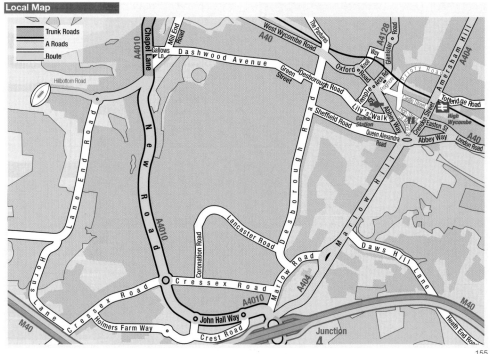

155

NEC Harlequins

Season Summary 2005/06 (National Division One)

Position	Won	Drawn	Lost	For	Against	Bonus Points	Total Points
1	25	0	1	1001	337	21	121

NEC Harlequins returned to the Premiership at the first attempt after completely dominating National Division One, losing only once along the way. Key to this success was the club's ability to retain the majority of their big name players, while the signing of former All Blacks legend Andrew Mehrtens gave Quins the direction and impetus they lacked during 2004/05's relegation season. With Dean Richards back at the helm of a Premiership club and a plethora of summer signings, Quins will be looking to challenge for silverware in their return season.

Director of Rugby: Andy Friend

Club Honours
John Player Cup / Pilkington Cup: 1988, 1991
European Shield / Parker Pen Challenge Cup: 2001, 2004
National Division One: 2006
Powergen National Trophy: 2006

Season Squad

Stats 2005-06

Position	Player	Height	Weight	Apps	Rep	Tries	Points	Position	Player	Height	Weight	Apps	Rep	Tries	Points
W	C.Amesbury	N/A	N/A	4	2	3	15	P	M.Lambert	6'3"	19st 1lb	-	3	-	-
BR	P.Bouza	6'4"	15st 10lb	2	10	1	5	C	T.Masson	N/A	N/A	8	2	3	15
FB	M.Brown	6'0"	14st 5lb	7	6	7	37	FH	A.Mehrtens	5'10"	13st 2lb	16	4	1	194
L	K.Burke	6'6"	19st 3lb	-	6	-	-	L	S.Miall	6'4"	16st 6lb	26	-	3	15
BR	D.Clayton	N/A	N/A	-	1	-	-	W	U.Monye	6'1"	13st 4lb	16	2	16	80
P	A.Croall	6'0"	16st 7lb	2	3	-	-	P	R.Nebbett	5'11"	17st 8lb	20	3	-	-
C	M.Deane	5'10"	13st 8lb	9	12	2	10	H	J.Richards	5'9"	15st 10lb	9	12	-	-
8	T.Diprose	6'5"	17st 8lb	5	1	1	5	W	K.Richards	N/A	N/A	-	1	-	-
FB	G.Duffy	6'1"	14st 2lb	24	1	6	30	BR	C.Robshaw	6'2"	14st 7lb	6	4	2	10
BR	N.Easter	6'4"	18st 2lb	23	2	16	80	L	G.Robson	N/A	N/A	-	3	-	-
L	J.Evans	6'7"	16st 2lb	24	1	6	30	P	A.Rogers	6'3"	18st 5lb	4	1	2	10
H	T.Fuga	5'11"	14st 8lb	16	3	3	15	FL	L.Sherriff	6'4"	15st 10lb	14	6	4	20
C	W.Greenwood	6'4"	15st 12lb	15	1	4	22	SH	S.So'oialo	5'10"	14st 6lb	19	1	6	30
BR	T.Guest	6'4"	16st 0lb	7	10	5	25	C	J.Turner-Hall	N/A	N/A	4	1	-	-
W/C	G.Harder	6'1"	14st 9lb	6	3	4	20	SH	I.Vass	5'11"	15st 2lb	7	7	1	5
H	J.Hayter	6'2"	15st 10lb	1	4	1	5	FL	A.Vos	6'5"	16st 1lb	23	-	1	5
L	J.Inglis	N/A	N/A	-	1	-	-	P	L.Ward	N/A	N/A	7	17	-	-
FH	A.Jarvis	6'2"	13st 0lb	10	9	3	138	FB/W	T.Williams	5'11"	13st 2lb	13	5	12	60
P	C.Jones	6'0"	16st 7lb	18	-	5	25	P	M.Worsley	6'0"	17st 2lb	1	1	-	-
SH/W	S.Keogh	5'9"	12st 9lb	24	1	18	90								

NEC Harlequins

Last Season Form 2005/06

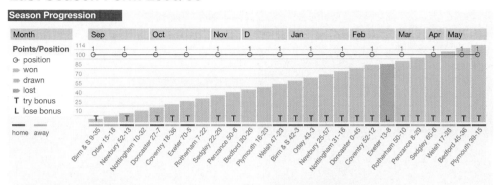

Season Progression

Month	Sep	Oct	Nov	D	Jan	Feb	Mar	Apr	May

Points/Position: 114, 100, 85, 70, 55, 40, 25, 10

- G position
- won
- drawn
- lost
- T try bonus
- L lose bonus

home away

Birm & S 9-35, Otley 15-18, Newbury 52-13, Nottingham 10-32, Doncaster 27-7, Coventry 18-36, Exeter 70-5, Rotherham 7-22, Sedgley 22-29, Penzance 50-6, Bedford 20-26, Plymouth 16-23, Welsh 47-23, Birm & S 42-3, Otley 43-3, Newbury 25-57, Nottingham 31-16, Doncaster 0-45, Coventry 52-12, Exeter 13-8, Rotherham 50-10, Penzance 8-29, Sedgley 65-8, Welsh 17-28, Bedford 45-36, Plymouth 39-15

Home Matches

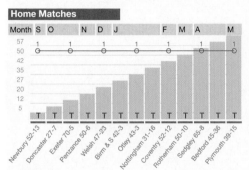

Month	S	O		N	D	J		F	M	A		M

57, 50, 42, 35, 27, 20, 12, 5

Newbury 52-13, Doncaster 27-7, Exeter 70-5, Penzance 50-6, Welsh 47-23, Birm & S 42-3, Otley 43-3, Nottingham 31-16, Coventry 52-12, Rotherham 50-10, Sedgley 65-8, Bedford 45-36, Plymouth 39-15

Away Matches

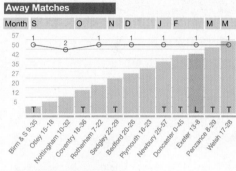

Month	S		O		N	D		J	F		M	M

57, 50, 42, 35, 27, 20, 12, 5

Birm & S 9-35, Otley 15-18, Nottingham 10-32, Coventry 18-36, Rotherham 7-22, Sedgley 22-29, Bedford 20-26, Plymouth 16-23, Newbury 25-57, Doncaster 0-45, Exeter 13-8, Penzance 8-29, Welsh 17-28

Division 1 Statistics

	Home	Away
Tries		
137	88	49
Coversions		
101	64	37
Penalty goals		
38	15	23
Drop goals		
0	0	0
Yellow/Red cards		
9/0	1/0	8/0
Powerplay tries		
18	13	5
Shorthand tries		
3	1	2

Powerplay tries are scored when your side are playing with a man or more advantage due to yellow or red cards.

Shorthand tries are scored when your side are playing with a man or more fewer due to yellow or red cards.

Team Performance

Position	Team	% total points won	% won at home	% won away
1	**Harlequins**			
2	Bedford			
3	Penzance			
4	Rotherham	47%	50%	43%
5	Plymouth			
6	Exeter			
7	Nottingham			
8	Otley			
9	Doncaster			
10	Coventry			
11	Newbury	53%	50%	57%
12	Welsh			
13	Sedgley			
14	Birm & S			

NEC Harlequins

Top Scorer – Andrew Mehrtens

Points Facts

Total points	% team points	Home	Away
▶ 194	▶ 19	▶ 84	▶ 110

Points by Time Period

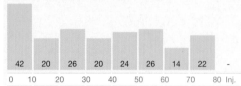

42	20	26	20	24	26	14	22	-
0	10	20	30	40	50	60	70	80 Inj.

Team Tries and Points

Tries by Time Period

▶ scored
▶ conceded

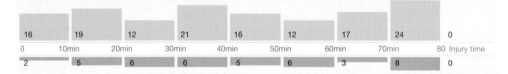

16	19	12	21	16	12	17	24	0
0	10min	20min	30min	40min	50min	60min	70min	80 Injury time
2	5	6	6	5	6	3	8	0

Tries by Halves

▶ scored
▶ conceded

▶ 137	▶ 68	▶ 69	▶ 50%	▶ 50%
Total	1st half	2nd half	1st half %	2nd half %
▶ 41	▶ 19	▶ 22	▶ 46%	▶ 54%

How Points were Scored

▶ tries:	685
▶ conversions:	202
▶ pen goals:	114
drop goals:	0

How Points were Conceded

▶ tries:	205
▶ conversions:	42
▶ pen goals:	87
drop goals:	3

Tries Scored by Player

▶ backs:	86
▶ forwards:	50

Tries Conceded by Player

▶ backs:	26
▶ forwards:	14

NEC Harlequins

Eight-Season Form 1998-2006

Season Progression

Season	98-99	99-00	00-01	01-02	02-03	03-04	04-05	05-06
Points/Position	33	18	38	35	44	54	38	121
○ position	4	10	11	9	7	6	12	1

Premiership
Division 1
Division 2

Games

Season	98-99	99-00	00-01	01-02	02-03	03-04	04-05	05-06
won	16	7	7	5	9	10	6	25
drawn	1			3		2	1	
lost	9	15	15	14	13	10	15	1

Points

Season	98-99	99-00	00-01	01-02	02-03	03-04	04-05	05-06
scored	690	441	440	434	461	502	416	1001
conceded	653	687	538	507	560	449	459	337

Points Difference

Season	98-99	99-00	00-01	01-02	02-03	03-04	04-05	05-06
points	+37	-246	-98	-73	-99	+53	-43	+664

Total Premiership Record

Largest win
▶ **43-6**
vs Saracens (H)
16.11.01

Largest defeat
▶ **19-77**
vs Bath Rugby (A)
29.04.00

Most tries scored in a game
▶ **7**
vs Sale Sharks (H)
25.10.97

Most tries conceded in a game
▶ **10**
vs Bath Rugby (A)
29.04.00

Top points scorer
▶ P.Burke 707

Top try scorer
▶ D.O'Leary 24

Top drop goal scorer
▶ P.Burke 16

Most appearances
▶ J.Leonard 110

Longest winning sequence
▶ **6 wins** from 17.10.98 to 21.11.98

Longest losing sequence
▶ **9 defeats** from 08.05.04 to 05.11.04

NEC Harlequins EFL

ENHANCED FIXTURE LIST
[does not include play-off data]

Guinness Premiership 2006-07 — Premiership History

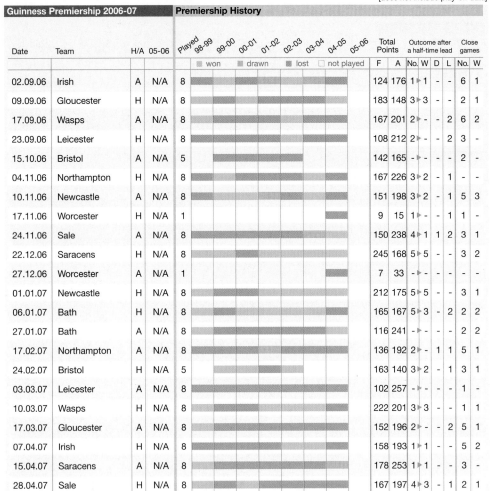

Date	Team	H/A	05-06	Played	98-99 99-00 00-01 01-02 02-03 03-04 04-05 05-06 (won / drawn / lost / not played)	Total Points F	A	Outcome after a half-time lead No.	W	D	L	Close games No.	W
02.09.06	Irish	A	N/A	8		124	176	1►1	-	-	6	1
09.09.06	Gloucester	H	N/A	8		183	148	3►3	-	-	2	1
17.09.06	Wasps	A	N/A	8		167	201	2►-	-	2	6	2
23.09.06	Leicester	H	N/A	8		108	212	2►-	-	2	3	-
15.10.06	Bristol	A	N/A	5		142	165	-►-	-	-	2	-
04.11.06	Northampton	H	N/A	8		167	226	3►2	-	1	-	-
10.11.06	Newcastle	A	N/A	8		151	198	3►2	-	1	5	3
17.11.06	Worcester	H	N/A	1		9	15	1►-	-	1	1	-
24.11.06	Sale	A	N/A	8		150	238	4►1	1	2	3	1
22.12.06	Saracens	H	N/A	8		245	168	5►5	-	-	3	2
27.12.06	Worcester	A	N/A	1		7	33	-►-	-	-	-	-
01.01.07	Newcastle	H	N/A	8		212	175	5►5	-	-	3	1
06.01.07	Bath	H	N/A	8		165	167	5►3	-	2	2	2
27.01.07	Bath	A	N/A	8		116	241	-►-	-	-	2	2
17.02.07	Northampton	A	N/A	8		136	192	2►-	1	1	5	1
24.02.07	Bristol	H	N/A	5		163	140	3►2	-	1	3	1
03.03.07	Leicester	A	N/A	8		102	257	-►-	-	-	1	-
10.03.07	Wasps	H	N/A	8		222	201	3►3	-	-	1	1
17.03.07	Gloucester	A	N/A	8		152	196	2►-	-	2	5	1
07.04.07	Irish	H	N/A	8		158	193	1►1	-	-	5	2
15.04.07	Saracens	A	N/A	8		178	253	1►1	-	-	3	-
28.04.07	Sale	H	N/A	8		167	197	4►3	-	1	2	1

Club Information

Useful Information

Founded
1866

Address
Twickenham Stoop
Langhorn Drive
Twickenham
Middlesex
TW2 7SX

Stadium capacity
12,400

Main switchboard
020 8410 6000

Website
www.quins.co.uk

Travel Information

Car
From the M4:
Leave the M4 at Junction 3. Take the 3rd exit of the Roundabout for the A312, towards Feltham (A3006). Continue along the A312 for 4.5 miles. At the A305 / A316 roundabout, turn left onto the A316. Follow the A316 Chertsey Road, over three roundabouts. Continue for 2 miles. With Twickenham Rugby Stadium on your left, Quins' ground is on the right.

U-turn at the RFU roundabout. Enter the Stoop via Langhorn Drive, 450 yards on your left.

Train
Twickenham station is served by trains from London Waterloo and Reading, with more services and routes accessible via Clapham Junction. After the match (and after a warming pint or two in the East Stand) there are plenty of trains to return you home safely. Upon leaving the station, turn right towards Twickenham Rugby Stadium and left at the mini-roundabout. Take the first left into Court Way and then turn left into Craneford Way and continue on until you reach the stadium. The Twickenham Stoop is at the end of the road on the right.

Maps

Area Map

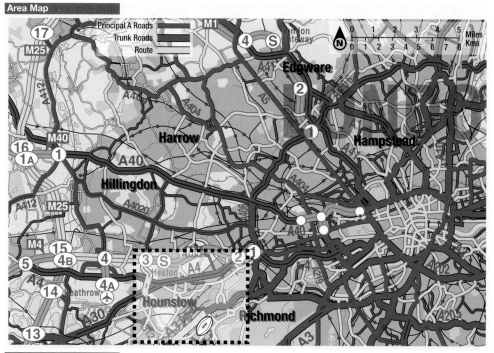

Local Map

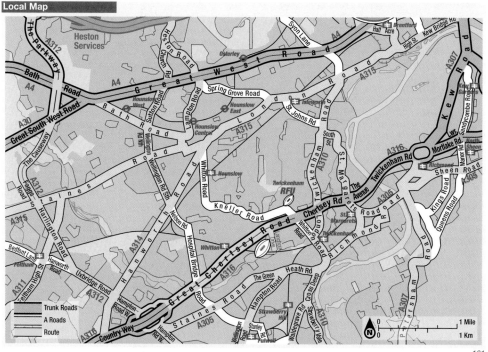

Newcastle Falcons

Season Summary 2005/06

Position	Won	Drawn	Lost	For	Against	Bonus Points	Total Points
7	9	1	12	416	433	9	47

The 2005/06 season was a landmark for long-serving Newcastle Falcon's director of rugby Rob Andrew, who celebrated 10 years at the helm of the club. Andrew, though, had little to celebrate, as his side once again flattered to deceive in the Premiership. Without the services of playmaker Jonny Wilkinson for most of the campaign and lacking in fire power, Newcastle were always going to struggle. However, it wasn't all doom and gloom. The coming-of-age of talented youngsters Toby Flood and Matthew Tait, the return of Wilkinson and the emergence of some promising young players gave reason for optimism.

Director of Rugby: Rob Andrew

Club Honours
Allied Dunbar Premiership: 1997-98
John Player Cup / Powergen Cup: 1976, 1977, 2001, 2004

Season Squad

Stats 2005-06

Position	Player	Height	Weight	Apps	Rep	Tries	Points
P	G.Anderson	6'0"	18st 8lb	1	-	-	-
L	A.Buist	6'6"	17st 0lb	8	4	-	-
FB	M.Burke	6'0"	14st 10lb	20	-	8	142
SH	H.Charlton	5'11"	14st 4lb	9	5	-	-
BR	C.Charvis	6'3"	16st 10lb	13	-	-	-
SH	L.Dickson	5'11"	12st 6lb	-	3	-	-
8	P.Dowson	6'3"	16st 10lb	2	-	-	-
W/FB	A.Elliott	6'3"	14st 9lb	12	1	8	42
FL/L	O.Finegan	6'6"	18st 12lb	13	4	1	5
FH/FB	T.Flood	6'2"	15st 0lb	12	4	1	7
L	S.Grimes	6'5"	17st 3lb	4	5	-	-
SH	J.Grindal	5'9"	13st 4lb	13	7	-	-
L	L.Gross	6'9"	19st 8lb	2	4	-	-
FL	C.Harris	6'0"	17st 0lb	12	1	1	5
W/C	J.Hoyle	6'1"	13st 4lb	3	-	1	5
8	G.Irvin	N/A	N/A	-	1	-	-
H	A.Long	5'11"	16st 3lb	17	4	1	5
W	T.May	5'10"	14st 5lb	18	-	4	23
C	M.Mayerhofler	6'0"	15st 2lb	14	1	-	-
FL	M.McCarthy	6'4"	17st 0lb	9	10	3	15
P	R.Morris	6'2"	18st 11lb	20	2	1	5
C	J.Noon	5'10"	13st 5lb	12	3	2	10
P	T.Paoletti	6'0"	20st 0lb	1	5	-	-
L/FL	G.Parling	6'5"	16st 5lb	16	2	1	5
P	I.Peel	5'11"	18st 0lb	1	1	-	-
L	A.Perry	6'7"	18st 7lb	19	-	-	-
W	O.Phillips	5'11"	14st 7lb	5	-	2	10
FB/C	J.Shaw	6'0"	15st 2lb	5	4	2	10
8	J.Smithson	6'2"	11st 13lb	2	1	-	-
C/W	M.Tait	5'11"	13st 4lb	16	-	2	10
H	M.Thompson	6'2"	18st 0lb	5	12	-	-
FH	D.Walder	5'10"	12st 9lb	11	2	2	56
P	M.Ward	5'11"	18st 9lb	19	3	-	-
FH	J.Wilkinson	5'10"	13st 5lb	4	3	1	56
C	M.Wilkinson	6'3"	17st 0lb	-	1	-	-
P	J.Williams	6'0"	15st 5lb	2	6	-	-
FL	E.Williamson	6'2"	14st 9lb	-	1	-	-
P	D.Wilson	6'1"	18st 7lb	-	7	-	-
FL	B.Woods	6'2"	16st 5lb	10	7	1	5

Newcastle Falcons

Last Season Form 2005/06

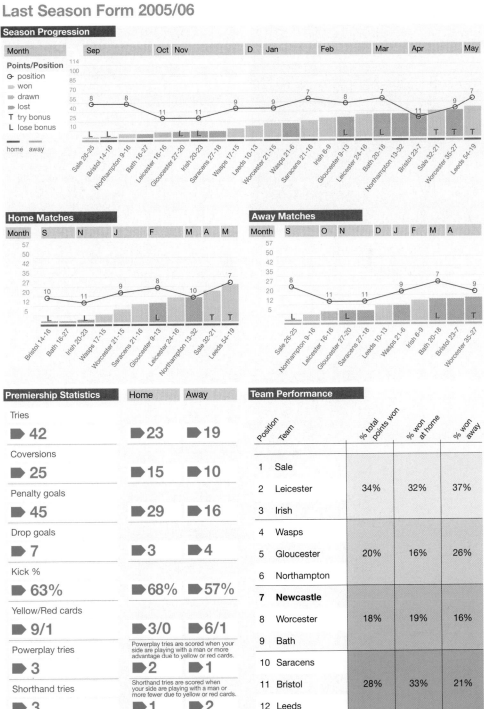

Season Progression

| Month | Sep | Oct | Nov | D | Jan | Feb | Mar | Apr | May |

Points/Position
- ⊖ position
- ➡ won
- ➡ drawn
- ➡ lost
- T try bonus
- L lose bonus

home away

Home Matches

| Month | S | N | J | F | M | A | M |

Away Matches

| Month | S | O | N | D | J | F | M | A |

Premiership Statistics

	Home	Away
Tries	➡ 42	➡ 23 ➡ 19
Coversions	➡ 25	➡ 15 ➡ 10
Penalty goals	➡ 45	➡ 29 ➡ 16
Drop goals	➡ 7	➡ 3 ➡ 4
Kick %	➡ 63%	➡ 68% ➡ 57%
Yellow/Red cards	➡ 9/1	➡ 3/0 ➡ 6/1
Powerplay tries	➡ 3	➡ 2 ➡ 1
Shorthand tries	➡ 3	➡ 1 ➡ 2

Powerplay tries are scored when your side is playing with a man or more advantage due to yellow or red cards.

Shorthand tries are scored when your side are playing with a man or more fewer due to yellow or red cards.

Team Performance

Position	Team	% total points won	% won at home	% won away
1	Sale			
2	Leicester	34%	32%	37%
3	Irish			
4	Wasps			
5	Gloucester	20%	16%	26%
6	Northampton			
7	**Newcastle**	18%	19%	16%
8	Worcester			
9	Bath			
10	Saracens			
11	Bristol	28%	33%	21%
12	Leeds			

Newcastle Falcons

Top Scorer – Matthew Burke

Points Facts

Total points	% team points	Home	Away
▶142	▶34	▶80	▶62

Points by Time Period

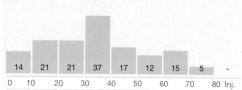

14	21	21	37	17	12	15	5	-
0	10	20	30	40	50	60	70	80 Inj.

Team Tries and Points

Tries by Time Period

▶ scored
▶ conceded

3	4	7	4	2	8	7	5	2
0	10min	20min	30min	40min	50min	60min	70min	80 Injury time
6	4	3	8	8	5	5	5	0

Tries by Halves

▶ scored
▶ conceded

	Total	1st half	2nd half	1st half %	2nd half %
scored	▶ 42	▶ 18	▶ 24	▶ 43%	▶ 57%
conceded	▶ 44	▶ 21	▶ 23	▶ 48%	▶ 52%

How Points were Scored

▶ tries:	210
▶ conversions:	50
▶ pen goals:	135
▶ drop goals:	21

How Points were Conceded

▶ tries:	220
▶ conversions:	60
▶ pen goals:	150
▶ drop goals:	3

Tries Scored by Player

▶ backs:	33
▶ forwards:	9

Tries Conceded by Player

▶ backs:	29
▶ forwards:	15

Newcastle Falcons

Eight-Season Form 1998-2006

Season Progression

Season	98-99	99-00	00-01	01-02	02-03	03-04	04-05	05-06

Points/Position
- ○ position
- Premiership
- Division 1
- Division 2

28 · 8 · 19 · 9 · 57 · 6 · 56 · 40 · 10 · 45 · 9 · 47 · 7 · 47 · 7

Games

Season	98-99	99-00	00-01	01-02	02-03	03-04	04-05	05-06
won	14	6	11	12	8	7	9	9
drawn		2				2	2	1
lost	12	14	11	9 · 1	14	13	11	12

Points

Season	98-99	99-00	00-01	01-02	02-03	03-04	04-05	05-06
scored	719	377	554	490	388	497	475	416
conceded	639	630	568	458	545	525	596	433

Points Difference

Season	98-99	99-00	00-01	01-02	02-03	03-04	04-05	05-06
points	+80	-253	-14	+32	-157	-28	-121	-17

Total Premiership Record

Largest win

▶ **56-10**
vs Rotherham Titans (H)
09.11.03

Largest defeat

▶ **10-83**
vs Leicester Tigers (A)
19.02.05

Most tries scored in a game

▶ **8**
vs Leeds Tykes (H)
06.05.06

Most tries conceded in a game

▶ **11**
vs Leicester Tigers (A)
19.02.05

Top points scorer

▶ J.Wilkinson 1307

Top try scorer

▶ G.Armstrong 35

Top drop goal scorer

▶ J.Wilkinson 19

Most appearances

▶ J.Noon 132

Longest winning sequence

▶ **12 wins** from 23.08.97 to 10.03.98

Longest losing sequence

▶ **7 defeats** from 03.11.02 to 03.01.03

Newcastle Falcons EFL

ENHANCED FIXTURE LIST
[does not include play-off data]

Premiership History

Date	Team	H/A	05-06	Played	98-99	99-00	00-01	01-02	02-03	03-04	04-05	05-06	Total Points F	A	Outcome after a half-time lead No.	W	D	L	Close games No.	W
03.09.06	Northampton	A	9-16	9									150	257	3►1	-	2		3	1
08.09.06	Worcester	H	21-15	2									37	36	1►1	-	-		2	1
17.09.06	Saracens	A	27-18	9									166	268	-►-	-	-		5	1
22.09.06	Irish	H	20-23	9									244	201	7►4	-	3		5	2
15.10.06	Wasps	A	21-6	9									182	252	1►-	1	-		6	1
03.11.06	Bristol	H	14-16	6									161	126	2►2	-	-		2	-
10.11.06	Harlequins	H	N/A	8									198	151	5►3	1	1		5	1
17.11.06	Sale	A	26-25	9									185	285	3►2	-	1		1	-
25.11.06	Bath	A	20-18	9									137	199	3►2	-	1		2	-
22.12.06	Gloucester	A	27-20	9									187	275	3►1	-	2		3	1
26.12.06	Sale	H	32-21	9									245	151	7►7	-	-		4	4
01.01.07	Harlequins	A	N/A	8									175	212	2►2	-	-		3	2
07.01.07	Leicester	H	24-16	9									180	191	4►3	-	1		5	2
27.01.07	Leicester	A	16-16	9									144	334	2►-	1	1		2	1
18.02.07	Bristol	A	23-7	6									109	159	1►1	-	-		-	-
23.02.07	Wasps	H	17-15	9									226	193	7►6	-	1		4	2
03.03.07	Irish	A	6-9	9									139	190	3►2	-	1		6	3
09.03.07	Saracens	H	21-16	9									254	171	6►6	-	-		6	4
16.03.07	Worcester	A	35-27	2									57	44	1►1	-	-		-	-
06.04.07	Northampton	H	13-32	9									230	215	4►4	-	-		3	3
13.04.07	Gloucester	H	9-13	9									245	189	5►4	-	1		5	1
28.04.07	Bath	H	16-27	9									175	161	6►4	-	2		7	4

Legend: ■ won ■ drawn ■ lost □ not played

Club Information

Useful Information

Founded
1995
(Gosforth formed in 1877)
Address
Kingston Park
Brunton Road
Kenton Bank Foot
Newcastle NE13 8AF
Capacity
10,000
Main switchboard
0191 214 5588
Website
www.newcastle-falcons.co.uk

Travel Information

Car
From South:
Take the M1 and turn right onto the M62 at junction 42, towards the A1. Follow the A1 all the way into Newcastle, heading for the junction for Newcastle Airport. When you reach that junction, take the Kingston Park exit then continue straight ahead over two mini roundabouts. After passing under a bridge, turn right into Brunton Road then continue until you see the ground on your left.
From West:
Follow the A69 until it joins the A1, and follow signs for the Newcastle Airport junction. Then as route for South.
Train
GNER and Virgin Trains run services to Newcastle Central. From there, catch the Tyne and Wear Metro to Kingston Park station.
Air
Newcastle International Airport is a short cab ride from the stadium.

Maps

Area Map

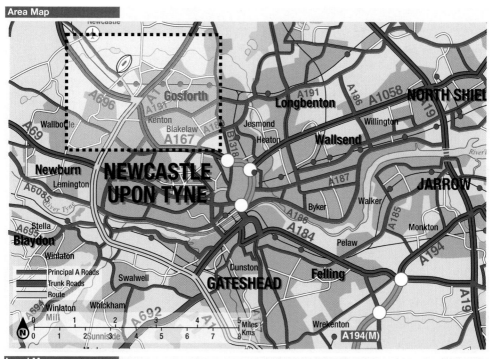

Local Map

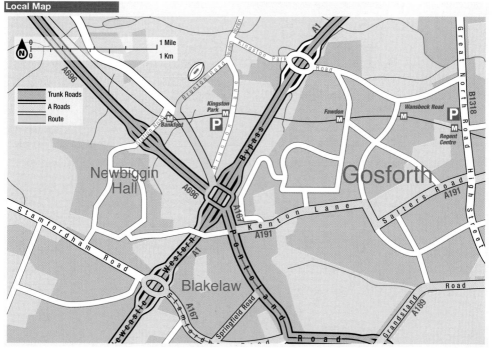

Northampton Saints

Season Summary 2005/06

Position	Won	Drawn	Lost	For	Against	Bonus Points	Total Points
6	10	1	11	464	488	11	53

Saints fans waited in anticipation for All Black Carlos Spencer to pull on a Northampton shirt and they certainly weren't disappointed, as Spencer wowed the Franklin's Gardens crowd with his electric pace and breathtaking skills, ensuring he was voted Saints Player of the Year. Despite inconsistent form in the Premiership, Saints rose to the occasion with perhaps the performance of the season against Saracens in February, where they put on an outstanding display of rugby. Northampton fans will enjoy Heineken Cup rugby at Franklin's Gardens next season and Saints will face French Champions and last season's beaten finalists Biarritz in the quest for European glory.

Head Coach: Budge Pountney

Club Honours
Heineken Cup: 1999-2000

Season Squad

Stats 2005-06

Position	Player	Height	Weight	Apps	Rep	Tries	Points	Position	Player	Height	Weight	Apps	Rep	Tries	Points
P	P.Barnard	6'0"	17st 8lb	9	1	1	5	L	M.Lord	6'4"	17st 2lb	17	5	-	-
L	S.Boome	6'3"	17st 0lb	1	2	-	-	C	S.Mallon	6'3"	14st 11lb	4	1	2	10
8	D.Browne	6'5"	16st 3lb	39	-	2	10	FH	L.Myring	6'0"	14st 3lb	1	-	1	5
P	C.Budgen	5'8"	17st 10lb	11	8	1	5	P	C.Noon	5'11"	18st 3lb	1	2	-	-
FB/W	J.Clarke	6'3"	14st 1lb	22	-	6	30	FB	J.Pritchard	5'9"	13st 5lb	1	1	-	4
W	B.Cohen	6'2"	15st 10lb	13	1	7	35	C	D.Quinlan	6'4"	16st 2lb	14	1	1	5
C	R.Davies	5'9"	14st 0lb	3	4	2	10	L	A.Rae	6'5"	15st 8lb	1	1	-	-
W	P.Diggin	5'8"	13st 2lb	3	1	-	-	FB	B.Reihana	6'0"	13st 7lb	21	-	5	206
BR	M.Easter	6'3"	16st 0lb	4	2	2	10	H	D.Richmond	5'11"	15st 6lb	10	4	-	-
P	S.Emms	5'11"	17st 8lb	1	7	-	-	SH	M.Robinson	5'10"	13st 8lb	18	4	2	10
FL	D.Fox	6'0"	15st 10lb	11	7	2	10	W	J.Rudd	6'2"	17st 0lb	11	3	1	5
L	D.Gerard	6'6"	19st 0lb	5	11	-	-	BR/L	G.Seely	6'4"	17st 0lb	2	1	-	-
H	M.Grove	6'3"	17st 2lb	-	1	-	-	P	T.Smith	5'10"	16st 3lb	19	-	-	-
P	L.Harbut	5'10"	17st 7lb	-	3	-	-	BR	M.Soden	6'2"	16st 4lb	2	2	-	-
FL	S.Harding	6'1"	16st 4lb	10	7	1	5	FH	C.Spencer	6'1"	15st 0lb	21	-	4	34
H	D.Hartley	6'1"	17st 11lb	4	8	-	-	P	B.Sturgess	6'1"	17st 10lb	3	3	-	-
SH	J.Howard	5'9"	12st 7lb	4	9	-	-	H	S.Thompson	6'2"	18st 2lb	9	4	3	15
C/FH	R.Kydd	5'11"	14st 3lb	3	3	-	-	BR	P.Tupai	6'4"	17st 10lb	11	1	1	5
W	S.Lamont	6'2"	15st 0lb	12	2	6	30	C	A.Vilk	5'11"	15st 6lb	3	4	1	5
FL	B.Lewitt	6'3"	15st 0lb	6	7	-	-								

Northampton Saints

Last Season Form 2005/06

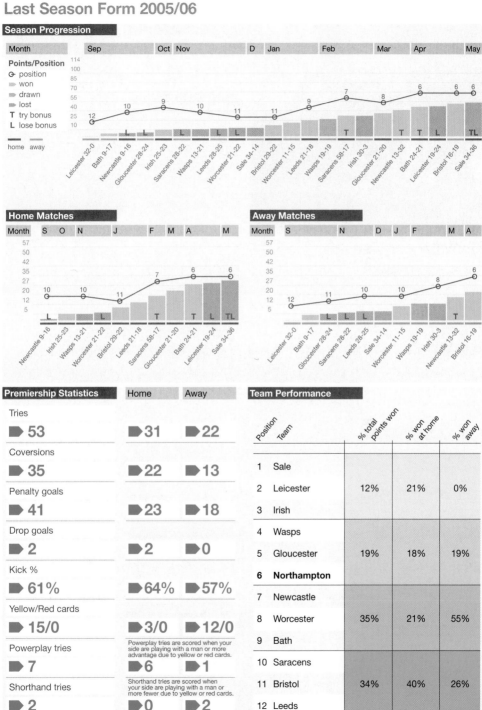

Season Progression

Month	Sep		Oct	Nov		D	Jan		Feb		Mar		Apr		May

Points/Position
- ⊖ position
- won
- drawn
- lost
- **T** try bonus
- **L** lose bonus

home away

Leicester 32-0, Bath 9-17, Newcastle 9-16, Gloucester 28-24, Irish 25-23, Saracens 28-22, Wasps 13-21, Leeds 28-25, Worcester 21-22, Sale 34-14, Bristol 29-22, Worcester 11-15, Leeds 21-18, Wasps 19-19, Saracens 58-17, Irish 30-3, Gloucester 21-20, Newcastle 13-32, Bath 24-21, Leicester 19-24, Bristol 16-19, Sale 34-36

Home Matches

Month	S	O	N		J		F	M	A		M

Newcastle 9-16, Irish 25-23, Wasps 13-21, Worcester 21-22, Bristol 29-22, Leeds 21-18, Saracens 58-17, Gloucester 21-20, Bath 24-21, Leicester 19-24, Sale 34-36

Away Matches

Month	S		N		D	J	F		M	A

Leicester 32-0, Bath 9-17, Gloucester 28-24, Saracens 28-22, Leeds 28-25, Sale 34-14, Worcester 11-15, Wasps 19-19, Irish 30-3, Newcastle 13-32, Bristol 16-19

Premiership Statistics

		Home	Away
Tries	53	31	22
Coversions	35	22	13
Penalty goals	41	23	18
Drop goals	2	2	0
Kick %	61%	64%	57%
Yellow/Red cards	15/0	3/0	12/0
Powerplay tries	7	6	1
Shorthand tries	2	0	2

Powerplay tries are scored when your side are playing with a man or more advantage due to yellow or red cards.

Shorthand tries are scored when your side are playing with a man or more fewer due to yellow or red cards.

Team Performance

Position	Team	% total points won	% won at home	% won away
1	Sale			
2	Leicester	12%	21%	0%
3	Irish			
4	Wasps			
5	Gloucester	19%	18%	19%
6	**Northampton**			
7	Newcastle			
8	Worcester	35%	21%	55%
9	Bath			
10	Saracens			
11	Bristol	34%	40%	26%
12	Leeds			

Northampton Saints

Top Scorer – Bruce Reihana

Points Facts

Total points	% team points	Home	Away
▸206	▸45	▸131	▸75

Points by Time Period

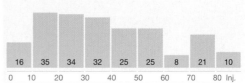

16	35	34	32	25	25	8	21	10
0	10	20	30	40	50	60	70	80 Inj.

Team Tries and Points

Tries by Time Period

▸ scored
▸ conceded

7	4	6	7	3	8	7	10	1
0	10min	20min	30min	40min	50min	60min	70min	80 Injury time
7	7	8	6	5	4	6	6	1

Tries by Halves

▸ scored
▸ conceded

	Total	1st half	2nd half	1st half %	2nd half %
scored	▸ 53	▸ 24	▸ 29	▸ 45%	▸ 55%
conceded	▸ 50	▸ 28	▸ 22	▸ 56%	▸ 44%

How Points were Scored

▸ tries: 265
▸ conversions: 70
▸ pen goals: 123
▸ drop goals: 6

How Points were Conceded

▸ tries: 250
▸ conversions: 64
▸ pen goals: 162
▸ drop goals: 12

Tries Scored by Player

▸ backs: 38
▸ forwards: 14

Tries Conceded by Player

▸ backs: 37
▸ forwards: 12

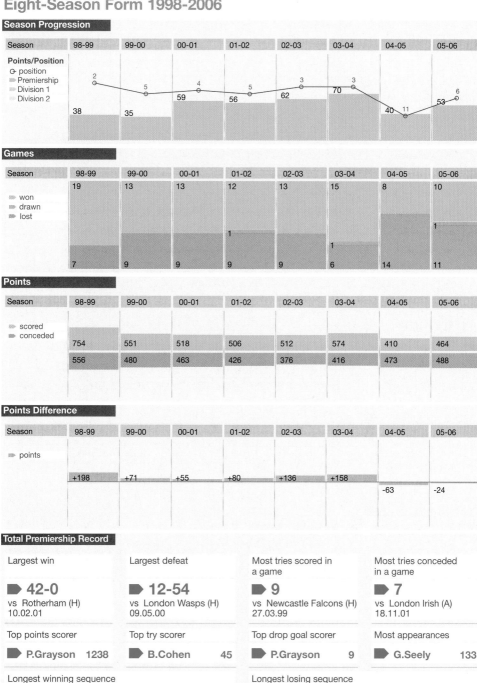

Northampton Saints

Eight-Season Form 1998-2006

Season Progression

Season	98-99	99-00	00-01	01-02	02-03	03-04	04-05	05-06
Points/Position ⚬ position ▸ Premiership ▸ Division 1 ▸ Division 2	2 / 38	5 / 35	4 / 59	5 / 56	3 / 62	3 / 70	11 / 40	6 / 53

Games

Season	98-99	99-00	00-01	01-02	02-03	03-04	04-05	05-06
▸ won	19	13	13	12	13	15	8	10
▸ drawn				1		1		1
▸ lost	7	9	9	9	9	6	14	11

Points

Season	98-99	99-00	00-01	01-02	02-03	03-04	04-05	05-06
▸ scored	754	551	518	506	512	574	410	464
▸ conceded	556	480	463	426	376	416	473	488

Points Difference

Season	98-99	99-00	00-01	01-02	02-03	03-04	04-05	05-06
▸ points	+198	+71	+55	+80	+136	+158	-63	-24

Total Premiership Record

Largest win	Largest defeat	Most tries scored in a game	Most tries conceded in a game
▸ **42-0** vs Rotherham (H) 10.02.01	▸ **12-54** vs London Wasps (H) 09.05.00	▸ **9** vs Newcastle Falcons (H) 27.03.99	▸ **7** vs London Irish (A) 18.11.01

Top points scorer	Top try scorer	Top drop goal scorer	Most appearances
▸ P.Grayson 1238	▸ B.Cohen 45	▸ P.Grayson 9	▸ G.Seely 133

Longest winning sequence	Longest losing sequence
▸ **7 wins** from 05.11.99 to 26.01.00	▸ **9 defeats** from 18.09.04 to 28.11.04

Northampton Saints EFL

ENHANCED FIXTURE LIST
[does not include play-off data]

Premiership History

Legend: ■ won ■ drawn ■ lost □ not played

Date	Team	H/A	05-06	Played	98-99	99-00	00-01	01-02	02-03	03-04	04-05	05-06	Total Points F	A	Outcome after a half-time lead No.	W	D	L	Close games No.	W
03.09.06	Newcastle	H	9-16	9									257	150	6	5	-	1	3	2
09.09.06	Sale	A	34-14	9									204	263	4	2	1	1	3	1
16.09.06	Bath	H	24-21	9									212	113	6	6	-	-	3	2
23.09.06	Gloucester	A	28-24	9									184	200	6	3	-	3	3	1
14.10.06	Leicester	H	19-24	9									168	136	5	4	-	1	2	-
04.11.06	Harlequins	A	N/A	8									226	167	5	5	-	-	-	-
11.11.06	Worcester	A	11-15	2									34	32	-	-	-	-	2	1
18.11.06	Saracens	H	58-17	9									252	179	6	5	-	1	3	-
26.11.06	Irish	A	30-3	9									218	179	5	5	-	-	3	2
22.12.06	Wasps	H	13-21	9									180	184	6	5	-	1	3	1
27.12.06	Saracens	A	28-22	9									176	241	2	-	-	2	4	1
01.01.07	Worcester	H	21-22	2									27	39	-	-	-	-	1	-
07.01.07	Bristol	A	16-19	6									152	158	4	2	-	2	1	1
27.01.07	Bristol	H	29-22	6									170	99	4	3	-	1	2	-
17.02.07	Harlequins	H	N/A	8									192	136	6	5	-	1	5	3
24.02.07	Leicester	A	32-0	9									156	217	2	2	-	-	2	-
03.03.07	Gloucester	H	21-20	9									221	164	4	4	-	-	4	1
10.03.07	Bath	A	9-17	9									135	188	5	4	-	1	1	1
17.03.07	Sale	H	34-36	9									256	172	5	4	-	1	2	1
06.04.07	Newcastle	A	13-32	9									215	230	5	3	-	2	3	-
15.04.07	Wasps	A	19-19	9									125	236	3	2	1	-	2	1
28.04.07	Irish	H	25-23	9									195	190	1	1	-	-	4	2

Club Information

Useful Information

Founded
1880
Address
Franklin's Gardens
Weedon Road
Northampton
NN5 5BG
Capacity
13,591 (11,500 seated)
Main switchboard
01604 751543
Website
www.northamptonsaints.
co.uk

Travel Information

Car
From North:
Approaching on the M1, exit at junction 16 and take the A45 onto Weedon Road, which is signposted 'Town Centre'. Turn left into Ross Road and follow signs for the car park.
From South:
Approaching on the M1, exit at junction 15a and follow signs for Sixfields. Turn left to join the A45 onto Weedon Road. Then as route for North.

Train
Silverlink trains run from Milton Keynes Central or Coventry to Northampton station.
Silverlink Trains also run directly from London Euston to Northampton station.
From Northampton station, turn right and continue walking until you pass the bus station and enter a shopping area. Turn left, then left again down Abbey Street into the Northampton Saints Car Park.

Maps

Area Map

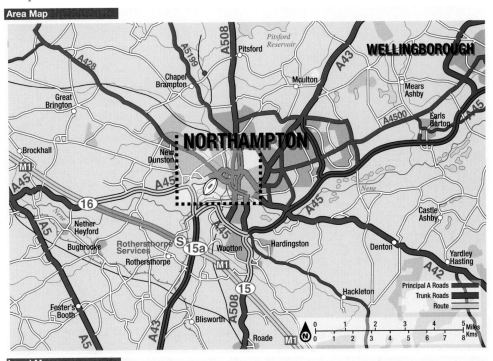

Local Map

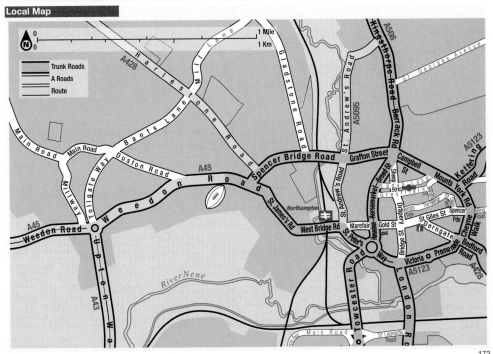

Sale Sharks

Season Summary 2005/06

Position	Won	Drawn	Lost	For	Against	Bonus Points	Total Points
1	16	1	5	573	444	8	74

An emphatic win over Tigers at Twickenham saw the north west side winning their first league title and making Premiership history finishing top of the league and going on to claim the Premiership title. Although Sharks were forced to play periods of the season without key players due to international commitments, they proved they had quality players to stand in for the likes of Charlie Hodgson and Mark Cueto, only losing five Premiership games throughout their campaign. Head Coach Kingsley Jones has retained all his key players and has recruited well for the coming season – including Newport Gwent's John Bryant and Leeds' Chris Bell – as he looks to emulate the success achieved in 2005/06.

Director of Rugby: Philippe Saint-Andre

Club Honours
Parker Pen Shield: 2002, 2005
Guinness Premiership Champions: 2006

Season Squad

Stats 2005-06

Position	Player	Height	Weight	Apps	Rep	Tries	Points
BR	P.Anglesea	6'3"	16st 4lb	-	4	-	-
8	N.Bonner-Evans	6'4"	18st 0lb	7	4	-	-
H	N.Briggs	5'10"	14st 13lb	-	1	-	-
H	S.Bruno	5'9"	16st 9lb	6	9	1	5
FL	J.Carter	6'3"	17st 0lb	2	1	-	-
8	S.Chabal	6'3"	17st 0lb	17	1	3	15
SH	V.Courrent	5'9"	13st 12lb	12	5	3	82
P	B.Coutts	6'3"	18st 0lb	9	2	-	-
W	M.Cueto	6'0"	14st 9lb	16	-	6	30
L	C.Day	6'6"	16st 10lb	9	10	-	-
P	L.Faure	6'1"	18st 0lb	6	4	-	-
L	I.Fernandez Lobbe	6'5"	17st 4lb	12	6	3	15
SH	B.Foden	6'0"	13st 7lb	1	7	1	5
W	S.Hanley	6'4"	15st 12lb	7	1	4	20
FL	M.Hills	6'1"	14st 7lb	-	2	-	-
FH	C.Hodgson	5'10"	12st 13lb	15	1	2	248
L/BR	C.Jones	6'7"	16st 1lb	19	1	2	10
P	M.Jones	5'7"	19st 0lb	-	1	-	-
FH	D.Larrechea	6'0"	14st 3lb	11	2	1	32
L/BR	B.Lloyd	6'5"	15st 13lb	-	1	-	-

Position	Player	Height	Weight	Apps	Rep	Tries	Points
FL	M.Lund	6'3"	16st 9lb	19	1	4	20
SH	S.Martens	5'11"	14st 7lb	14	2	3	15
C/W	C.Mayor	6'2"	15st 0lb	5	10	5	25
W	M.Riley	6'2"	14st 4lb	-	1	-	-
W	O.Ripol Fortuny	5'9"	12st 6lb	13	2	4	20
P	E.Roberts	N/A	N/A	1	2	-	-
FB	J.Robinson	5'8"	13st 4lb	23	-	4	29
L	D.Schofield	6'6"	18st 0lb	17	3	3	15
C/W	E.Seveali'i	5'10"	14st 0lb	14	-	3	15
P	A.Sheridan	6'5"	18st 10lb	8	2	-	-
P	B.Stewart	6'2"	18st 0lb	14	9	-	-
C/W/BR	E.Taione	6'4"	19st 6lb	1	4	-	-
C	M.Taylor	6'1"	15st 0lb	20	-	1	5
H/FL	A.Titterrell	5'8"	14st 9lb	19	5	2	10
C	R.Todd	5'11"	16st 0lb	11	4	1	5
P	S.Turner	6'0"	17st 9lb	10	12	-	-
W/C	N.Wakley	6'2"	15st 0lb	-	2	-	-
FL/L	J.White	6'5"	18st 6lb	16	2	-	-
SH	R.Wigglesworth	5'9"	13st 3lb	6	12	1	19

Sale Sharks

Last Season Form 2005/06

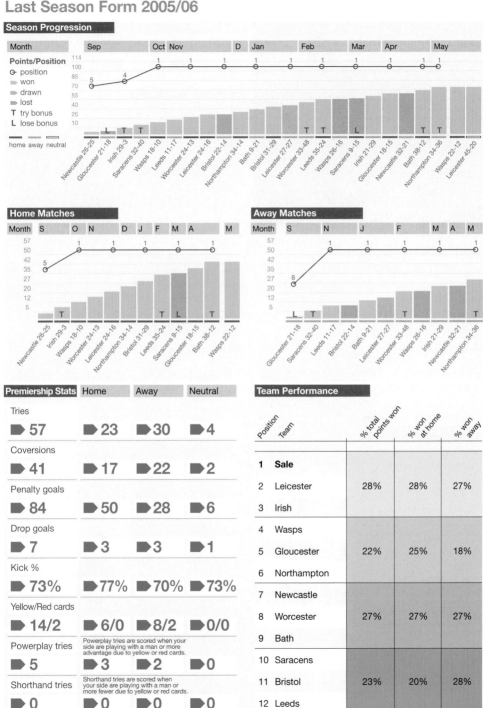

Season Progression

| Month | Sep | Oct | Nov | D | Jan | Feb | Mar | Apr | May |

Points/Position
- ⊖ position
- won
- drawn
- lost
- T try bonus
- L lose bonus

home away neutral

Newcastle 26-25, Gloucester 21-18, Irish 29-3, Saracens 32-40, Wasps 18-10, Leeds 11-17, Worcester 24-13, Leicester 24-16, Bristol 22-14, Northampton 34-14, Bath 9-21, Bristol 31-29, Leicester 27-27, Worcester 33-48, Leeds 35-24, Wasps 26-16, Saracens 9-15, Gloucester 18-15, Newcastle 32-21, Bath 38-12, Northampton 34-36, Wasps 22-12, Leicester 45-20

Home Matches

| Month | S | O | N | D | J | F | M | A | M |

Newcastle 26-25, Irish 29-3, Wasps 18-10, Worcester 24-13, Leicester 24-16, Northampton 34-14, Bristol 31-29, Leeds 35-24, Saracens 9-15, Gloucester 18-15, Bath 38-12, Wasps 22-12

Away Matches

| Month | S | N | J | F | M | A | M |

Gloucester 21-18, Saracens 32-40, Leeds 11-17, Bristol 22-14, Bath 9-21, Leicester 27-27, Worcester 33-48, Wasps 26-16, Irish 21-29, Newcastle 32-21, Northampton 34-36

Premiership Stats

	Home	Away	Neutral
Tries			
57	23	30	4
Coversions			
41	17	22	2
Penalty goals			
84	50	28	6
Drop goals			
7	3	3	1
Kick %			
73%	77%	70%	73%
Yellow/Red cards			
14/2	6/0	8/2	0/0
Powerplay tries	Powerplay tries are scored when your side are playing with a man or more advantage due to yellow or red cards.		
5	3	2	0
Shorthand tries	Shorthand tries are scored when your side are playing with a man or more fewer due to yellow or red cards.		
0	0	0	0

Team Performance

Position	Team	% total points won	% won at home	% won away
1	**Sale**			
2	Leicester	28%	28%	27%
3	Irish			
4	Wasps			
5	Gloucester	22%	25%	18%
6	Northampton			
7	Newcastle			
8	Worcester	27%	27%	27%
9	Bath			
10	Saracens			
11	Bristol	23%	20%	28%
12	Leeds			

Sale Sharks

Top Scorer – Charlie Hodgson

Points Facts

	Total points	% team points	Home	Away	Neutral
	▶248	▶39	▶157	▶68	▶23

Points by Time Period

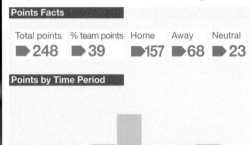

29	30	28	31	50	16	28	31	5
0	10	20	30	40	50	60	70	80 Inj.

Team Tries and Points

Tries by Time Period

- scored
- conceded

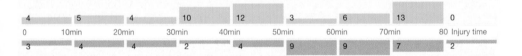

4	5	4	10	12	3	6	13	0
0	10min	20min	30min	40min	50min	60min	70min	80 Injury time
3	4	4	2	4	9	9	7	2

Tries by Halves

- scored
- conceded

▶ 57	▶ 23	▶ 34	▶ 40%	▶ 60%
Total	1st half	2nd half	1st half %	2nd half %
▶ 44	▶ 13	▶ 31	▶ 30%	▶ 70%

How Points were Scored

- tries: 285
- conversions: 82
- pen goals: 252
- drop goals: 21

How Points were Conceded

- tries: 220
- conversions: 58
- pen goals: 186
- drop goals: 12

Tries Scored by Player

- backs: 39
- forwards: 18

Tries Conceded by Player

- backs: 33
- forwards: 10

Sale Sharks

Eight-Season Form 1998-2006

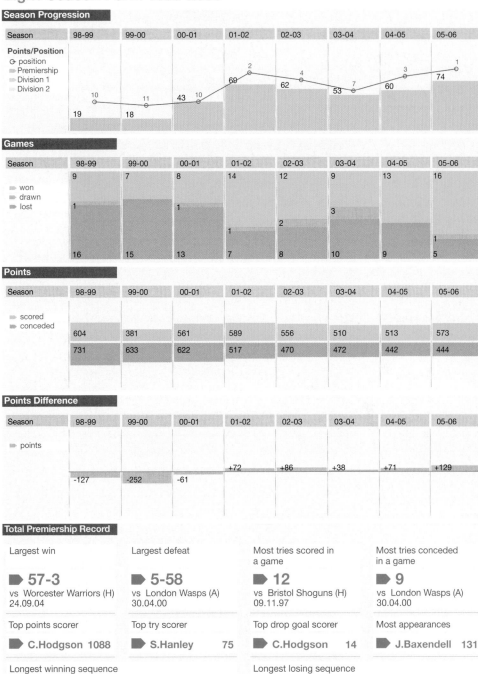

Season Progression

Season	98-99	99-00	00-01	01-02	02-03	03-04	04-05	05-06

Points/Position
- ○ position
- ▬ Premiership
- ▬ Division 1
- ▬ Division 2

| | 19 | 18 | 43 | 69 | 62 | 53 | 60 | 74 |
| position | 10 | 11 | 10 | 2 | 4 | 7 | 3 | 1 |

Games

Season	98-99	99-00	00-01	01-02	02-03	03-04	04-05	05-06
▬ won	9	7	8	14	12	9	13	16
▬ drawn	1		1	1	2	3		1
▬ lost	16	15	13	7	8	10	9	5

Points

Season	98-99	99-00	00-01	01-02	02-03	03-04	04-05	05-06
▬ scored	604	381	561	589	556	510	513	573
▬ conceded	731	633	622	517	470	472	442	444

Points Difference

Season	98-99	99-00	00-01	01-02	02-03	03-04	04-05	05-06
▬ points	-127	-252	-61	+72	+86	+38	+71	+129

Total Premiership Record

Largest win	Largest defeat	Most tries scored in a game	Most tries conceded in a game
▶ **57-3**	▶ **5-58**	▶ **12**	▶ **9**
vs Worcester Warriors (H) 24.09.04	vs London Wasps (A) 30.04.00	vs Bristol Shoguns (H) 09.11.97	vs London Wasps (A) 30.04.00

Top points scorer	Top try scorer	Top drop goal scorer	Most appearances
▶ C.Hodgson 1088	▶ S.Hanley 75	▶ C.Hodgson 14	▶ J.Baxendell 131

Longest winning sequence	Longest losing sequence
▶ **6 wins** from 08.05.04 to 03.10.04	▶ **7 defeats** from 20.12.98 to 14.02.99

ENHANCED FIXTURE LIST
[does not include play-off data]

Guinness Premiership 2006-07 | Premiership History

Legend: won | drawn | lost | not played

Date	Team	H/A	05-06	Played	F	A	No.	W	D	L	No.	W
03.09.06	Leicester	A	27-27	9	139	282	3	1	1	1	2	1
09.09.06	Northampton	H	34-14	9	263	204	5	5	-	-	3	1
15.09.06	Worcester	A	33-48	2	58	56	1	1	-	-	-	-
22.09.06	Saracens	H	9-15	9	187	214	7	5	-	2	1	-
15.10.06	Irish	A	21-29	9	173	178	3	3	-	-	5	4
03.11.06	Wasps	H	18-10	9	198	234	1	1	-	-	4	1
10.11.06	Bristol	A	22-14	6	132	128	3	3	-	-	-	-
17.11.06	Newcastle	H	26-25	9	285	185	6	5	-	1	1	1
24.11.06	Harlequins	H	N/A	8	238	150	4	4	-	-	3	1
22.12.06	Bath	A	9-21	9	151	212	2	1	-	1	4	-
26.12.06	Newcastle	A	32-21	9	151	245	1	-	-	1	4	-
01.01.07	Bristol	H	31-29	6	228	156	5	4	-	1	3	2
06.01.07	Gloucester	H	18-15	9	221	215	5	3	2	-	3	1
27.01.07	Gloucester	A	21-18	9	152	277	2	1	-	1	2	1
18.02.07	Wasps	A	26-16	9	217	273	3	2	-	1	1	1
23.02.07	Irish	H	29-3	9	264	173	3	3	-	-	4	1
04.03.07	Saracens	A	32-40	9	230	348	2	1	-	1	1	-
09.03.07	Worcester	H	24-13	2	81	16	2	2	-	-	-	-
17.03.07	Northampton	A	34-36	9	172	256	4	2	-	2	2	1
06.04.07	Leicester	H	24-16	9	167	218	4	3	1	-	2	-
13.04.07	Bath	H	38-12	9	224	167	5	4	-	1	6	3
28.04.07	Harlequins	A	N/A	8	197	167	2	2	-	-	2	1

Table column groups: Played (98-99, 99-00, 00-01, 01-02, 02-03, 03-04, 04-05, 05-06) · Total Points (F / A) · Outcome after a half-time lead (No. / W / D / L) · Close games (No. / W)

Club Information

Useful Information

Founded
1861

Address
Edgeley Park
Hardcastle Road
Edgeley
Stockport
SK3 9DD

Capacity
10,641 (3,132 seated)

Main switchboard
0161 283 8888

Website
www.salesharks.com

Travel Information

Car

From South:
Leave the M6 at junction 19 (towards Manchester Airport, Stockport A55), then turn right at the roundabout onto the A556. After approx four miles you reach a roundabout, turn right onto the M56 (towards Manchester). After approx a further seven miles, exit the M56 and join the M60 (signposted Stockport, Sheffield). Leave the M60 at junction 1 and follow the signs to Cheadle and Stockport County FC at the roundabout. Continue straight ahead at the first set of traffic lights, then right at the next set (keep following signs for Stockport County FC). After a mile, turn left onto the B5465 Edgeley Road, then after another mile turn right into Dale Street. Take the second turning on the left into Hardcastle Road to reach the stadium.

From North:
From the M62 join the M60 and continue south. Leave the M60 at junction 1, then as route for South.

Train
Stockport station is approx half a mile from the stadium. Arriva Trains Northern run services from Sheffield to Stockport. From London, Virgin Trains run from London Euston to directly to Stockport.

Maps

Area Map

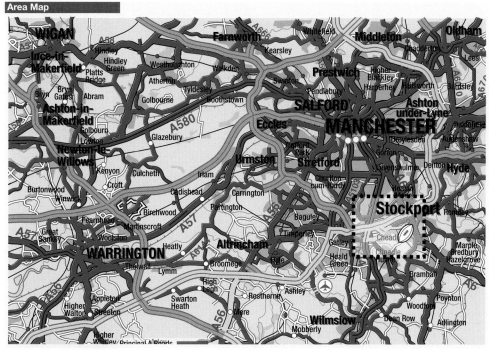

Local Map

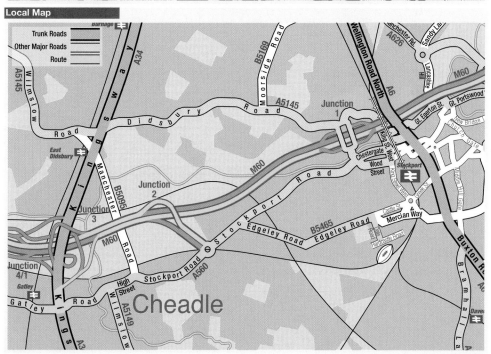

Saracens

Season Summary 2005/06

Position	Won	Drawn	Lost	For	Against	Bonus Points	Total Points
10	8	1	13	433	483	12	46

Eight successive Premiership defeats saw Saracens plunge to 11th in the league and only four points above bottom club Leeds in February, ending Steve Diamond's reign. However, thanks to the arrival of Australian coach Eddie Jones, the Vicarage Road side pulled themselves from the brink of relegation, finding some form during the latter part of the season. A memorable win against Sale marked a turning point in their campaign, triggering a run of four successive wins for the men in black, easing them into 10th place. The Watford side was boosted by the news that French international Thomas Castaignede had signed a one-year contract extension.

Director of Rugby: Alan Gaffney

Club Honours
Pilkington Cup: 1998

Season Squad

Stats 2005-06

Position	Player	Height	Weight	Apps	Rep	Tries	Points	Position	Player	Height	Weight	Apps	Rep	Tries	Points
FL	S.Armitage	5'9"	16st 8lb	2	1	3	15	P	N.Lloyd	6'0"	16st 9lb	4	10	-	-
C	P.Bailey	6'0"	12st 8lb	6	1	-	-	P	H.Mitchell	N/A	N/A	2	2	1	5
8	D.Barrell	6'4"	15st 0lb	-	1	-	-	C	A.Powell	5'11"	14st 4lb	2	5	2	10
C	M.Bartholomeusz	5'9"	13st 8lb	12	-	2	10	L	S.Raiwalui	6'6"	18st 13lb	17	2	-	-
SH	K.Bracken	5'11"	13st 0lb	12	4	-	-	BR	T.Randell	6'2"	17st 4lb	7	5	-	-
P	B.Broster	5'11"	16st 9lb	6	9	-	-	SH	M.Rauluni	5'10"	13st 7lb	2	13	1	5
H	S.Byrne	5'10"	15st 6lb	12	5	-	-	BR	B.Russell	6'3"	15st 10lb	9	9	1	5
H	M.Cairns	5'11"	16st 0lb	10	11	2	10	L	T.Ryder	6'5"	16st 9lb	7	2	-	-
FH	T.Castaignede	5'9"	13st 3lb	9	1	4	20	BR	A.Sanderson	6'2"	16st 1lb	4	1	-	-
L	K.Chesney	6'6"	18st 4lb	14	8	1	5	FB	D.Scarbrough	6'1"	13st 3lb	19	1	7	35
SH	A.Dickens	5'10"	12st 9lb	8	5	-	-	BR	D.Seymour	5'11"	14st 2lb	9	7	-	-
L	I.Fullarton	6'7"	16st 12lb	6	1	-	-	BR	B.Skirving	6'4"	16st 12lb	14	1	2	10
C	D.Harris	5'10"	15st 12lb	4	6	1	5	C	K.Sorrell	5'11"	13st 8lb	21	-	2	10
W	R.Haughton	6'2"	13st 7lb	9	2	3	15	W	T.Vaikona	6'2"	16st 2lb	15	1	2	10
FH	G.Jackson	5'11"	13st 6lb	22	-	3	238	P	C.Visagie	6'1"	18st 0lb	14	1	-	-
C	B.Johnston	6'3"	16st 7lb	13	1	3	15	BR	H.Vyvyan	6'6"	16st 0lb	21	-	-	-
H	A.Kyriacou	5'11"	15st 2lb	-	3	-	-	P	K.Yates	5'11"	17st 12lb	18	2	-	-
FH	N.Little	6'0"	15st 0lb	-	1	-	-								

Last Season Form 2005/06

Season Progression

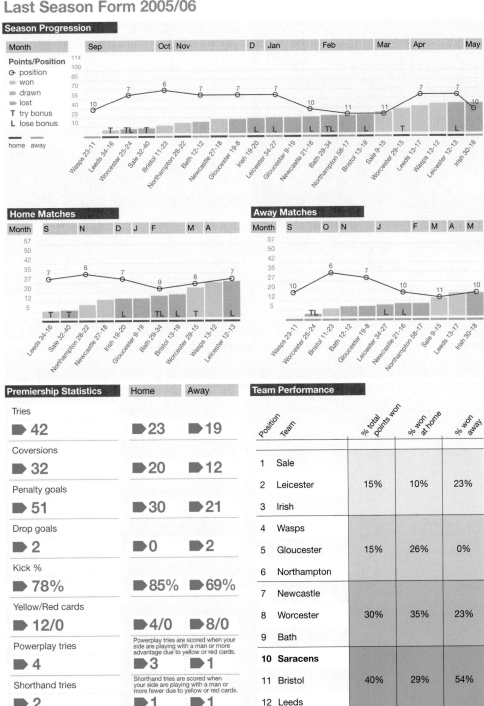

| Month | Sep | | Oct | Nov | | | D | Jan | | Feb | | | Mar | | Apr | | May |

Points/Position
- ⊙ position
- won
- drawn
- lost
- T try bonus
- L lose bonus

home away

Positions: 10, 7, 6, 7, 7, 7, 10, 11, 11, 7, 7, 10

Matches: Wasps 23-11, Leeds 34-16, Worcester 25-24, Sale 32-40, Bristol 11-23, Northampton 28-22, Bath 12-12, Newcastle 27-18, Gloucester 19-8, Irish 19-20, Leicester 34-27, Gloucester 9-19, Newcastle 21-16, Bath 29-34, Northampton 58-17, Bristol 13-19, Sale 9-15, Worcester 29-15, Leeds 13-17, Wasps 13-12, Leicester 12-13, Irish 30-18

Home Matches

| Month | S | N | | D | J | F | | M | A | |

Positions: 7, 6, 7, 9, 8, 7

Matches: Leeds 34-16, Sale 32-40, Northampton 28-22, Newcastle 27-18, Irish 19-20, Gloucester 9-19, Bath 29-34, Bristol 13-19, Worcester 29-15, Wasps 13-12, Leicester 12-13

Away Matches

| Month | S | O | | J | | F | M | A | M |

Positions: 10, 6, 7, 10, 11, 10

Matches: Wasps 23-11, Worcester 25-24, Bristol 11-23, Bath 12-12, Gloucester 19-8, Leicester 34-27, Newcastle 21-16, Northampton 58-17, Sale 9-15, Leeds 13-17, Irish 30-18

Premiership Statistics

		Home	Away
Tries	42	23	19
Coversions	32	20	12
Penalty goals	51	30	21
Drop goals	2	0	2
Kick %	78%	85%	69%
Yellow/Red cards	12/0	4/0	8/0
Powerplay tries	4	3	1
Shorthand tries	2	1	1

Powerplay tries are scored when your side are playing with a man or more advantage due to yellow or red cards.

Shorthand tries are scored when your side are playing with a man or more fewer due to yellow or red cards.

Team Performance

Position	Team	% total points won	% won at home	% won away
1	Sale			
2	Leicester	15%	10%	23%
3	Irish			
4	Wasps			
5	Gloucester	15%	26%	0%
6	Northampton			
7	Newcastle			
8	Worcester	30%	35%	23%
9	Bath			
10	**Saracens**	40%	29%	54%
11	Bristol			
12	Leeds			

Saracens

Points Facts

Total points	% team points	Home	Away
▶238	▶56	▶135	▶103

Points by Time Period

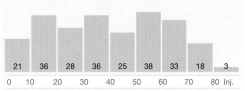

21	36	28	36	25	38	33	18	3
0	10	20	30	40	50	60	70	80 Inj.

Team Tries and Points

Tries by Time Period

- ▶ scored
- ▶ conceded

5	5	1	6	6	6	8	5	0
0	10min	20min	30min	40min	50min	60min	70min	80 Injury time
4	5	8	9	3	4	2	12	1

Tries by Halves

- ▶ scored
- ▶ conceded

	Total	1st half	2nd half	1st half %	2nd half %
scored	▶42	▶17	▶25	▶40%	▶60%
conceded	▶48	▶26	▶22	▶54%	▶46%

How Points were Scored

- ▶ tries: 210
- ▶ conversions: 64
- ▶ pen goals: 153
- drop goals: 6

How Points were Conceded

- ▶ tries: 240
- ▶ conversions: 60
- ▶ pen goals: 168
- drop goals: 15

Tries Scored by Player

- ▶ backs: 30
- ▶ forwards: 10

Tries Conceded by Player

- ▶ backs: 37
- ▶ forwards: 9

Eight-Season Form 1998-2006

Season Progression

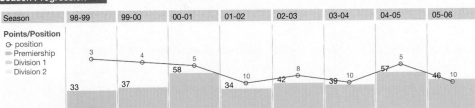

Season	98-99	99-00	00-01	01-02	02-03	03-04	04-05	05-06

Points/Position
- ⊙ position
- ▬ Premiership
- ▬ Division 1
- ▬ Division 2

position: 3, 4, 5, 10, 8, 10, 5, 10

points: 33, 37, 58, 34, 42, 39, 57, 46

Games

Season	98-99	99-00	00-01	01-02	02-03	03-04	04-05	05-06
won	16	14	12	7	8	8	12	8
drawn	1					1	2	1
lost	9	8	10	15	14	13	8	13

Points

Season	98-99	99-00	00-01	01-02	02-03	03-04	04-05	05-06
scored	748	729	589	425	499	397	384	433
conceded	583	514	501	671	587	543	428	483

Points Difference

Season	98-99	99-00	00-01	01-02	02-03	03-04	04-05	05-06
points	+165	+215	+88	-246	-88	-146	-44	-50

Total Premiership Record

Largest win	Largest defeat	Most tries scored in a game	Most tries conceded in a game
▶ **59-5**	▶ **13-55**	▶ **9**	▶ **7**
vs Rotherham (H) 24.09.00	vs London Irish (H) 22.11.01	vs Bedford Blues (A) 16.04.00	vs Newcastle Falcons (A) 15.05.02

Top points scorer	Top try scorer	Top drop goal scorer	Most appearances
▶ G.Johnson 363	▶ T.Castaignede 25	▶ A.Goode 9	▶ K.Chesney 153

Longest winning sequence		Longest losing sequence	
▶ **7 wins**	from 29.04.98 to 11.10.98	▶ **9 defeats**	from 26.11.05 to 26.02.06

Saracens EFL

ENHANCED FIXTURE LIST
[does not include play-off data]

Guinness Premiership 2006-07 | Premiership History

Date	Team	H/A	05-06	Played 98-99 99-00 00-01 01-02 02-03 03-04 04-05 05-06	F	A	No.	W	D	L	No.	W
				won drawn lost not played	Total Points		Outcome after a half-time lead				Close games	
02.09.06	Wasps	H	13-12	9	175	241	2►1	-	1		6	4
10.09.06	Bristol	A	11-23	6	186	151	4►3	-	1		1	1
17.09.06	Newcastle	H	27-18	9	268	166	9►8	-	1		5	4
22.09.06	Sale	A	9-15	9	214	187	2►2	-	-		1	1
15.10.06	Bath	H	29-34	9	229	202	4►4	-	-		1	-
04.11.06	Gloucester	A	19-8	9	132	246	2►1	-	1		4	1
12.11.06	Leicester	H	12-13	9	171	184	3►1	-	2		4	1
18.11.06	Northampton	A	58-17	9	179	252	2►2	-	-		3	3
26.11.06	Worcester	H	29-15	2	45	25	1►1	-	-		1	1
22.12.06	Harlequins	A	N/A	8	168	245	2►2	-	-		3	1
27.12.06	Northampton	H	28-22	9	241	176	7►5	-	2		4	3
01.01.07	Leicester	A	34-27	9	137	291	1►-	-	1		2	1
07.01.07	Irish	A	30-18	9	188	211	3►2	-	1		3	2
28.01.07	Irish	H	19-20	9	214	250	5►2	-	3		4	-
18.02.07	Gloucester	H	9-19	9	240	178	5►5	-	-		2	2
24.02.07	Bath	A	12-12	9	172	178	3►3	-	-		1	-
04.03.07	Sale	H	32-40	9	348	230	7►7	-	-		1	1
09.03.07	Newcastle	A	21-16	9	171	254	3►1	1	1		6	1
18.03.07	Bristol	H	13-19	6	148	95	5►4	-	1		3	1
08.04.07	Wasps	A	23-11	9	123	268	1►-	-	1		3	1
15.04.07	Harlequins	H	N/A	8	253	178	6►5	1	-		3	2
28.04.07	Worcester	A	25-24	2	43	43	1►-	-	1		2	1

Club Information

Useful Information

Founded
1876
Address
Vicarage Road Stadium
Vicarage Road
Watford
Herts
WD1 8ER
Capacity
22,100 (all seated)
Main switchboard
01923 475222
Website
www.saracens.com

Travel Information

Car
From North:
Leave the M1 at junction 5, taking the third exit from the roundabout and follow signs to Watford Town Centre. When joining the ring road get into the middle lane, before moving into the left lane after the second set of traffic lights. Follow signs for Watford General Hospital, which is next to Vicarage Road.

From West:
Leave the M25 at junction 19, and follow the A411 Hempstead Road, signposted Watford. Go straight over the first roundabout, then left at the second. Follow the signs towards Watford General Hospital, which is next to Vicarage Road.

Train
Watford High Street station is approx 10 minutes walk from the stadium. North London Railway trains run from London Euston station.

Tube
Watford tube station is approx 20 minutes walk from the stadium, on the Metropolitan Line.

Maps

Area Map

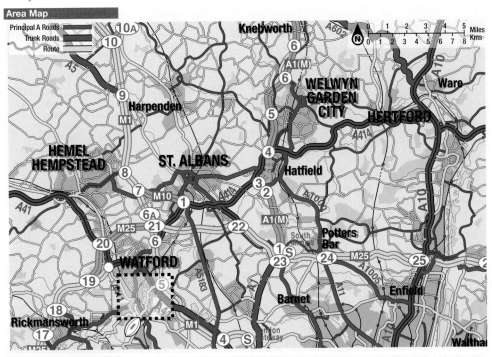

Local Map

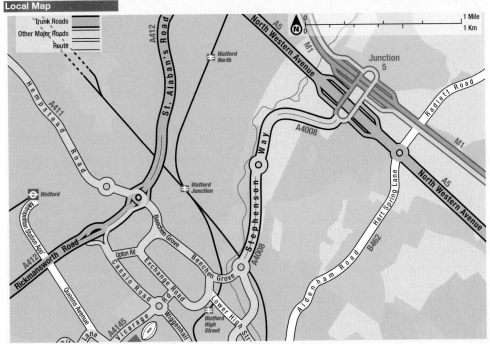

Worcester Warriors

Season Summary 2005/06

Position	Won	Drawn	Lost	For	Against		Bonus Points	Total Points
8	**9**	**1**	**12**	**451**	**494**		**9**	**47**

In their second season in the top flight and under the watchful eye of John Brain and new head coach Anthony Eddy, Worcester were fourth in the league at Christmas and on course for finishing in the top half. However, with Pat Sanderson sidelined for much of the season with a back injury, Warriors struggled to replicate that kind of form in the second half of the season, winning only three league games in 2006. Andy Gomarsall jostled for a place with Matt Powell to form the half back pairing with Shane Drahm, with Powell ending the season the favoured of the two. Warriors finished the season in a creditable eighth position, one place higher than their first year in the Premiership.

Head Coach: Anthony Eddy
Director of Rugby: John Brain

Club Honours
N/A

Season Squad

Stats 2005-06

Position	Player	Height	Weight	Apps	Rep	Tries	Points	Position	Player	Height	Weight	Apps	Rep	Tries	Points
P	C.Black	5'11"	17st 2lb	-	1	-	-	FB/W	N.Le Roux	5'8"	11st 13lb	13	1	2	10
L	R.Blaze	6'7"	18st 0lb	1	2	-	-	C	T.Lombard	6'2"	13st 5lb	21	-	2	10
FH	J.Brown	5'10"	11st 2lb	5	2	-	30	P	M.MacDonald	6'1"	20st 5lb	1	3	-	-
L	T.Collier	6'6"	21st 3lb	1	5	-	-	W/C	M.Maguire	6'1"	14st 11lb	1	-	-	-
FB	T.Delport	6'2"	14st 6lb	16	2	4	20	L	P.Murphy	6'7"	17st 6lb	21	1	1	5
FH	S.Drahm	5'9"	12st 10lb	17	3	3	233	L	E.O'Donoghue	6'6"	17st 4lb	1	8	-	-
H	C.Fortey	5'11"	17st 8lb	15	4	-	-	W	U.Oduoza	6'3"	14st 4lb	3	-	-	-
P	L.Fortey	5'10"	16st 3lb	2	6	-	-	SH	M.Powell	5'10"	13st 9lb	7	10	-	-
L	C.Gillies	6'7"	17st 8lb	20	-	-	-	C	D.Rasmussen	6'2"	14st 12lb	17	2	2	10
SH	A.Gomarsall	5'10"	14st 4lb	13	5	1	5	SH	N.Runciman	5'9"	11st 11lb	2	-	1	5
W	C.Hallam	N/A	N/A	-	1	-	-	BR	P.Sanderson	6'2"	14st 8lb	11	-	2	10
FL	T.Harding	6'0"	15st 4lb	7	4	1	5	P	T.Taumoepeau	6'0"	18st 0lb	14	5	-	-
W	A.Havili	5'7"	15st 10lb	14	-	6	30	C	G.Trueman	6'0"	14st 2lb	4	4	1	5
BR	D.Hickey	6'3"	15st 12lb	17	2	2	10	BR	J.Tu'amoheloa	5'10"	14st 6lb	7	-	-	-
H	G.Hickie	5'10"	15st 10lb	1	8	-	-	C/W	M.Tucker	6'0"	15st 10lb	7	-	-	-
C	B.Hinshelwood	6'2"	15st 10lb	7	-	-	-	BR	S.Vaili	6'4"	17st 6lb	5	11	2	10
P	C.Horsman	6'2"	17st 6lb	6	-	-	-	H	A.Van Niekerk	5'10"	16st 12lb	6	3	-	-
BR	K.Horstmann	6'3"	16st 9lb	19	2	3	15	FH/C	S.Whatling	5'10"	15st 0lb	3	6	-	3
W	J.Hylton	6'0"	13st 5lb	4	3	-	-	P	T.Windo	6'0"	16st 12lb	21	-	3	15
H	A.Keylock	N/A	N/A	-	-	-	-								

Worcester Warriors

Last Season Form 2005/06

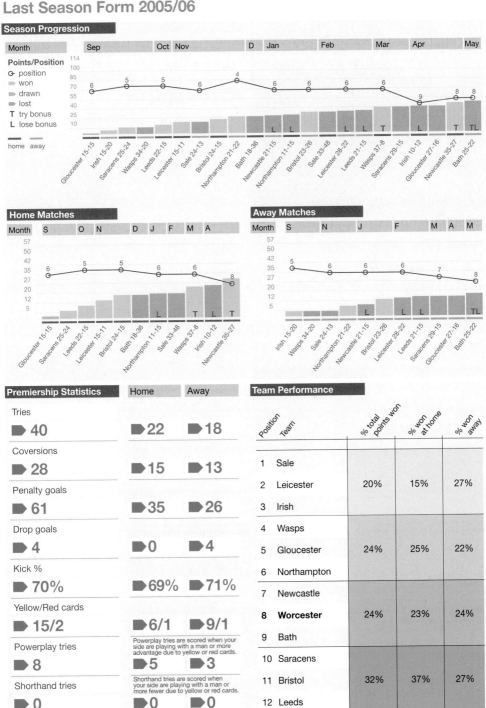

Season Progression

| Month | Sep | | Oct | Nov | | D | Jan | | Feb | | Mar | | Apr | | May |

Points/Position
- position
- won
- drawn
- lost
- T try bonus
- L lose bonus

home away

Matches: Gloucester 15-15, Irish 15-20, Saracens 25-24, Wasps 34-20, Leeds 22-15, Leicester 15-11, Sale 24-13, Bristol 24-15, Northampton 21-22, Bath 18-36, Newcastle 21-15, Northampton 11-15, Bristol 23-26, Sale 33-48, Leicester 28-22, Leeds 21-15, Wasps 37-8, Saracens 29-15, Irish 10-12, Gloucester 27-16, Newcastle 35-27, Bath 25-22

Home Matches

| Month | S | O | N | | D | J | F | M | A | |

Matches: Gloucester 15-15, Saracens 25-24, Leeds 22-15, Leicester 15-11, Bristol 24-15, Bath 18-36, Northampton 11-15, Sale 33-48, Wasps 37-8, Irish 10-12, Newcastle 35-27

Away Matches

| Month | S | | N | | J | | F | | M | A | M |

Matches: Irish 15-20, Wasps 34-20, Sale 24-13, Northampton 21-22, Newcastle 21-15, Bristol 23-26, Leicester 28-22, Leeds 21-15, Saracens 29-15, Gloucester 27-16, Bath 25-22

Premiership Statistics

		Home	Away
Tries	40	22	18
Coversions	28	15	13
Penalty goals	61	35	26
Drop goals	4	0	4
Kick %	70%	69%	71%
Yellow/Red cards	15/2	6/1	9/1
Powerplay tries	8	5	3
Shorthand tries	0	0	0

Powerplay tries are scored when your side is playing with a man or more advantage due to yellow or red cards.

Shorthand tries are scored when your side is playing with a man or more fewer due to yellow or red cards.

Team Performance

Position	Team	% total points won	% won at home	% won away
1	Sale			
2	Leicester	20%	15%	27%
3	Irish			
4	Wasps			
5	Gloucester	24%	25%	22%
6	Northampton			
7	Newcastle			
8	**Worcester**	24%	23%	24%
9	Bath			
10	Saracens			
11	Bristol	32%	37%	27%
12	Leeds			

Worcester Warriors

Top Scorer – Shane Drahm

Points Facts

Total points	% team points	Home	Away
▶ 233	▶ 54	▶ 117	▶ 116

Points by Time Period

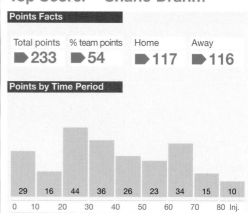

29	16	44	36	26	23	34	15	10
0	10	20	30	40	50	60	70	80 Inj.

Team Tries and Points

Tries by Time Period

- scored
- conceded

5	3	6	6	5	4	4	7	0
0	10min	20min	30min	40min	50min	60min	70min	80 Injury time
7	5	6	7	9	9	7	5	1

Tries by Halves

- scored
- conceded

	Total	1st half	2nd half	1st half %	2nd half %
scored	▶ 40	▶ 20	▶ 20	▶ 50%	▶ 50%
conceded	▶ 56	▶ 25	▶ 31	▶ 45%	▶ 55%

How Points were Scored

- tries: 200
- conversions: 56
- pen goals: 183
- drop goals: 12

How Points were Conceded

- tries: 280
- conversions: 64
- pen goals: 144
- drop goals: 6

Tries Scored by Player

- backs: 22
- forwards: 14

Tries Conceded by Player

- backs: 41
- forwards: 15

Worcester Warriors

Eight-Season Form 1998-2006

Season Progression

Season	98-99	99-00	00-01	01-02	02-03	03-04	04-05	05-06
Points/Position ⊙ position ➡ Premiership ➡ Division 1 — Division 2	34	38	112	108	114	125	42	47
position	3	3	2	2	2	1	9	8

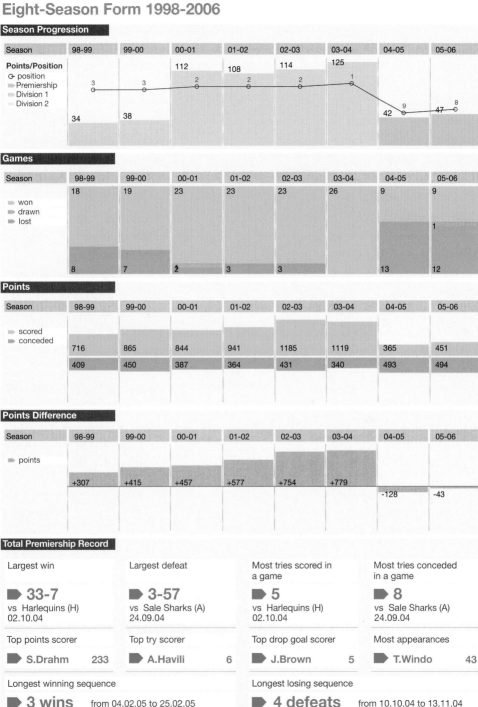

Games

Season	98-99	99-00	00-01	01-02	02-03	03-04	04-05	05-06
won	18	19	23	23	23	26	9	9
drawn								1
lost	8	7	2	3	3		13	12

Points

Season	98-99	99-00	00-01	01-02	02-03	03-04	04-05	05-06
scored	716	865	844	941	1185	1119	365	451
conceded	409	450	387	364	431	340	493	494

Points Difference

Season	98-99	99-00	00-01	01-02	02-03	03-04	04-05	05-06
points	+307	+415	+457	+577	+754	+779	-128	-43

Total Premiership Record

Largest win	Largest defeat	Most tries scored in a game	Most tries conceded in a game
➡ **33-7** vs Harlequins (H) 02.10.04	➡ **3-57** vs Sale Sharks (A) 24.09.04	➡ **5** vs Harlequins (H) 02.10.04	➡ **8** vs Sale Sharks (A) 24.09.04

Top points scorer	Top try scorer	Top drop goal scorer	Most appearances
➡ **S.Drahm** 233	➡ **A.Havili** 6	➡ **J.Brown** 5	➡ **T.Windo** 43

Longest winning sequence	Longest losing sequence
➡ **3 wins** from 04.02.05 to 25.02.05	➡ **4 defeats** from 10.10.04 to 13.11.04

Guinness Premiership 2006-07 / Premiership History

Date	Team	H/A	05-06	Played	98-99	99-00	00-01	01-02	02-03	03-04	04-05	05-06	Total Points F	A	Outcome after a half-time lead No.	W	D	L	Close games No.	W
02.09.06	Bristol	H	24-15	1									24	15	1	1	-	-	-	-
08.09.06	Newcastle	A	21-15	2									36	37	1	1	-	-	2	1
15.09.06	Sale	H	33-48	2									56	58	1	1	-	-	-	-
23.09.06	Bath	A	25-22	2									32	43	1	-	-	1	1	-
13.10.06	Gloucester	H	15-15	2									28	33	1	-	-	1	2	-
04.11.06	Leicester	A	28-22	2									29	78	-	-	-	-	1	-
11.11.06	Northampton	H	11-15	2									32	34	1	1	-	-	2	1
17.11.06	Harlequins	A	N/A	1									15	9	-	-	-	-	1	1
26.11.06	Saracens	A	29-15	2									25	45	1	-	-	1	1	-
22.12.06	Irish	H	10-12	2									26	18	1	1	-	-	1	-
27.12.06	Harlequins	H	N/A	1									33	7	1	1	-	-	-	-
01.01.07	Northampton	A	21-22	2									39	27	2	2	-	-	1	1
07.01.07	Wasps	A	34-20	2									37	66	1	-	-	1	-	-
26.01.07	Wasps	H	37-8	2									64	32	2	2	-	-	1	1
17.02.07	Leicester	H	15-11	2									26	49	1	1	-	-	1	1
24.02.07	Gloucester	A	27-16	2									32	55	-	-	-	-	-	-
03.03.07	Bath	H	18-36	2									40	62	1	-	-	1	1	-
09.03.07	Sale	A	24-13	2									16	81	-	-	-	-	-	-
16.03.07	Newcastle	H	35-27	2									44	57	1	1	-	-	-	-
08.04.07	Bristol	A	23-26	1									26	23	1	1	-	-	1	1
15.04.07	Irish	A	15-20	2									35	40	-	-	-	-	1	1
28.04.07	Saracens	H	25-24	2									43	43	1	-	-	1	2	1

Legend: ■ won ■ drawn ■ lost ☐ not played

Club Information

Useful Information

Founded
1871

Address
Sixways
Pershore Lane
Hindlip
Worcester
WR3 8ZE

Capacity
10,000 (3,700 seated)

Main switchboard
01905 454183

Website
www.wrfc.co.uk

Travel Information

Car
M5 Junction 7 (Worcester South) and follow AA signs for Park & Ride, County Hall (Countryside Centre). For a 15:00 kick off, buses start at 12:30 then every few minutes until 14:25. For a 20:00 kick off, buses start at 18:20 then every few minutes until 19:25.
M5 Junction 6 (Worcester North) and follow AA signs for Park & Ride, Blackpole (Blackpole East Trading Estate). For a 15:00 kick off, buses start at 12:30 then every few minutes until 14:25. For a 20:00 kick off, buses start at 18:20 then every few minutes until 19:25.
M5 Junction 6 (Worcester North) and follow AA signs for Park & Walk, Shire Business Park.

Train
Worcester Shrub Hill Station. Orange Bus Route 31 to City Bus station (every 10 minutes), then transfer to Rugby Special Service at frequent intervals (Stand F). A taxi to Sixways is about £8.00.
Worcester Foregate Street Station. Rugby Special Bus Service from outside the station every 10 minutes. For a 15:00 kick off, buses start to leave the station at 12:30 then every few minutes until 14:05 to the ground. For a 20:00 kick off, buses leave the station at 18:00 then every few minutes until 19:05.

Worcester Warriors

Maps

Area Map

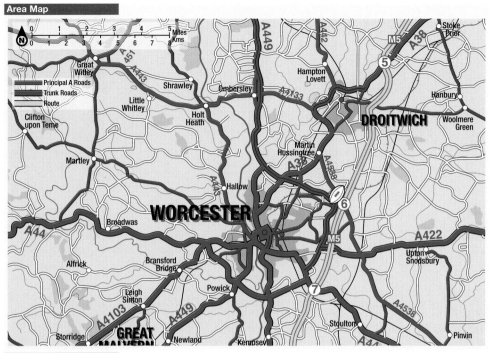

Local Map

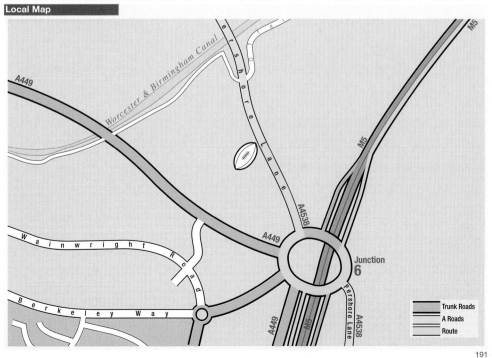

Premiership Fixture Grid 2006/07

Worcester	Saracens	Sale Sharks	Northampton	Newcastle	NEC Harlequins	London Wasps	London Irish	Leicester Tigers	Gloucester	Bristol Rugby	Bath Rugby	HOME / AWAY
3-Mar	15-Oct	13-Apr	16-Sep	28-Apr	6-Jan	12-Nov	17-Feb	17-Mar	2-Sep	27-Dec		Bath Rugby
2-Sep	18-Mar	1-Jan	27-Jan	3-Nov	24-Feb	4-Mar	16-Sep	22-Dec	28-Apr		17-Nov	Bristol Rugby
13-Oct	18-Feb	6-Jan	3-Mar	13-Apr	9-Sep	26-Dec	10-Nov	16-Sep		24-Nov	7-Apr	Gloucester
17-Feb	12-Nov	6-Apr	14-Oct	7-Jan	23-Sep	26-Nov	26-Dec		10-Mar	15-Apr	9-Sep	Leicester Tigers
22-Dec	28-Jan	23-Feb	28-Apr	22-Sep	7-Apr	8-Sep		18-Nov	1-Jan	10-Mar	4-Nov	London Irish
26-Jan	2-Sep	3-Nov	22-Dec	23-Feb	10-Mar		18-Mar	28-Apr	18-Nov	24-Sep	1-Jan	London Wasps
27-Dec	15-Apr	24-Nov	17-Feb	10-Nov		17-Sep	2-Sep	3-Mar	17-Mar	15-Oct	27-Jan	NEC Harlequins
16-Mar	17-Sep	17-Nov	3-Sep		1-Jan	15-Oct	3-Mar	27-Jan	22-Dec	18-Feb	25-Nov	Newcastle
11-Nov	27-Dec	9-Sep		6-Apr	4-Nov	15-Apr	26-Nov	24-Feb	23-Sep	7-Jan	10-Mar	Northampton
15-Sep	4-Mar		17-Mar	26-Dec	28-Apr	18-Feb	15-Oct	3-Sep	27-Jan	10-Nov	22-Dec	Sale Sharks
28-Apr		22-Sep	18-Nov	9-Mar	22-Dec	8-Apr	7-Jan	1-Jan	4-Nov	10-Sep	24-Feb	Saracens
	26-Nov	9-Mar	1-Jan	8-Sep	17-Nov	7-Jan	15-Apr	4-Nov	24-Feb	8-Apr	23-Sep	Worcester